The Lost Frontier

The Lost Frontier

Reading Annie Proulx's *Wyoming Stories*

Mark Asquith

BLOOMSBURY
NEW YORK • LONDON • NEW DELHI • SYDNEY

Bloomsbury Academic
An imprint of Bloomsbury Publishing Inc

1385 Broadway 50 Bedford Square
New York London
NY 10018 WC1B 3DP
USA UK

www.bloomsbury.com

Bloomsbury is a registered trade mark of Bloomsbury Publishing Plc

First published 2014

© Mark Asquith, 2014

All rights reserved. No part of this publication may be reproduced or transmitted in any form or by any means, electronic or mechanical, including photocopying, recording, or any information storage or retrieval system, without prior permission in writing from the publishers.

No responsibility for loss caused to any individual or organization acting on or refraining from action as a result of the material in this publication can be accepted by Bloomsbury or the author.

Library of Congress Cataloging-in-Publication Data
A catalog record for this book is available from the Library of Congress.

ISBN: HB: 978-1-6235-6147-5
PB: 978-1-6235-6819-1
ePub: 978-1-6235-6335-6
ePDF: 978-1-6235-6016-4

Typeset by Fakenham Prepress Solutions, Fakenham, Norfolk NR21 8NN

To Alan Asquith: in gratitude for all the early guidance

Contents

Acknowledgements		viii
Introduction		1
1	Landscape	29
2	Pioneers	57
3	Ranchers	85
4	Cowboys	107
5	Indians	141
6	Losers	163
Conclusion		185
Notes		191
Bibliography		211
Index		225

Acknowledgements

I would like to thank Ross King for reading various drafts of the book and offering sage advice. I would also like to thank Eric Patterson for his insightful comments and helpful suggestions concerning avenues of research. A special thanks to Alistair Doyle for all his practical support and dry humour. I would also like to thank the editorial team at Bloomsbury, especially Haaris Naqvi and Laura Murray, for taking on the project in the first place and seeing it through painlessly to its conclusion. Thanks also to Nick Fawcett, Gregory Evans, Theresa Mikuriya, Tom Durno, Nicolas Raynaud, Clara Story and Dave Klempner for their perceptive reading of the manuscript and valuable advice. My main debt, however, is to my wife, Anne-Marie, without whose patience, affection and common sense, this book would not have been completed.

Introduction

She stares at you with 'dark, watchful eyes … Eyes to fit that old Wyoming character, the former gunfighter who reckons on dying peaceably.' Not my words, but those of David Thomson in his evocatively entitled profile of Annie Proulx: 'The Lone Ranger'.[1] Epithets such as 'gnarled', 'grizzled' and 'chiselled' are ubiquitous in descriptions of Proulx, while her eyes are invariably described as fixed on some point in the middle distance. Nicci Gerrard described her as a 'frontier woman' in an early review in *The Observer* – 'weather-worn, life-worn, as if she has spent years walking on hard earth against bitter winds'; while in *The Independent* Ros Wynne-Jones imagined her as an older character in one of her own stories: 'At 86, she had a skin like a slipcover over a rump-sprung sofa, yet her muscled forearms and strong fingers suggested she could climb a sheer rock-face.'[2]

Proulx has rejected such labels as the product of 'commercialization', but nevertheless seems happy to cultivate such a persona. The photograph of the author that stares out from the dust-jacket of her novels establishes the element of choreographed authenticity that Proulx brings to the management of her image: it is both posed and natural; she is a rural woman and happy to project herself as such, bringing the same degree of care and attention to the creation of her literary persona as to her fictional characters. Complementing this hardy western persona has grown the myth of Proulx the no-nonsense interviewee. Katharine Viner of *The Guardian* has noted: 'There is no other way to approach an interview with E. Annie Proulx except with fear.'[3] She hates small talk and, as David Thomson found to his cost, to stray onto topics that she regards as personal is to be left 'leaning into the gunfighter's intransigence'. Aida Edemariam recorded just such a look when she asked an intimate question during an early profile for *The Guardian*: 'Her face hardens with a joke that's not quite a joke: "it's a good thing I put the guns away".' To some extent all are playing a game which allows Proulx to perform a role while being deadly serious: the character she projects allows her to be evasive while conforming to the role of the western writer who 'tells it as it is'.[4]

Proulx's most high-profile performance to date followed the 2006 Academy Awards in which Ang Lee's adaptation of *Brokeback Mountain* lost out to the film *Crash* in the category of Best Picture. Her response in *The Guardian*, menacingly entitled 'Blood on the Red Carpet', deliberately presents herself as the common-sense voice of the western outsider railing against an LA metropolitan elite dangerously out of touch with 'contemporary culture'. Her position is laced with contradictions, since the rural persona she adopts is representative of that rural constituency with which the film sat most uneasily. Nevertheless, Proulx pulls it off with a tone of gentle mockery and defiance, disarming her critics with a closing foray which is at once deprecatory and self-consciously western: 'For those who call this little piece a Sour Grapes Rant, play it as it lays.'[5]

To some extent, Proulx's most enduring character creation is her own persona, which emerges as the product of careful mediation between author, publisher and journalists. That character, as befits the author of three volumes of Wyoming short stories, is unashamedly western. This is no mean feat for a single mother with an academic background in Renaissance Studies, who had not set foot in the West until she was in her sixties. Indeed, prior to her move in 1995, Proulx had lived a remarkably un-western lifestyle.[6] She was born in Norwich, Connecticut in 1935, the eldest of five daughters, to a French-Canadian immigrant father called George Napoleon who worked in a textile factory. Her mother, Lois Gill, was an amateur naturalist and painter who furnished her daughter with visual sensitivity and a love of reading. She grew up in New England and North Carolina and entered Colby College in Waterville, Maine, in 1957, but dropped out to marry the first of her three husbands. Her private life, over which she is fiercely protective, reads like one of her more dramatic narratives; two marriages Proulx has described as 'terrible', noting, perhaps sardonically, that she has 'a talent for choosing the wrong people'.[7] After gaining an MA at Sir George Williams University (now Concordia University) in Montréal in 1973, Proulx enrolled for a PhD in Renaissance economic history, but, having passed the oral requirements, was forced to leave her studies in order to look after her three sons. She moved to Canaan, on the US–Canada border, and was immediately faced with the problem of how to support a family while living in a remote rural retreat. She turned to journalism, living in the woods like a latter-day Henry Thoreau producing 'How To' articles for local magazines on rural subjects such as cooking, fishing, hunting and gardening. They were not, however, esoteric exercises in nostalgia for the urban market, but part of Proulx's attempt to keep alive country traditions for future generations. She made a good living for a number of years, dabbling with short stories on aspects of rural life which were published in *Gray's Sporting Journal*.

And so it would have remained, had not Tom Jenks at Charles Scribner's Sons invited her in 1982 to collect some of her short stories together into a collection. The resulting *Heart Songs* (an old name for country and western music) was published in 1988. It focuses on the humdrum lives of the residents of Chopping County as they go about their daily routines of hunting, shooting and fishing. Beneath the veneer of bucolic cheeriness, however, she reveals a community brutalized by the harsh landscape and isolation, and a gallery of eccentric characters bearing ancient grudges, hidden secrets and under continual threat from outsiders: it is the kind of terrain that Proulx has been mining ever since. Critics were unanimous in their belief that the hard-bitten narrative tone, stacked metaphors, present-tense terseness, elliptical sentences and mixture of realism with surrealism heralded the arrival of a new and distinctive literary voice. Proulx's rural tales may have appeared stylistically fresh and crisp, but thematically they looked back to an older tradition of 'regional writers' such as Frank Norris and John Steinbeck who sought to trace the ways in which the lives of ordinary individuals are moulded by the limitations of a specific landscape.

Reviewing the work in *The Boston Globe*, Tim Gautreaux suggested that Proulx seemed to be doing for New England what Cormac McCarthy was doing for the Tex-Mex borders.[8] But McCarthy's bloody yet heroic vision of a passing West is a world away from the petty jealousies and uncomfortable sexual secrets that interest Proulx. Furthermore, it is clear that her stories do not emerge from her attachment to a particular geographical location, but rather from an historical methodology; one which takes as its starting point communities under threat. On this point, Proulx has claimed that:

> I try to define periods when regional society and culture, rooted in location and natural resources, start to experience the erosion of traditional ways, and attempt to master contemporary, large-world values. The characters in my novels pick their way through the chaos of change.[9]

Essentially, although *Heart Songs* was very definitely the chronicle of a community moulded by its relationship with a specific location, neither the characters nor the landscape were essential to the evolution of her writing. What was central was Proulx's training as a historian, particularly her interest in the French *Annales* School – an avant-garde group popular in the first half of the twentieth century. Three aspects of their methodology are pertinent to Proulx's development. Of primary importance is the *Annales*' rejection of history as the linear record of great feats by great men in favour of a more fragmentary and egalitarian approach (a position which fits in with the postmodern rejection of the grand narrative in favour of competing voices). The history of a community begins with the careful analysis of present conditions before determining how such factors as landscape, climate, economic trends and social conditions may have combined to allow the people to evolve into this state. It is history built upon the communal behaviour of ordinary people rather than legislators, in which shopping lists, marriage certificates and death records replace the political memoir as a source for material. It is perhaps no surprise, therefore, that so much of Proulx's fiction derives from and is abetted by hours of detailed research in local libraries and much more:

> I read manuals of work and repair, books of manners, dictionaries of slang, city directories, lists of occupational titles, geology, regional weather, botanists' plant guides, local histories, newspapers. I visit graveyards, collapsing cotton gins, photograph barns and houses, roadways. I listen to ordinary people speaking with one another in bars and stores, in laundromats. I read bulletin boards, scraps of paper I pick up from the ground.[10]

Her theoretically inspired interest is complemented by her earlier career as a writer of 'How To' articles for local magazines, a job which forced her to observe what ordinary people were doing to 'make things work in rural situations'.[11] These people, living in a reciprocal relationship with the land, tell a different story to that created by regional historians, federal bureaucrats or even writers.

One result of Proulx's historical training is that her particular brand of regionalism has proved remarkably portable. This is made apparent by the geographical breadth of her oeuvre: in her first novel, *Postcards* (1992), she traces the collapse of the New England dairy industry in the years immediately following the Second World War; in *The Shipping News* (1993), it is a frozen Newfoundland fishing community threatened by over-fishing and government legislation; in *That Old Ace in the Hole* (2002) she moves to the Texas and Oklahoma panhandles and a ranching community pressurized by corporate hog-farming; and in *Accordion Crimes* (1996), it is the whole of America, as Proulx explores the erosion of the cultural traditions of American immigrants during the process of cultural assimilation.

In many ways Wyoming is simply another endangered region that took Proulx's fancy. She herself has noted that 'writing about the American West is just like writing about the American East or wherever'.[12] However, it is also clear that when in 1995 she left the region that had been the family home since the seventeenth century in order to move to the tiny mountain village of Centennial near Laramie in the southeast part of Wyoming, she found herself face to face with a region that challenged her creative imagination. Her initial reaction, like so many entering the West for the first time, focused on the endless landscape: 'What an enormous help the sight lines were, and the room to walk. There's something about being able to shoot your eyes very far ahead. In northern New England the trees got in the way.'[13] Proulx captures something of her astonishment in the story 'Man Crawling Out of Trees' (*BD*), in which we meet Mitchell Fair, another refugee from the dark shadows cast by New England's trees:

> Mitchell was stunned by the beauty of the place, not the over-photographed jags of the Grand Tetons, but the high prairie and the luminous yellow distance, which pleased his sense of spatial arrangement. He felt as though he had stumbled into a landscape never before seen on the earth and at the same time that he had been transported to the *ur*-landscape before human beginnings. The mountains crouched at every horizon like dark sleeping animals, their backs whitened by snow. He trod on wildflowers, glistening quartz crystals, on agate and jade, brilliant lichens … His heart squeezed in, and he wished for a celestial eraser to remove the fences, the crude houses, the one he bought included, from this place. (106)

Mitchell's initial reaction evokes nineteenth-century notions of the sublime, before he congratulates himself on distinguishing between an 'authentic' and a 'popular' version of nature. It is a landscape that provokes not only aesthetic appreciation but atavistic yearning, a reaction, according to geographer Yi-Fu Tuan, familiar to those who experience the 'first glimpse of the desert through a mountain pass or the first plunge into forested wilderness.'[14] It is a brief but intense experience that nullifies the past while preparing the viewer to be reborn into a promised land. This is certainly how Mitchell, recovering from a kidney transplant (an operation that introduces the theme of transplantation and rejection), would like to see it. It is a landscape that bears the scars of its ancient history, like hieroglyphs of a lost language that defies the comprehension and even conceptual awareness of the modern viewer. Mitchell's reaction serves as a warning to those seeking to make sense of it, for despite his seeming sensitivity, he judges the 'prairie' in terms of a 'spatial arrangement' to be apprehended aesthetically in the same way that he looks at his wife's designer kitchen. The mountain metaphors are clichéd, while the detailed description of what is under his feet is apparent rather than real; it is clearly generic and has less to do with the reality of the ground than what his imagination tells him should be there. Indeed, Mitchell's epiphany has little to do with expansiveness and merely serves to validate his own narrow-mindedness, which includes the erasure by 'celestial eraser' of anything that does not conform to his idea of what a primeval landscape should look like.[15]

Proulx's extract clearly dramatizes the problem of conceptualizing the western wilderness. William Fox argues that our normal cognitive and cultural habits prove unequal to a landscape lacking the 'verticals' which provide the 'middle ground' where 'normally our vision, hence our imagination, spends most of its time'.[16] Proulx echoes this conclusion in her introduction to the collection of essays *Red Desert: History of a Place*, in which she observes that in such an empty space the individual is forced to perform 'a kind of psychological double-think' as the point of focus shifts between what is 'close at hand to the far horizon line'.[17] Perhaps because of this existential crisis, it is, according to contemporary Wyoming novelist and journalist Tom Rea, a problem that still fixates writers: 'In Wyoming, we're still arguing about what this emptiness actually is, and whether and how to fill it.'[18] One way of dealing with the emptiness, of course, is to stop seeing it as absence. As Rea makes clear: 'The state's already full: with sky, sagebrush, rocks, antelope, cattle. Scraps of water. Here and there a highway, a tree, a house. Once in a long while, a town' – the kind of plenitude that makes a virtue of emptiness.[19] Another way of dealing with it, is to lose yourself. Wyoming has long been a rest cure for those facing domestic tragedy: an empty space where the psyche can be reconfigured. Ten years before Proulx's move, the writer Gretel Ehrlich arrived in Wyoming seeking *The Solace of Open Spaces* (1985) following the death of her partner. And one hundred years before Ehrlich, a young Owen Wister arrived in the region searching for a cure for his depression. What he found, he claims, was a landscape 'like what scenery on the moon must be', dotted with oases of green that made him think of 'Genesis'.[20] Like Mitchell and Ehrlich, he experienced the Wyoming landscape as combining desolation with the promise of redemption and growth. Unlike them, however, he was not content to find solace. When faced with the wilderness he sought to fill it up: with stories.

To some extent the emptiness of the West has always invited storytelling. Leslie Fiedler has argued that the idea of a western kingdom in which white men could confront their dark 'other' has long satisfied a deep-seated need in the European psyche. According to his reading, Plato's myth of Atlantis or the Celtic dream of Avalon are replaced by the narrative of a people sailing in the wake of the Mayflower in search of economic and religious freedom and a confrontation in the woods.[21] Even as the first settlers arrived on the east coast (the western limit of their world), their eyes were straying towards a new West, which both threatened and promised with the allure of a new Eden. The West that emerges from early accounts establishes the way that the region has been viewed ever since. For Michel Montaigne it was a region of pastoral innocence free from the vices of the East: even the Indians (shady figures of fear for the New England Puritans), once reappraised through the lens of European Romanticism (particularly the advocacy of Jean-Jacques Rousseau) and the political philosophy of John Locke, emerged as 'Noble Savages'. This process of idealization can be found in the canvases of Thomas Cole and Albert Bierstadt, the Transcendentalist movement of the mid-nineteenth century, and, more recently, Deep Green Ecology movements and those seeking alternative lifestyles. It was to take a Frenchman, Hector Crèvecoeur, to carve out a new identity for the 'western' farmers surrounding his farm in Orange County, New York. There is, as Leo Marx has observed of Crèvecoeur's *Letters from an American Farmer* (1782), no mention of Arcadia, no stock of poeticisms derived from Virgil in his creation of a Pastoral Republic. There is just the plain-speaking, hard-working pioneer fleeing the corruption of the urban East.[22] And yet still in 1800 two-thirds of the citizens of the new Republic lived within 50 miles of the Atlantic. This changed with the Lewis and Clark expedition of 1804-6, which, although primarily an exercise in mapping territory, had the effect of re-orientating the collective imagination. As Henry Smith Nash, one of the earliest historians of the region, has claimed: the importance of their journey 'lay on the level of imagination: it was drama, it was the enactment of a myth that embodied the future'.[23]

The West would have been opened up without them, but Lewis and Clark fulfilled the empty region's unquenchable thirst for heroes. For, as Theodore Roosevelt, one of the first politicians to understand the region's symbolic importance, observed: 'close on their tracks followed the hunters, trappers, and fur traders who themselves made ready the way for the settlers whose descendants were to possess the land'.[24] It was this latter group, motivated by paradoxical dreams of freedom and ownership, that was to inspire America's very own creation story. Except that, in the hands of Frederick Jackson Turner, the first great historian of the West, it was not a 'story' at all. When in 1893 he presented his account of how the struggle of western migration created tough, self-reliant and democratic Americans to members of the American Historical Association at the Columbian Exposition, Chicago, it was as a 'thesis' – a title that confers academic respectability and authority. What he proposed was radical: no longer was the real America to be found on the east coast, or even in the southern states, but in the West.

And, we might add, in the past. For the irony of the 1893 World's Columbian Exposition celebration of the future – exhibits included a Mercedes Benz, the hamburger and Thomas Edison's Kinetoscope – is that it gave birth to a vision of American identity rooted firmly in nostalgia.[25] Turner's thesis wove together concepts of environmental determinism and social Darwinism to reassure his audience that America would be great not simply because it was ordained by Manifest Destiny, but because of evolutionary science. Taking his cue from the popular 'germ theory' of the period, he argued that America could be conceived of as a host colonized by hard-working 'European germs'.[26] Whereas contemporaries focused on the stoic qualities of the old world, Turner sought to emphasize the evolution in character experienced by migrants during their struggle with a hostile environment. At a stroke, notions of American identity based on war with Europe and America's slave past were replaced by a creation myth based on evolutionary biology.[27] What's more, he did it with theatrical style. In a touch worthy of Buffalo Bill Cody, he not only conjured up the concept of the frontier out of dry statistical data, but he also drew the curtain down on this crucially formative period, thereby casting the pall of whimsical regret over all future engagement with the region.

Perhaps this theatrical gesture had been inspired by the proximity of the great impresario himself, for Cody's Wild West Extravaganza was in full swing a few blocks down the road from Turner's Chicago venue. Turner declined an invitation to attend on the afternoon of 12 July in order to finish his own conference paper; if he had gone he would have been exposed to a very different vision of the West and the business of making history. For where Turner's West was empty, Cody's was full of Indians waiting to be scripted into a more murderous drama; a drama dominated not by honourable, but ultimately dull, homesteaders, but by brave scouts and the US cavalry fending off carefully choreographed Indian attacks. Like Turner's vision, this was not presented by Cody as mere theatre, but as 'history' – a claim based upon his deployment of authentic props. As Philip Deloria has observed, because 'real Indians, decked out in real feathers and buckskins, led the attack on the real stagecoaches and homesteads', this version of the West must be 'real'.[28] The logic is unimpeachable, and yet it creates a vision of the West in which performance and history are so intertwined that the region becomes detached from any notion of reality. For Jean Baudrillard, Cody's presentation of a series of 'signifiers' – buckskins, battleaxes, etc. – transforms the West into an example of a *simulacrum*: it is not a copy of something real, but something that becomes real (or hyperreal) in its own right. And as such it becomes the perfect symbol for all America, which is a constructed reality in which 'everything is destined to reappear as simulation… . Things seem only to exist by virtue of this strange destiny.'[29]

The twists and turns of this fraught relationship are illustrated clearly by the extraordinary fact that Sitting Bull, architect of Custer's defeat at Greasy Grass, later toured with the show with some of his Sioux braves charging Custer on a nightly basis. Cody himself worked as a scout for the 5th cavalry, in which role he donned his theatrical costume. In June 1876 he killed a 'real' Indian, Yellow Hand, an event that was enacted nightly in the show by Cody wearing the same costume.[30] Thus, as Richard Slotkin has observed, Cody's arena becomes the ultimate 'mythic space in which past and present, fiction and reality, could co-exist; a space in which history, translated into myth, was re-enacted as ritual'. The audience leaving the canvas arena at the end of a performance will have been aware that their experience differed from that when consuming a play: with no script or cohesive plot, and 'actors' who never emerged from role, the audience really had seemingly witnessed 'history' rather than 'fiction'.[31]

For those not lucky enough to get ringside seats, Cody's vision was replicated and amplified in the dime novel market which, due to cheap paper and improved manufacturing techniques, exploded in the latter half of the century. The West was a popular subject, partly because its heyday (1860–90) aligned with the chronology of settlement, but also because the industrialized slaughter of the Civil War found America looking West in search of a new pastoral narrative of bravery and conquest. The West, as it had done for the first emigrants, once again became a geography of hope. The aim was to produce escapist fiction for eastern audiences, particularly young men emasculated by the drudge of office life. The novels may have been set in the West, but they were manufactured in the East (all major publishers were headquartered in New York) on an industrial scale (the celebrated Prentiss Ingraham authored over 600 novels) by authors who had seldom been out of the city. The much-feted Gilbert Patten earned his sobriquet 'Wyoming Bill' from having once travelled through the state on a train. The speed of production and lack of first-hand experience meant that authors relied on the work of one another and an increasingly codified set of caricatures, symbols and events. The result is that the dime novel market augmented Cody's process of fictionalization to produce a fantasy West.[32]

Just as in the latter part of the nineteenth century the popularity of the Western began to diminish, a saviour rode out of the mountains to transform the story of the West forever: the cowboy. Here was a reaffirmation of the spirit of gritty pioneer self-reliance packaged in a more glamorous wardrobe. Cody was quick off the mark, introducing 'Buck Taylor: King of the Cowboys' into his Wild West Extravaganza in 1887, his choreographed rituals – horse breaking, gunslinging, lassoing – complementing this highly theatrical version of the West. With his clinking spurs and ten-gallon hat the cowboy proved a publisher's dream: he may have been a home-grown hero, but he slipped easily into narrative conventions that had proved successful for centuries. If, as French structuralist Claude Lévi-Strauss argued in *Structural Anthropology* (1968), the potency of narrative derives from the conflict and resolution of simple binary relationships – then the Western, with its oppositions of cowboy vs Indian; wilderness vs city; freedom vs restriction, is the structuralist form *par excellence*. Add to this the recycling of stock characters (sheriff, gunslinger) in familiar landscapes (desert, saloon) engaged in familiar activities (shoot-outs, cattle drives) accoutred with the same visual signifiers (guns, spurs) and you have the structure for an enduring myth.[33] Nobody understood this better than Theodore Roosevelt, the first in a long line of American presidents (a group which includes Ronald Reagan and George W. Bush) who harnessed the image of the cowboy to political effect.

Roosevelt first travelled West in 1884 to come to terms with the death of his wife. What he found in the 'never ending plains' was, as he confessed to his sister, the fulfilment of a childhood fantasy; an empty land that his imagination peopled with the heroes of pulp fiction. But Roosevelt was no mere observer; the West transformed the pale, dyspeptic eastern politician into the rugged westerner, allowing Roosevelt to become a personification of the Turner thesis, with additional cowboy glamour. In his written works (particularly his multi-volume *Winning of the West* (1889–96)) he adopted a faux-cowboy folksiness to herald the birth of a new ideal of American masculinity, his own body (frequently photographed in cowboy garb), a testament to the value of clean living.[34] It is this body that, during the 1903 election campaign, rode out of Wyoming's Black Hills and into Cheyenne to be greeted by reporters from the *Tribune*: 'Down the mountain valley he came in a whirl of dust. ... The West was written in every line of his frame and clothes and bearing.' The presidential hopeful transforms himself into the storybook cowboy, in the process, according to the novelist Owen Wister, becoming a 'pioneer in taking the cowboy seriously'.[35]

Wister should know; his own Wyoming novel, *The Virginian* (1902), was published the year before Roosevelt's ride (to whom the novel is dedicated) and is so skilful in its manipulation of the accepted genre that Bernard DeVoto heralded it as the 'birth of an art'.[36] So successful was Wister in establishing the template of the serious cowboy novel, that when in 1949 Jack Schaefer allowed his eponymous *Shane* to ride out of the mountains and into Wyoming to stand up for the small man, he was following a script that had altered little from Wister's. Indeed, so formulaic had the cowboy conventions become that western commentator Wallace Stegner recalls that after reading Schaefer's manuscript (he was an editor at Houghton Mifflin at the time), he could not decide whether it was the best Western ever written, or a parody.[37]

In the year following the publication of *The Virginian*, audiences gathered in cheap theatres across America to watch yet another Wyoming cowboy drama. *The Great Train Robbery* was a 12-minute film by Edwin Porter depicting a raid by the Hole-in-the-Wall Gang on a Union Pacific train in

Wyoming in August 1900.³⁸ Hushed audiences were mesmerized by the magic of this new technology, ironically harnessed to bring to life a vision of the West with which they were reassuringly familiar. For the 'dime West', constructed out of easily recognizable archetypes engaged in activities which emphasized action over words – shoot-outs, horse chases, saloon brawls – was tailor-made for the early days of silent cinema. Porter's film is significant not only because it offered a visual reinforcement of the Western conventions but, in re-enacting a historical event, it blurred the distinction between fiction and reality. As did so many early cinematic ventures in which directors sought to transform 'real' cowboys still riding the plains – such as Kit Carson and Wyatt Earp – into 'reel' cowboys before they, like the entire frontier, passed away. Hollywood, like Cody, offered a simplified vision of America based on an unambiguous moral code. Thus, when in 1953, Alan Ladd rode into Wyoming in the title role of George Stevens' film of *Shane*, America may have passed through the Depression, two world wars and entered the nuclear age, but it was as if nothing had changed.

The upshot of all this activity is that when Proulx arrived in the West in 1995, the emptiness that faced her was apparent rather than real: the sight lines may have been long, but they all converged on the myth. Western commentator William Kittredge has described the myth as 'an insidious trap for those who would write about the American West, a box for the imagination'.³⁹ Not only does it appear to provide an endless supply of easily reworked archetypes and stories, but it also seems impervious to postmodern revision. He should know. His *Cord* series of novels – with such titles as *The Nevada War* (1982) and *Brimstone Basin* (1986) – was designed to offer a slightly feminist, self-reflexive subversion of the traditional western novel. But such nuances were missed by his loyal readership, which took his novels at face value and accused him of selling out. Larry McMurtry, self-proclaimed scourge of the mythical West (hence his suitability to co-author the screenplay for *Brokeback Mountain*), experienced similar reactions to his most popular work, *Lonesome Dove* (1985) (turned into a popular TV mini-series). He thought that he was writing the ultimate 'anti-western' in the form of a realistic account of latter-day cowboys attempting a heroic, coming-of-age cattle drive. Both readers and viewers alike received it as a historical vindication of the myth, leaving a rueful McMurtry to concede: 'The romance of the West is so powerful, you can't really swim against the current. Whatever truth about the West is printed, the legend is always more potent.'⁴⁰

If the West is a trap, then a cursory glance at Proulx's *Wyoming Stories* would suggest that she has fallen into it; for within them we find a gallery of traditional characters pressed into service – pioneers, ranchers, cowboys and Indians (there are no accountants, police officers and school teachers in her Wyoming) – living in the shadows of a John Ford landscape. However, as the title of her first collection makes clear, she is rejecting the long sight lines that have produced a mythologized West, to study the region at *Close Range*. She is taking a long, hard look at stock western characters (caricatures within the constraints of the genre), to reveal 'real' rather than 'reel' people whose character, as the subtitle to the trilogy intimates, has been moulded by a relationship with a specific landscape over generations. This is not the landscape of sublime magnificence, but, as the title to her third collection makes clear, the *Bad Dirt* of absolute indifference. For, as the pun on *Close Range* suggests, the mythical free range seems to have been 'closed' and there is nothing 'open' about a range carved up by competing petro-chemical companies, extractive industries, and suitcase ranchers. It is not a glamorous view of the West, and she concedes that some Wyomingites – who believe that the state is *Fine Just the Way It Is* – 'object mightily to my stories which do not always project upright, noble, pure characters'. However, it is a West whose only debt to mythology is its burdensome weight.[41]

Proulx's western vision differs from that held by Kittredge and McMurtry because it is that of a middle-aged woman impervious to the allure of the region's male bravado. In many ways Proulx sees herself as both observer and 'historian' of the West, a position that allows her to explore the relationship between history, fiction and the role of imaginative recreation in the stories people tell about themselves. Proulx has stated that 'almost every single one of the stories that I write about in Wyoming are founded on historical fact', an observation she enforces either intra-textually (through references to real events or people) or through the presence of detailed acknowledgements at the beginning of each collection.[42] Even the horrific 'People in Hell Just Want a Drink of Water' (*CR*), which ends in the castration of a character grotesquely maimed in a car crash, can be traced back to 'a few disturbing paragraphs' found in a regional Wyoming history by Helena Thomas Rubottom.[43] Significantly, such is the balance of journalistic reportage with historical notation (a legacy of her working past and training as a historian) combined with her forensic attention to detail (the result of all those hours spent in libraries) that most of the stories – even those which spiral into magic realism – sound as if they are based on real-life events. The voice that narrates Proulx's fairy tale of a man-eating plant, 'The Sagebrush Kid' (*FJW*), adopts a register of historical exposition augmented by the intra-textual verisimilitude derived from reference to real historical characters and events. In 'The Indian Wars Refought' (*BD*) Proulx uses the discovery of Cody's lost film of the battle of Wounded Knee to explore the role of 'authenticity' and 'imagination' in the construction of history. Here, as elsewhere in her work, fictional characters jostle with historical figures in towns drawn from the imagination but situated within the vicinity of cities locatable on a map. Their stories may be continuously punctuated by references to historical events, but their lives remain curiously detached from reality. It is a narrative ploy that reminds us of the tenuousness of our grasp on the distinction between 'fiction' and 'reality' and proves the wider implications of the collection's tagline: 'Reality's never been of much use out here.'

Proulx's approach to the West chimes with a far more wide-ranging reassessment of western history gaining currency when she arrived in Wyoming. The 'Trails: Towards a New Western History' symposium, which took place in Santa Fe in 1986, launched Patricia Limerick, Richard White and the 'New Historians' onto a collision course with the linear history of the Turner thesis.[44] Limerick offered a new vision of western history, in which ideology and myth give way to plurality and complexity.[45] For the problem with myth, as Roland Barthes has argued, is that it 'abolishes the complexity of human acts ... it does away with dialectics ... [it] organises a world which is without contradictions because it is without depth, a world wide open and wallowing in the evident'.[46] Reintroducing subtlety into western history means getting rid of the concept of frontier – the dreaded 'F Word' according to Limerick, which is shorthand for 'the place where white people get scarce'. If an account of western conquest is to make sense, she argues, then it is essential to stop seeing it as a frozen region 'with Indian people and Hispanics waiting like stage furniture for the play to begin when the white men came out'.[47] Figuratively, for literary critic Neil Campbell, this means rejecting the West as a space conceived in terms of linear growth out of rootedness (symbolized by the tree), and seeing it instead as a 'complex space of migratory, hybrid cultures that extends both within and without the region (symbolized by the complex underground horizontal root system, the rhizome).[48] The West conceived by the New Historians, therefore, is a region in which the linearity of an imposed voice of authority gives way to the many voices left out by Turner – the Native Americans, ethnic minorities, women – which, when they are heard, often reveal uncomfortable and contradictory histories.

This is not to say that one simple narrative has been replaced by a new binary and equally rigid distinction between what might be considered a 'real' and an 'imaginary' West. The myth has remained durable in the postmodern world, precisely because it is easily reducible to a set of identifiable symbols that are dislocated from their historical and geographical context. The myth, as historian Robert Athearn has observed, acts as a 'spare tire, a numbered emotional bank account, a fall-back position that is reassuring, comforting', for westerners struggling with the real world.[49] Accordingly, Neil Campbell has invoked the idea of the West as 'a third space' made up of competing dialogues, the most important of which is that of the contemporary West with its mythical past. The West becomes a dynamic environment which acknowledges that nostalgia for the old West and the lives lived by contemporary westerners are not fixed in a relationship of historical influence, but bleed into each other. In this West causal relationships are replaced by an acknowledgement that some things happen simultaneously.[50]

The West is a complex interplay of myth making and marketing that modern western inhabitants have been experiencing ever since Cody's original extravaganza. Popular culture represents the region as sublime in its harshness and westerners as free, independent and self-reliant, which is the way they like to see themselves. The reality is that in Wyoming – the self-proclaimed 'cowboy state' – ranching now accounts for only 2 per cent of the state's income, and an outdoors job is more likely to be landscape gardening than cow-punching.[51] The men who worked the land now find employment in Wal-Mart and DVD rental stores and as a consequence find it increasingly difficult to live up to the archetype of Shane. Like the Indians participating in Cody's Wild West Extravaganza they suffer by comparison with the western vision that inhabits their imagination. As Stegner observes: 'A lot of clerks and soda jerks in western cities are partly what fact and history have made them, and partly what the romantic imagination and traditional stereotypes tell them to be.'[52] The more they feel marginalized in a West that has no need of western dreams, the more fervently they cling to the world of their imagination. *Close Range* is prefaced by a quotation from a Wyoming rancher, the full text of which reads: 'It's more a tension between myth and people struggling to live up to that myth ... Reality's never been of much use out here.'[53] It is this tension that provides the grim comedy underlying Proulx's *Wyoming Stories*.

In her trilogy, Proulx's intention is to provide a corrective to the myth by giving voice to the previously marginalized – Native Americans, female pioneers, gay cowboys – while simultaneously exploring the trauma suffered by contemporary Wyomingites living in its shadow. She is not alone in this: Elaine Showalter has noted that Proulx is one of the new female western voices – which includes Terry Tempest Williams, Pam Houston, Barbara Kingsolver and Gretel Ehrlich – who have sought to claim male territory as their own. By 'territory' she seems to be looking past considerations of a male narrative and psychology to a literal male geography: the deserts and high plains of the West. She observes that Proulx 'writes about cowboys, ranchers, and drifters in ways that seem natural and unforced, and puts her version of the American West next to that of Cormac McCarthy'.[54] McCarthy makes an apt comparison for, rather like McMurtry, his best revisionist intentions seem to have been stifled by a deep-seated imaginative sympathy with the mythological West. Joyce Carol Oates has noted that both he and Proulx share an 'aesthetic wonderment for the physical terrain of the West and the big skies above', combined with a horror at the brutality of the lives of those forced to scratch out an existence on its margins.[55] But whereas McCarthy's tone of biblical declamation continually dignifies the suffering of his characters, raising it to a level commensurate with the landscape, Proulx is more interested in the incongruity between the sublime environment and the difficult lives of ordinary people living in it. The heroes of McCarthy's *Border Trilogy*, like so many of the characters inhabiting Proulx's Wyoming, are struggling to come to terms with the conflict between an idealized vision of the West and the reality they see around them. Indeed, the border in question is less geographical than imaginative. As such they are continually in search of 'authenticity' (a term freighted with contradictions), which they believe they have found in Mexico, where they can behave like the tough, taciturn cowboy heroes that fill their Hollywood-inspired imaginations.[56] In some ways John Grady and Billy Parnam would not look out of place if they rode into Proulx's Wyoming, but for all their troubled dislocation from both the landscape and contemporary society, there is still a questing masculinity and lack of interiority that lends to them a heroic stature. The grime of the contemporary West is something that they ride through on the way to somewhere else, their dreams intact. Their vision of the West, despite some tarnishing, remains noble. For Proulx, by contrast, it is the suspect nature of the dream that corrupts her cowboys, who tend to be vulnerable young men working in dead-end jobs, trapped by a shared mythology. For most it only emerges on a Saturday night when they don a pair of jeans and tight boots and yodel along to Dwight Yoakam.

This, however, is just one group that forms Proulx's focus in her *Wyoming Stories*; at the other end of the economic spectrum there are the multi-millionaires taking advantage of the state's lack of taxation to play cowboy.[57] These are, according to Limerick, the baby boomers who bought the Gene Autry lunch box and the Roy Rogers chaps and the Hopalong crayons and who now, as 50-year-olds, can afford to buy the whole ranch.[58] These men, because it is always men, are Proulx's neighbours at her Bird Cloud home – the heirs to fortunes in 'Ciba-Geigy, Anschutz, Wal-Mart, Campbell's Foods'.[59] Neighbourliness, however, does not prevent her from parodying them mercilessly through fictional creations like Wyatt Match ('Tits-Up in a Ditch', *FJW*) – whose name announces his Western pretensions – and also the science fiction actor Frank Fane ('A Pair of Spurs', *CR*), whose conception of the 'authentic' West proves every bit as fictional as his science fiction world. Another group of incoming western fantasists is the growing population of young professionals and retirees in search of the simple life away from the suburbs with its attendant crime and pollution. Geographer Jack Lessinger has coined the term 'Penturbia' to describe a new West of log 'ranchettes' with a horse in the paddock and a 4×4 in the driveway.[60] These are families like the Fairs ('Man Crawling Out of Trees', *BD*), whose laughable attempts to adapt to western ways becomes the focus of a biting satire first deployed against the 'urban bumpkins' of *Heart Songs*. Wyoming has also become a haven for those seeking alternative lifestyles. Local writer Warren Adler has observed that 'there are numerous clannish sub-cultures of people here who revel in mountain climbing or devote themselves to … other disciplines, who wouldn't or couldn't live anyplace else on the planet'.[61] Proulx fictionalizes this new western migration through her 'spandex pioneers' Caitlin and Marc ('Testimony of a Donkey', *FJW*), who have swapped leather chaps for lycra, a trusty horse for a titanium mountain bike, and the cattle trail for cross-country skiing. In the pony-tailed character Harold Batts ('A Pair of Spurs', *CR*), Proulx explores the more offbeat attraction of the region: only in the West can the production-line metal worker grow into the artist, satisfying his interest in cult religions by making spiritually inspired spurs.

Proulx's *Wyoming Stories* tell the stories of these incomers and, perhaps more tellingly, their impact upon local communities, which can be devastating. For not only do rich arrivals push up land prices and tax rates, they also introduce predatory business ethics which sit uneasily with the more old-fashioned community values of the West. Locals can find themselves 'dispossessed, disenfranchised strangers' as the local drugstore turns 'into a Ralph Lauren factory outlet, the local café into a fern bar, the coffee shop into a cappuccino bar'.[62] Wyoming novelist Tim Sandlin has observed that contemporary Wyoming is replaying *Shane*, but 'instead of ranchers against homesteaders, we have those who worked for the Western way of life against those who would buy it', while Shane plays the part of 'the tourist who only wants to be left alone'.[63] For isolated ranchers struggling to make ends meet, the pressure is to 'sell up' and 'sell out' their western heritage, thus condemning themselves to the role of support actors in somebody else's western fantasy. As western commentator Jack Hitt observes: 'The wealthy often buy a ranch and let the owner run it, turning the former rancher, his former cowboys, and his former cows into living lawn ornaments.'[64] It is a perfect example of how the real becomes hyperreal according to Baudrillard's conception. For Wyomingites, already trying to live up to a suspect mythology, the need to play the cowboy in this new version of Cody's show can be psychologically overwhelming. And yet when the 'imagined' West overwhelms the real locality and regional culture gives way to stereotypes, local inhabitants find themselves more dependent, both economically and psychologically, on the myth.[65]

To some extent, of course, Wyomingites are victims of their own success. Historian Liza Nicholas observes that very early on 'Wyomingites took note of the powerful cultural tales circulating about its region and articulated this popular culture view of the West through a tourist industry that highlighted the cowboy, the Old West, and the "western" character traits of self-sufficiency and independence.'[66] Each year, around seven million people visit Wyoming – the self-styled 'Forever-West' state with a population of less than 500,000 – where they are given the full western experience.[67] The state has over 35 Dude ranches, while its streets throng to rodeos and pageants (such as the Cheyenne Frontier Days) in which the locals dress up and play the part of caricature westerners. Cheyenne resident Carina Evans explains: 'You're encouraged to dress western during the summer because that's when the tourists come.'[68] Towns such as Jackson resemble film sets, while to take a stroll with writer JoAnn Wypijewski through the streets of Laramie is to enter a cowboy theme park:

> Wild Willie's Cowboy Bar anchors one corner downtown; a few feet away is The Rancher. Farther up the same street is the Ranger Lounge and Motel; down another, the legendary Buckhorn Bar, with its mirror scarred by a bullet hole. ... Around the corner stands the Cowboy Saloon, with its tableau of locomotives and thundering horses, lightning storms and lassos, portraits of grand old men who'd graced the town in history (Buffalo Bill Cody) and in dreams (Clint Eastwood).[69]

This is typical of Proulx's western towns, which similarly blur the distinction between the 'authentic' and the 'imaginative'. Redsled is a tourist town in which 'the pawnshop, the Safeway, the Broken Arrow bar, Custom Cowboy, the vacuum cleaner shop' jostle with incongruity ('The Mud Below', *CR*, 67). When we follow Sutton Muddyman through the streets of Signal he is confronted with two visions of the West: a computer store selling 'sunfaded boxes of obsolete software' sits next to Harold Batts' shop selling spurs. As he bends his '4× Cattleman crease' against the Wyoming wind, we, and indeed he, are unsure to which world he belongs. He is an authentic rancher, a 'Dude rancher' and also part of the decorative background: a triplet that undermines the very notion of 'authenticity' ('A Pair of Spurs', *CR*, 178). Characters who occupy similar conflicted space are those who make a living selling a commodified version of the West back to itself. Kaylee Felts has left her parents' ranch to run 'HIGH WEST – *Vintage Cowboy Gear, Western Antiques, Spurs, Collectibles*' ('The Mud Below', *CR*, 54); while Roany Hemp makes a good living selling tailored cowboy shirts and other outfits to rich ranchers ('The Governors of Wyoming', *CR*). Proulx highlights some of the conceptual ironies resulting from such merchandising through the visit to a western town made by Vergil Wheelwright in 'The Colors of Horses' (*Accordion Crimes*). Following a visit to the local supermarket, he tries on cowboy costumes at the Kowboy Korner store, before retiring to a local bar: 'Everybody in the place was wearing a message, words and images on belt buckles, t-shirts, leather labels on their jeaned rumps, names woven into hat bands, billed caps stamped KING ROPES.'[70] This is where small-town western values converge with postmodern consumer capitalism, where an 'authentic' regional identity can be purchased off the peg rather than moulded by interaction with a local landscape.

The demeaning reality facing contemporary Wyomingites is brought to surreal life in the western parade that traps rancher Gilbert Wolfscale in his car at the end of 'What Kind of Furniture would Jesus Pick?' (*BD*):

> Behind the band came two teenage boys dressed as Indians, breech-clouts over swim trunks, a load of beads around their necks, black wigs with braids and feathers... . Then two men whom he recognized as Sheridan car mechanics slouched along in buckskin suits and fur hats, carrying antique flintlocks... . Now came two horses, both bearing kids dressed as cowboys, heavy woolly chaps, pearl-button western shirts, limp bandannas, big hats, and boots... . The last of all was a CPC pickup, three hard-hatted methane gas workers sitting in the back smoking cigarettes and joking with one another. (85–6)

Here the local community consciously performs in a synthetic version of their past while also acknowledging their present and future. It is a parade worthy of Bill Cody's Wild West show, or, perhaps more pertinently, Disneyland. Jean Baudrillard understood Disneyland: it didn't offer escapism but a simpler vision of a 'real' America, the authenticity of which, like Cody's vision, rested on details. The parade is not a copy of something real, but something that has become real (or hyperreal) in its own right. Gilbert is appalled by 'the whole hokey Wild West treatment', however it represents a pared-down view of westerness to which he himself subscribes (85). Ironically, he resents the fact that there are no ranchers, but recognizes that he, like the cowboy and the Indian, needs to pass into history before he can be resurrected through the lens of nostalgia.

This moment of meta-narrative is an apt symbol of Proulx's West: a combination of self-conscious performers and bewildered onlookers struggling to come to terms with their notion of an authentic western experience. In many ways Proulx's *Wyoming Stories* offer the reader an opportunity to peek behind the scenes of Gilbert's western charade and to take in the grimness beneath the folksy entertainment. For within these stories we find retirees reinvented as pioneers; breakfast food moguls playing rancher;

tractor salesmen masquerading as cowboys; and hospital nurses finding their roots as Indians. Proulx's focus on a limited number of clichéd western characters informs the methodology of this study, which eschews a formal assessment of each collection in favour of an analysis of particular western archetypes – the Pioneer, Rancher, Cowboy and Indian. The book opens with an assessment of arguably the most important character of them all in Proulx's fiction – the Landscape – and ends with a study of those stories concerned with the Losers in the contemporary West. The three collections – *Close Range* (1999), *Bad Dirt* (2004), *Fine Just the Way It Is* (2008) – do have distinctive features of tone and subject interest, but studying them sequentially would lead to awkward repetition, hence the need for a more thematic approach. Within this broad thematic division, however, every effort has been made to deal with the stories separately. In an interview with the *Missouri Review*, Proulx noted that 'if the writer is trying to illustrate a particular period or place, a collection of short stories is a good way to take the reader inside a house of windows, each opening onto different but related views – a kind of flip book of place, time and manners'.[71] This study remains faithful to this aesthetic, taking in the view without smashing the windows.

Each collection, as intimated, does have distinctive features through which it is possible to chart Proulx's relationship with her adoptive state and her stylistic development. In *Close Range* she combines gritty realism with a strain of magical realism to catalogue the lives of Wyoming's contemporary cowboys and ranchers. Like *Heart Songs* before, these are tales of hardscrabble lives in which unfulfilled dreams, violent struggle and sexual deviance are brought to life with a taut, mutilated prose. If, as Proulx's British publisher, Christopher Potter, has noted, *Close Range* 'is about people damaged by and leaving Wyoming', then *Bad Dirt*, which followed five years later, 'is about people moving to Wyoming'.[72] These are both the urban rich and trailer trash; all those who are either seeking authentic 'bad dirt' or mired in it. This is a collection that deals with waste and excess, in which the leftovers are prominent. The great Wyoming plains evoked in *Close Range* have become littered with large-scale cattle enterprises and trailer parks, and much of the action centres on the bar-room. Critical reaction was mixed, leading some to claim that the West was written out.[73] *Fine Just the Way It Is*, as the title implies, seems a riposte to such accusations, unconscious or otherwise. It focuses on Wyoming's past – whether ancient (one story concerns a Stone Age buffalo hunt), or the pioneer experience of the nineteenth and early twentieth century. It gives voice to those who had previously remained silent: pioneer and ranching women, and the old. The tales are bleak and we are left with the impression that Wyoming is certainly not 'fine just the way it is', but there is little to be done other than suffer and endure.

One element that remains fairly constant across the trilogy (despite some diminishment in its expressive force in *Bad Dirt*) is Proulx's narrative voice. Gretel Ehrlich's observations concerning Wyoming's speech patterns are of interest here:

> The solitude in which westerners live makes them quiet. They telegraph thoughts and feelings by the way they tilt their heads and listen; pulling their Stetsons into a steep dive over their eyes.... Conversation goes on in what sounds like a private code; a few phrases imply a complex of meanings.... Sentence structure is shortened to the skin and bones of a thought. Descriptive words are dropped, even verbs.... People hold back their thoughts in what seems to be a dumbfounded silence, then erupt with an excoriating perceptive remark. Language, so compressed, becomes metaphorical.[74]

This could be a review of Proulx's collection, which is narrated by a voice characterized by compressed sentences, elliptical phrasing, missing pronouns and mutilated syntax: these are sentences written to be mumbled out of the side of the mouth around a half-smoked roll-up. Proulx creates a faux-cowboy narrative voice, which is generally ambivalent, but seems to gravitate towards the central character of a scene through diction, syntax and, indeed, tone. Proulx has suggested that the potency of this voice comes from her listening to conversations in local Wyoming bars, a practice that western writer Ivan Doig has called eavesdropping at the 'geezer table'.[75] However, perhaps Proulx's narrative voice has less to do with real Wyomingites and everything to do with the emulation of a style of writing traceable from Jack London through Ernest Hemingway to Norman Mailer. It is a style that, like Proulx's, announces its virility in its slang, choppy rhythms and bitten-off fragments; a style in which grammar is inherently feminine.[76] Furthermore, Proulx's voice has clearly been influenced by the classic Western, in which verbiage is suspect, and in which silence only gives way to laconic epigrams – of which Proulx is a master. Of course, in the zone of cultural interplay that comprises the contemporary West, we are also left to wonder about the degree to which those Wyomingites observed by Ehrlich and overheard by Proulx took their cue not from the weather, but from TV cowboys.

Across the collection, Proux's characters are constructed from an assemblage of metaphors around a name – Chad Grills, Chay Slump, Harp Daft – that seems a parody of their westerness. They are as narrow-minded as their surroundings are expansive, character traits reinforced by our limited interior access. Even when they are at their most emotionally vulnerable, we learn about their feelings not through access to their reflections, but from their actions (usually violent and animalistic); their speech patterns (raw, economical and hopelessly inarticulate); pathetic fallacy (their interior lives are moulded by landscape); assorted metaphors and recurring symbols (images of fire, mud and water dominate the emotional landscape); and the cruelly laconic observations of a disinterested narrator. They are as taciturn as their narrators, their raw edges dulled by a life of struggle within a hostile environment. Some are individualized through their own idiolects; there is a circumlocution about the speech of Horm Tinsley (often hedged with apologetic clauses), through which Proulx indicates his unfitness to ranch ('People in Hell', *CR*); the anonymous narrator of 'A Lonely Coast' (*CR*) draws her story from a dark lexis and imagery only lightened by the explosive behaviour of the central character. In a world in which verbosity may seem suspect, even effeminate, they face the harshness of their environment with stoicism and understatement. Verl Lister confronts all disaster with the listless observation: 'I had me some luck today' ('Tits-Up in a Ditch', *FJW*).

The Wyoming that Proulx conjures up in the *Wyoming Stories* lies at the intersection of reality and the imagination and is presented to us in a narrative voice that combines gritty realism with flights of magical realism. We are constantly reminded that the present is built upon and fed by the legacy of the past; a pioneer mythology constructed upon a people's struggle with a hostile landscape. It is this recurring theme that forms the bedrock of her fiction and resonates throughout the following overview of the chapters making up this study. Proulx herself claims that 'every single thing I write comes from landscape', a deceptively simple statement that aligns her with an older tradition of regional writers (Willa Cather, O. E. Rolvaag) in which the landscape performs the function of a brooding presence shaping the lives of those who live upon it.[77] Quite what Proulx means by this elusive term, and how it might differ from 'scenery' and concomitant terms such as 'wilderness', dominates the opening theoretical discussion of Chapter One of this study. It questions how landscape description can be presented as an important fictional device when it plays so little role in the lives of contemporary readers. It asks how Proulx has liberated the landscape from its reduction to tourist kitsch, and how she has transformed it from environmental victim to a brooding presence in the lives of those who live upon it. It argues that Proulx's *Wyoming Stories* offer a new *Annales*-inspired 'neo regionalism' that rejects notions of landscape as static and shrinking in favour of a more dynamic relationship with man. Familiar concepts of beauty and squalor become blurred: for Proulx landscape is both the Yellowstone Park and the Coke cans lying in the car park.

The chapter moves to an analysis of how Proulx puts theory into practice in the stories 'The Sagebrush Kid' (*FJW*), 'The Half-Skinned Steer' (*CR*) and 'Testimony of a Donkey' (*FJW*). Central to them all is the tragedy of complacent westerners undone by their failure to acknowledge the brutal landscape beneath their contemporary vision of it. 'The Sagebrush Kid' covers 150 years of Wyoming history – from stagecoach to tourist attraction – during which time the man-eating plant becomes emblematic of a landscape which, despite its apparent capitulation, will swallow up (literally) whatever man has to throw at it. In 'The Half-Skinned Steer' the cursed sagebrush is transformed into the steer of the title, which, despite its eviscerated appearance, punishes the unwary. The story explores how landscapes conform to cultural expectation; the connection between the male conquest of the land and the domination of women; and the relationship between landscape, maps and memory. 'Testimony of a Donkey' focuses on a new generation of spandex pioneers actively seeking the dangers of the landscape with which their ancestors struggled. This is a story that returns the characters to an Ur-landscape before the presence of man, a process that enables Proulx to explore the conceptual difference between European and American attitudes to landscape.

Chapter Two moves to an exploration of the pioneer experience, which Proulx characterizes as a state of mind rather than an historical event. She divides pioneers into four groups distinguished by their mode of transport – prairie schooners, railroad cars, ramshackle trucks, and luxury cars – a broad classification that she works out in her pioneer stories – 'Them Old Cowboy Songs' (*FJW*), 'The Great Divide' (*FJW*) and 'Man Crawling Out of Trees' (*BD*). The stories are set during different historical periods and concern characters of different social backgrounds and ages, but they are united in Proulx's determination to give voice to the female experience. The female pioneer, like the cowboy, is a complex interplay of myth and reality, which Proulx seeks to deconstruct in these stories. To understand her presentation fully, the chapter begins with a survey of the work of recent feminist criticism, focusing particularly on whether the move West led to greater or lesser female emancipation. Discussion then moves to an exploration of the conceptually gendered nature of the pioneer project (particularly the tendency to equate conquest of the virgin land with power over the female body), and its impact on the married couples in Proulx's stories.

The chapter then focuses on an analysis of the stories. The schooner emigrant only appears in the *Wyoming Stories* in the occasional compressed biographies that add contextual ballast to the histories of the main characters. However Proulx does write about them in 'The Goat Gland Operation' (*Accordion Crimes*), which offers a fascinating and enriching prequel to the larger collection. The title refers to a medical procedure to increase fertility, which becomes the overarching metaphor to explore emigrant themes of acceptance and rejection; the correlation between the fertility of the soil and sexual fertility; and, once again, the relationship between mastery of the land and sexual exploitation. 'Them Old Cowboy Songs' (*FJW*) draws out a comparison between the heroic but fictional suffering of men encoded in traditional cowboy ballads, and the silent suffering of women living with a conception of gentle, feminine behaviour (the 'cult of true womanhood') dangerously at odds with their harsh environment. In 'The Great Divide' (*FJW*), Proulx fast-forwards to the automotive age to explore the divisions implied by her title. It applies most obviously to the frontier, but it is also applicable to the division pioneering produces between male and female experiences, and the margin between success and failure in Proulx's Darwinian West. 'Man Crawling Out of Trees' (*BD*) brings the pioneer experience up to date as focus shifts to interstate retirees in search of the good life. Despite the passage of time, Proulx's pioneers suffer the same problems of acceptance and rejection, combined with the existential difficulty of living in an overwhelming landscape. It is, however, essentially a domestic drama in which the notion of the West becomes a means of probing the fault lines of married life.

Chapter Three moves to Proulx's ranchers. There is an ideological war being fought in the contemporary West between the rancher, who believes that he is the custodian of traditional values, and detractors who accuse him of invoking western nostalgia to mask a litany of environmental abuses. In the middle are Proulx's ranchers – men like Gilbert Wolfscale ('What Kind of Furniture', *BD*), Car Scrope ('A Pair of Spurs', *CR*), and Verl Lister ('Tits-Up in a Ditch', *FJW*) – small-scale cattlemen who find themselves threatened by federal taxes, environmentalists and suitcase ranchers. They are reactionary, violent and misogynistic, yet Proulx writes about them with great sympathy. They are presented as bemused victims of betrayal: the betrayal of an economy that does not need ranchers; of wives and children who prefer urban comforts to the austerity of the ranch; of a landscape that wants to return to desert; and a western mythology that told them they were the good guys. 'A Pair of Spurs' deals with the same themes, but this story is not simply an elegy for a certain way of life, but an exploration of the alternatives offered in the New West. The narrative's gritty realism gives way to a rich vein of magic realism as Proulx, with mocking detachment, addresses the different ranching futures envisioned by the various owners of the titular spurs. The story also explores notions of 'authenticity' when applied to the West, which it does through focus on Dude ranching and various environmental schemes committed to returning ranch land to a 'state of nature'. The latter issue is so controversial in contemporary western environmental politics that Proulx's thoughts on the subject are dealt with in a discrete section.

Focus shifts to the future of ranching, and in particular the role of the female rancher. Discussion covers the female cowboy (not to be confused with the eroticized cowgirl), embodied most clearly in the character of Mrs Freeze ('A Pair of Spurs', *CR*), before considering how the emancipated spirit of the tough-as-boots female pioneer translates into the ranching world of contemporary Wyoming. Proulx's answer is unpromising. In 'Tits-Up in a Ditch' (*FJW*) she uses the simple device of a shared name – Dakotah Lister – to demonstrate the evolution from feted prairie matriarch to scorned, single-mother granddaughter. This is a story about frontiers to female emancipation, both historical and the new 'frontier' presented by the war in Iraq. The answer suggested in 'The Bunchgrass Edge of the World' (*CR*) is hardly more positive. For despite the happy ending, which sees the successful succession of a female rancher, Proulx has to leave a recognizable Wyoming and resort to the fairy tale of Cinderella to achieve it.

In Chapter Four attention shifts to the icon of the American West – the cowboy. Proulx's interest does not lie with the historical figure – this she leaves to her essay 'How the West Was Spun' – rather she is concerned with the impact of cowboy mythology upon vulnerable young men growing up in contemporary Wyoming.[78] The chapter begins by charting the emergence of a code of masculinity detached from the reality of western lives: a code personified by the character Shane. Proulx's confused, young men want to be Shane, but create instead a version of the West that is nostalgically puerile and deeply conflicted. Nowhere is this confusion clearer than in their sexual development, for which Jack Schaefer's character, despite all his macho posturing, provides a remarkably poor role model. Proulx's stories set out to explore the sexual dysfunction that can arise in the shadow of Shane, with some surprisingly dark results. There is none darker than her western reworking of the legend of *Bluebeard* – '55 Miles to the Gas Pump' (*CR*) – which, despite its page-length brevity, introduces the core theme that dominates the presentation of her cowboys: the fabled isolation and rugged independence of the cowboy is more likely to lead to behaviour (particularly sexual) running counter to social norms than the moral elevation suggested by the mythology.

In 'People in Hell' (*CR*) Proulx updates *Shane*, but here the dark, silent figure who rides the plains is not Schaefer's romanticized gunslinger, but Rasmussen Tinsley, a character so disfigured by a car crash that he becomes a grotesque distortion of cowboy masculinity: the cowboy drawl reduced to dribbling grunts, his sexual prowess to his 'flashing' local ranch women. In 'The Mud Below' (*CR*) Proulx tells the story of Diamond Felts, an anxious, sexually naïve young man, who takes up rodeo as a model of masculinity to replace his absent father. In a story of family dysfunction, bull riding becomes an apt metaphor for exploring sexual deviance, with the result that Diamond becomes a man as disfigured on the inside by cowboy mythology as Tinsley is on the outside. In 'Brokeback Mountain' Proulx's interest is with the homoeroticism that is an unspoken part of the cowboy's historical past and his literary/screen representation. The chapter begins with a discussion of the historical evidence for cowboy homosexuality, before moving to an analysis of the homoerotic within cowboy literature and classic Westerns. It then moves to the shifting signification of the term 'Brokeback Mountain' (it has spawned numerous websites, chat rooms and entered common speech as a noun, adjective and verb), which has become a fictional space brimming with interpretative potential. Focus then centres on a close reading of Proulx's text, augmented by reference to both the screenplay and Ang Lee's film where appropriate. This reading begins with an analysis of Proulx's inspiration for the story, before proceeding to a discussion of the relationship between landscape and sexuality; the link between the cowboy myth and the homoerotic; and the relationship between cowboys and domesticity. The chapter ends with an appraisal of the story's legacy, including a discussion of the film's failure at the 2006 Academy Awards.

Chapter Five moves to a discussion of the cowboy's high plains nemesis, the Indian. Native American characters are marginal in Proulx's work, appearing mostly in subplots and forming the focus of only one of her stories. They are not, however, mere footnotes to the *Wyoming Stories*, but help to explore its central themes. As with the chapters on 'Pioneers' and 'Cowboys', this one begins with a deconstruction of the Indian archetype (charting his evolution from Montaigne's 'Noble Savage', through Cody's 'bloodthirsty warrior', to his rehabilitation as ecological sage), augmented by Proulx's academic interest in challenging many of the assumptions surrounding the pre-contact period. Her corrective vision emerges in the short story 'Deep-Blood-Greasy-Bowl' (*FJW*), an exercise in imaginative recreation that redefines the historical parameters of the notional 'Indian'. Discussion moves to consideration of some of the key questions dominating Native American intellectual politics. It traces the evolution of the Native American voice itself, beginning with the work of the early revisionist historians, through the most influential writers of the Native literary renaissance, to the voices of those contemporaries whose work has bearing on Proulx's writing. Despite the varied scope of much Native American writing, at its core is the particularly western (and very Proulxian) tragedy of the removal of a people from the land that gave them their identity. This sense of dislocation heightens the difficulty of separating the notional 'authentic' Native American identity from the culturally constructed archetype of the Indian, leading to the deceptively simple question: what is an Indian? It is a question that dominates Proulx's presentation.

There follows an analysis of Proulx's Indian characters, their marginality announced by their narrative representation as hitchhikers. In the novel

Postcards we are invited to piece together the life of Joe Blue Skies through allusions on postcards, the strange episodes recounted in the body of the text, or the hearsay of others. It is a reconstructive process that challenges our cultural expectations, while also mimicking the disruptive narrative style shared by much Native American literature. In 'The Governors of Wyoming' (*CR*), Proulx uses Wyoming's contemporary eco-terrorist campaigns to explore the correlation between the rape of the land by the first white settlers and the simultaneous rape of its female Indian inhabitants. In *That Old Ace in the Hole*, Proulx introduces the shambling figure of Moony Brassleg, whose life lies at the intersection of the spiritualized Indian world and the contemporary world of consumer culture. In the former mode, his gnomic utterances explore the difference between mapped and imaginative space; the difficulties of discovering or recreating cultural roots; and the despair of reservation life. Throughout, however, his utterances border on parody, inviting us to consider the role of Hollywood in the construction of an authentic Indian identity. Proulx returns to this theme in 'The Indian Wars Refought' (*BD*), a story devoted entirely to questions of cultural identity, assimilation and lost heritage. The title alludes to Bill Cody's lost film of the massacre of Wounded Knee (1876), which acts as a symbolic focus for the wars fought throughout the narrative. The film raises questions of bias and authenticity and, most importantly, the role of the imagination when reconstructing the past.

Chapter Six explores a very different Wyoming to that presented in *The Solace of Open Spaces*, as Proulx turns to those living on the economic margins. These are Proulx's losers: those left out during the construction of a successful economic model, condemned to a difficult life in a trailer park and a complex negotiation with their cowboy heritage. The chapter begins with a brief outline of the economic policies that have, according to one of Proulx's more vociferous characters, transformed the state into a '97,000-square-mile dog's breakfast of outside exploiters, Republican ranchers and scenery' ('The Governors of Wyoming', *CR*, 236). The characters which interest Proulx amidst this catastrophic economic mismanagement are the ranch sons dispossessed of their western legacy, and the cash-rich, culturally poor incoming roughnecks. Their narratives are located at the intersection between global economics and small-town western culture, and reflect the difficulty of adapting a cowboy culture to the realities of the global marketplace. The chapter moves to discussion of 'Job History' (*CR*), which, as the title suggests, offers a pared-down 'history' of a couple's turbulent working lives. It also explores the related issue of the survival of western regionalism in the interconnected, postmodern world. The humorous antics of Deb Sipple in 'The Trickle Down Effect' (*BD*) allow Proulx to draw a contrast between the 'cowboy capitalism' of Ronald Reagan's presidency and the community values of the West. In 'Florida Rental' (*BD*) Proulx updates Wyoming's Johnson County War to a struggle between a corporate rancher and his trailer neighbour, in the process exploring the politically explosive question of who owns the cultural capital of the West.

A detailed discussion of two stories follows: 'A Lonely Coast' (*CR*) and 'The Wamsutter Wolf' (*BD*). They, despite being focused on Wyoming's trailer community, return us to Proulx's determinist contention that characters are moulded by their interaction with a specific environment over time. These characters are, as one of them concedes, evidence that Wyoming's gene pool dried up long ago; they are losers in a brutal universe governed by Darwinian notions of 'adaptation' and 'the survival of the fittest'. In the former, Proulx employs a rare female first person narrative to explore the dysfunctional lives of a group of waitresses whose drug abuse and predatory sexuality are vindicated by a dissipated and feminized form of the cowboy myth. In the latter, Proulx introduces the narrative device of the ingénue who is unable to distinguish between cliché and authenticity to explore notions of winners and losers among Wyoming's trailer park roughnecks. This is a story full of predatory wolves – both pack and lone / corporate and sexual – Proulx's narrative inviting us to consider whether it is possible to be one while seeming the other.

Proulx's *Wyoming Stories* offer windows onto a region in which a people is defined not only by its relationship with the land but also by the myth that has grown out of that land. They may be idealistic pioneers, bemused old ranchers, displaced Indians, confused cowboys, or Trailer Rednecks, but they are united by their subordination to a crushing myth carved out by a people's struggle with a hostile landscape. The Proulx that draws back the curtain on these lives does not condemn, nor does she moralize or give in to sentimentality; she adopts the narrative pose of the outsider (a position that invites historical detachment), but writes about them with great tenderness and sympathy. She emerges from these stories as a 'true westerner': despite the transient nature of her fiction, it is quite clear that she has fallen in love with Wyoming, its brutal history and its rich gallery of eccentric characters. It only remains for us to enter the house, mount the stairs and take in the view from one of the windows: a view that will give out onto a landscape like no other: the landscape of *The Lost Frontier*.

1

Landscape

'Every single thing I write comes from landscape', Proulx claims.[1] The assertion is bold and simple and masks the complexity entailed by the conceptually slippery term 'landscape'. To the contemporary ear it implies an aesthetic appreciation of the land with possible moral undertones; a term to be employed by observers enjoying a view from which they can depart, rather than an inhabitant struggling to make a living. It recalls the awe that characterized Proulx's first reactions to Wyoming, subsequently articulated with great narrative irony by Mitchell Fair. For Proulx, however, this is scenery: landscape reduced to postcard sublimity and deployed by 'localist' writers to give a sense of exoticism and place to their dramas.[2] And there are fewer regions as rich in scenic iconography as the West. The early western novels of Bret Harte and Mary Hallock Foote are easily locatable through the description of endless plains, hoodoos, rolling tumbleweed, and cowboys in leather chaps. It is a visual grammar easily transferable to the screen: a shot of Monument Valley overlaid with a scratchy harmonica not only transports an audience West, but also evokes a hundred years of cowboy history.[3]

For Proulx, landscape is not something her characters move through, it is something they experience. As such there is a strong relationship between landscape and identity: 'I am something of a geographic determinist', she has claimed, 'Geography, geology, climate, weather, the deep past, immediate events, shape the characters and partly determine what happens to them.'[4] The story, in effect, grows out of the environment: her characters are moulded by the geography, climate and history of the region, allowing landscape to become the dominant character in her fiction. It is a view at odds with the modern penchant for the psychological novel, in which landscape is simply the mat unrolled by the acrobat before he commences his act. Consequently, critics have aligned her with an older tradition of 'naturalist' writers, such as Willa Cather, Ole Edvart Rolvaag and John Steinbeck, chroniclers of the rural dispossessed whose stories are set against brooding landscapes. For Cather and Rolvaag the story of the West *is* the story of man's confrontation with an inhospitable environment; a struggle transformed by Turner into a process by which pioneers are transformed into Americans. In Rolvaag's *The Giant in the Earth* (1927), the giant in question is not man, but rather a character trait of the plains; a conclusion reinforced by the novel's full title: *A Saga of the Prairie*. It is the land that speaks first: the rustle of the grass crushed by the wheels of the pioneer wagons is simultaneously a voice of complaint and defiance, reminding us that the plains will be there long after man has disappeared. It is a message that echoes throughout Proulx's fiction.

Such writing, Proulx argues, belongs to the 'Golden Age' of American landscape fiction (a period that fell roughly in the first half of the twentieth century) when the plot of a story was intimately tied to the location in which it was set. This period came to an end with Norman Mailer's *The Naked and the Dead* (1948), in which the characters' contempt for the authority of the natural world revealed a widening gap between urban and rural America: 'a gap that is now a vast chasm'. Since this time, landscape description has fallen out of fiction because it has fallen out of everyday American lives. Most contemporary Americans, she observes, only come into contact with the natural world as they drive through it and then 'the landmarks we look for and at are motels, signs, eateries, gas stations. The larger landscape is simply amorphous background.' As a consequence, fiction writers have turned their backs on 'what is *out there*' in favour of 'exploring the personal interior landscape'.[5]

There is, as there tends to be with such sweeping generalizations, nostalgia in Proulx's evocation of a 'Golden Age' which ignores the huge interest in landscape writing that emerged in the mid-1990s under the umbrella term 'ecofiction'. Its importance is signalled by the simultaneous rise of 'ecocriticism' (the inaugural meeting of the Association for the Study of Literature and the Environment (ASLE) took place in 1992 at the conference Western Literature Association, held that year at The Sands Hotel and Casino in Reno, Nevada – the year that Proulx's essay was published) as an academic discipline designed to remind readers that human relationships with nature are not marginal, but at the core of many texts.[6] Furthermore, as Proulx herself concedes, although landscape description has been disappearing from fiction it has re-emerged in the essays and non-fiction of writers such as Edward Abbey, Wendell Berry, Barry Lopez and Gary Snyder. These are not escapist works; rather they are concerned with man's relationship with his environment. Berry and Snyder, the latter influenced by his interest in eastern religions, offer a spiritual relationship with the landscape (one in keeping with Native American tradition), which traces the disease of modern society to man's dislocation from the land. Michael Kowalewski and Cheryll Glotfelty explain this unexpected popularity by pointing to the success of the environmental movement in increasing ordinary Americans' awareness of the natural world, combined with an interest in 'regional writing' (writing which emphasizes its connection to a certain geography) as a reaction to increasing disenchantment with national politics.[7]

This, however, is not the kind of landscape fiction that Proulx is talking about. To begin with, the term 'regional writer' does not connote a brave new world of expansive landscape fiction in the style of Steinbeck, but rather a provincialism that is the literary kiss of death to writers seeking to engage a larger audience. As Kowalewski notes: '"Regional fiction at its best" is a blurb emblazoned on any number of remaindered novels.'[8] Proulx is well aware of the 'regional writer trap', but inverts it to claim that she is in fact a 'writer of many regions', which, as it happens, are not that different in terms of 'the economic situations and the beliefs of the people who live in them'.[9] More significantly, as the term *eco* suggests, the landscape that appears in contemporary fiction is more likely to be the victim of human behaviour than its determinant. It has, as Proulx observes, been transformed from dangerous ground to fragile earth.[10] To Montanan writer, Rick Bass, the destruction of the natural environment is the defining issue of our times. Yet his critique is small scale and domestic. His targets in stories like the ironically titled 'Days of Heaven' are urban outsiders who, like the 'urban bumpkins' lampooned in both *Heart Songs* and *The Wyoming Stories*, leave a trail of destruction in their wake.[11] Other writers, by contrast, have sought to highlight much broader abuses. Edward Abbey's *The Monkey Wrench Gang* (1975) and Sharman Apt Russell's *Kill the Cowboy* (1993) have been instrumental in drawing attention to the environmental costs of unsustainable ranching methods. Others have confronted the implications of the 'nuclear West'. Leslie Silko's *Ceremony* (1977) compares the Native American spiritual relationship with the white world's pursuit of uranium for nuclear weapons; while more recently, Terry Tempest Williams' *Refuge: An Unnatural History of Family and Place* (1992) has offered an account of her mother's struggle with cancer (which she blames on nuclear testing), set against the gradually rising water levels of the Great Salt Lake: essentially the feminine body of both mother and mother nature has been contaminated and has now turned in upon itself.

The result of the 'regional' and 'eco' revolution is that writers hoping to re-establish the importance of landscape in their fiction are struggling with its cultural shift from oppressor to victim, combined with the danger of their work being branded 'regional'. There have been plenty of attempts, but Proulx argues that even novels which seem to foreground the environment in the development of plot, such as Jane Smiley's *A Thousand Acres* (1991) (in which she relocates King Lear's division of his kingdom between his three daughters to a Iowa farm), present the land as little more than 'a vague substance to be worked by agricultural machinery'.[12] More successful, perhaps, has been the use of the physical environment in Marilynne Robinson's *Housekeeping* (1981), which traces the lives of three generations of the Stone family living on the shores of lake Fingerbone. The town, like so many western towns, is dominated by its geography; the brooding mountains and the bottomless lake remind the residents of the fragility of their situation. The futility and transience of human endeavour is symbolized by the abandoned mines and quarries that ring the town: 'There was not a soul there but knew how shallow-rooted the whole town was ... anyone, on a melancholy evening, might feel that Fingerbone was a meager and difficult place.'[13] It is the lake that claims the lives of the grandfather and mother of the novel's narrator, Ruth; a symmetry that highlights Robinson's aim of offering a feminist critique of the traditional western narrative. For where the grandfather's pioneering legacy is inscribed in the landscape and looms over the lives of his daughters, the mother's contribution has remained silent and unremarked: women have no place in either the landscape or the West's conception of itself.

In the novels of Montana writer, Ivan Doig, whose work seems particularly relevant to Proulx, it is possible to chart the transformation of the landscape from the brutal taskmaster to victim. The former is presented in his western writer *This House of Sky* (1978) and the first two parts of the Montana trilogy – *English Creek* (1984) and *Dancing at Rascal Fair* (1987); the latter is depicted in the final part of the trilogy, *Ride with Me, Mariah Montana* (1990). Like Proulx, he is a trained historian and his earliest work reflects the naturalist credo that people's lives are irrevocably bound up with their environment. However, although the plot of the autobiographical *House of Sky* may read like a Cather novel, the landscape is made relevant to the contemporary reader through the avoidance of cliché and abstraction. Instead, he engages in close observation combined with the kind of linguistic vitality – compressed and inverted syntax, neologism, noun-verbs – that brings to life the sinister semi-anthropomorphized landscape familiar in Proulx's writing. When the contemporary West makes its appearance in *Ride with Me, Mariah Montana*, it is viewed with a mixture of nostalgia and pity rather than fear. Set in 1989, Jick McCaskill, the narrator of *English Creek*, is a retired rancher who is taken around Montana by his daughter and her estranged husband. The landscape of Jick's youth is now eviscerated by mining companies, overgrazed by agribusiness, and poisoned by chemical companies. The independent ranchers have sold up, their children (like Jick's son-in-law) unwilling to take on the hardship and responsibility of ranches, which now lie deserted. Their struggle is memorialized in ghostly cabins and the epithet 'place' – as in the 'Catlin place' – which become in Doig's work part of an imaginative map that ties a family's struggle and defeat to a particular piece of land.[14]

In many ways, Proulx's *Wyoming Stories* set out to tell the family story behind Doig's vacant 'places', while simultaneously acknowledging the parlous state (the pollution, pipelines and power cables) of Wyoming's present. This requires a new conception of landscape, which is not a return to the pastoral nostalgia of the localists, who simply validate western mythology through the employment of clichéd symbols; nor is it a recreation of the magnificent, but culturally evasive descriptions of McCarthy; rather it is a more inclusive conceptual understanding that seems appropriate for the postmodern world. The problem is that we are fixated upon false dialectics – landscape/cityscape; beauty/squalor; past/present – without acknowledging, Proulx argues, that it is only possible to isolate the 'wilderness' in the mind. Everything, she argues, is linked – geography, bulldozers, black squirrels and jet trails – and nothing is 'pure nor static'.[15] According to this understanding, landscape becomes a social player rather than a backdrop; a protagonist in a dynamic form of cultural practice; a 'verb' rather than a 'noun'; an agent of power, rather than a symbol of power relations.[16] It becomes a dynamic cultural product, existing in a state of reciprocity with the inhabitants who live upon it: it moulds their lives even while they alter it. This more dynamic interpretation, however, implies a less selective view of landscape, one that recognizes that beauty and squalor are often held in a delicate balance; that landscape is both the Yellowstone Park and the Coke cans lying in the visitors' car park.

Once we have acknowledged this broader definition, landscape ceases to be simply a picturesque but narratively irrelevant background and once again moves to the foreground as a major fictional presence helping to define both plot and character. It is easy to see the influence of the *Annales* School here; any community comprises a cultural landscape determined by factors such as geography, climate, economic trends and social conditions, which bring about slow, incremental change. This rejects a top-down explanation of social evolution in favour of the study of ordinary people interacting with each other and their environment over the *longue durée*. We can also see the influence of Proulx's interest in contemporary photography, particularly the work of 'topographers' like Robert Adams and Mark Klett, whose panoramas combine traditional scenic views with unsightly features that remind us of man's presence, such as billboards and oil pipelines.[17] The latter's mid-1970s project, re-photographing images captured in the original photographic

Land Survey (a nineteenth-century attempt to capture Manifest Destiny through the lens), is of particular interest. It undermines the historical authority of the former by going 'beyond the idea of the West as an exotic place out there', representing it instead as 'a place where millions of people live'.[18] We can see the full implications of Proulx's new approach to landscape in her treatment of U.S. Route 1 on the southern New England coast. Today it is a particularly depressing stretch of road, characterized by disfiguring signage and cheap motels. But it follows the more romantic wooded Indian Pequot path, a trail resonant with a history of conflict and betrayal. This landscape is not manicured to conform to the expectations of the viewer, but is a dynamic environment in which history, imagination and reality are in tension. The work of the writer, Proulx argues, is to remind the viewer of this more romantic past without falsifying the present.[19]

This intention can be observed in action in her panoramic description at the beginning of 'People in Hell' (*CR*); an opening that acts as a preface to the *Wyoming Stories* as a whole:

> YOU STAND THERE, BRACED, CLOUD SHADOWS race over the buff rock stacks as a projected film, casting a queasy, mottled ground rash. The air hisses and it is no local breeze but the great harsh sweep of wind from the turning of the earth. The wild country – indigo jags of mountain, grassy plain everlasting, tumbled stones like fallen cities, the flaring roll of sky – provokes a spiritual shudder. It is like a deep note that cannot be heard but is felt, it is like a claw in the gut.
>
> Dangerous and indifferent ground: against its fixed mass the tragedies of people count for nothing although the signs of misadventure are everywhere. No past slaughter nor cruelty, no accident nor murder that occurs on the little ranches or at the isolate crossroads with their bare populations of three or seventeen, or in the reckless trailer courts of mining towns delays the flood of morning light. Fences, cattle, roads, refineries, mines, gravel pits, traffic lights, graffiti'd celebration of athletic victory on bridge overpass, crust of blood on the Wal-Mart loading dock, the sun-faded wreaths of plastic flowers marking death on the highway are ephemeral. Other cultures have camped here a while and disappeared. Only earth and sky matter. Only the endlessly repeated flood of morning light. (107–8)

Proulx's breakdown of dialectics begins with the aesthetic distancing of the reader. In 'Dangerous Ground' she takes issue with John Brinckerhoff Jackson's old-fashioned but surprisingly persistent definition of landscape as: 'a portion of the earth's surface that can be comprehended at a glance'. She quotes approvingly the argument put forward by Native American novelist

Leslie Silko that such a definition 'assumes the viewer is somehow outside or separate from the territory he or she surveys. Viewers are as much a part of the landscape as the boulders they stand on.'[20] In the passage above we are at a moment when, according to Proulx, the viewer (who may be a character), the reader and writer 'stand metaphorically in both the unwritten and the written landscapes and enter the territory on the page at the same time it is created in the mind'.[21] Significantly, as the second person pronoun indicates, we are not an outsider viewing a landscape from a comfortable distance; we are in the midst of the weather and wind and planted firmly on the rocks, our response orchestrated by a narrator who possesses both acuity of vision and insider's knowledge unavailable to the static reader.

Proulx seems to take her cue from Cather, 'The wild country' reminding us of the description of 'The Wild Land' at the beginning of *O Pioneers!* (1913): 'The great fact was the land itself, which seemed to overwhelm the little beginnings of human society that struggled in its sombre wastes.'[22] There is an epic cadence to her description that momentarily raises us to a height suspended above the grime of the domestic tragedy about to unfold. The wind is not regional but the product of the rotating earth, and we experience a 'spiritual shudder' at the immensity of the distances contemplated. This is not a landscape to be viewed, but felt, the syntax and lexical structures mirroring the harshness of the description: it claws at the stomach, while a lexis of adverbs and adjectives – 'shudder', 'queasy', 'rash' and 'mottled – suggest sickness rather than awe. This is 'dangerous' but 'indifferent' land; it provides the tragic context in which a life of struggle gains meaning, but no moral context. While it endures, other cultures have lived, suffered and disappeared. It is not, however, a historical landscape with the expected monuments to western suffering – the graves of pioneers or the stone carvings of Native Americans – because that would be an evasion of the present. It is a landscape evocative of a romanticized legacy now dotted with 'trailer courts', 'graffitied bridges', and 'traffic lights'. As the narrative eye magnifies the contemporary scene, signs of personal suffering are deliberately small scale and mundane: the blood left on a 'Wal-Mart loading dock' or 'the sun-faded wreaths of plastic flowers' – their sun-faded appearance reminding us that no amount of grief 'delays the flood of morning light'.

There is, however, in Proulx's mixture of overwrought prose and brutal realism, combined with her narrative telescoping from planetary movements to blood stains, a giddying effect which leaves the reader with the sense that although she is evoking a specific landscape, it is grotesquely distorted. It is, as her reference to the 'projected film' implies, the West in Technicolor; indeed, it is this evocation of a landscape that is both 'familiar and strange' that makes up a Proulxian version of Baudrillard's hyperreal.[23] As the passage drifts between narrative genres (film Western, classical tragedy, domestic drama) underpinned by a narrative register which combines realism with the gravity of the epic, it seems that Proulx is deliberately drawing our attention to landscape as a mediated, cultural product rather than an objective, abstract presence. Essentially, she is conjuring a scene that says less about a specific landscape than the reader's cultural expectations. And the grandiose western landscape we expect – a vision moulded by our exposure to the descriptions of Cather and Rolvaag, classic Westerns, kitsch picture postcards, wildlife documentaries, and our occasional drive through it – is a fantasy deliberately shattered by the inclusion of the trailer parks and Wal-Marts that make up the contemporary West. Through this blurring of Wyoming's cowboy past with its superstore present, Proulx invites us to see a landscape description in terms of a whole history of man's engagement with it. Hence, despite Proulx's insistence on the solidity of the rocks upon which the reader stands, the landscape acts as a palimpsest revealing a legacy of both human interaction and cultural perception.

It is Proulx's desire to remind us that landscape is a complex cultural product that allows it to become the imaginative starting point for the flights of magical realism that permeate the entire collection. It is not simply that the fantastic landscape (endless vistas, 90-mile-an-hour winds, visible scars of an ancient past) gives rise to fantastic stories of human suffering and endurance, but also that the legacy of the West has always been a compromise between history and fiction. Indeed, the aesthetic dynamism offered by magical realism, which combines elements of social realism with magical interludes to provide a recognizable but absurd version of reality, seems an entirely appropriate response to the West. Proulx's Wyoming may be populated by ranchers and cowboys, but their stories are often mediated through the genre of the fairy tale. Some are clearly referenced – such as 'Porgier's bull' or 'Otik' (in which the western desert replaces the shadowy European woods) – but many others are simply contemporary updates of well-known fairy tales. One that falls into the latter category is 'The Bunchgrass Edge of the World' (*CR*), in which a ranch daughter's loneliness on an isolated ranch leads her to strike up a relationship with a John Deere tractor, in what turns out to be a re-framing of Cinderella. It is a story that falls out of the landscape, Proulx herself describing it in her acknowledgements as a 'vague region' where 'elements of unreality, the fantastic and improbable' converge with real life.[24] Proulx makes its importance apparent in an opening paragraph, which quietly echoes that of 'People in Hell':

> THE COUNTRY APPEARED AS EMPTY GROUND, Big sagebrush, rabbitbrush, intricate sky, flocks of small birds like packs of cards thrown

up in the air, and a faint track drifting toward the red-walled horizon. Graves were unmarked, fallen house timbers and corrals burned up in old campfires. Nothing much but weather and distance, the distance punctuated once in a while by ranch gates, and to the north the endless murmur and sun-flash of semis rolling along the interstate. (131)

Once again, Proulx appears to be taking her cue from Cather. When young Jim Burden first surveys the Nebraska plains that are to be his family's home at the beginning of *My Antonia*, he notes: 'There seemed to be nothing to see; no fences, no creeks or trees, no hills or fields ... There was nothing but land: not a country at all, but the material out of which countries are made.'[25] In her own opening description, Proulx's focus is on Jim Burden's dilemma: how the individual can make sense of such an empty, isolated environment. This is not free range – a crucible capable of sustaining the American Dream – but a landscape oppressive in its emptiness. Modernity, in the shape of the 'sun-flashes' and the 'endless murmur' of the semis as they 'roll' wavelike through the landscape, simply reminds the viewer that the ocean once covered this land, and therefore reinforces the sense of man's ephemerality. This is a land upon which man makes little impression: houses and corrals have gone up in smoke, while the graves are unmarked, the land having taken back both the inhabitants and the signs of their existence. There is a path, but the fact that it is both 'faint' and 'adrift' reminds us of the difficulty of navigating such an empty space. And yet, despite the strangeness of the ground, it only 'appears' empty; the ranches may have disappeared, but their skeletal gates remind us of the obsession with ownership that precipitated the western movement. These are families prepared to play out dynastic dramas of inheritance and legacy against the backdrop of a landscape surreal in its ambivalence.

One of the consequences of foregrounding landscape of such extremities is the danger of the diminishment of character. The classic Western pan shot of cowboys dwarfed by the rocky outcrops of Monument Valley may set the tone of a heroic struggle of man with the environment, or it may simply remind us of the futility of man's actions, even if that man is the Lone Ranger. Alan Weltzien has observed that: 'It doesn't inherently follow that big landscapes nurture little people, but Proulx emplots that formula. There are no giants in her earth, only pygmies; landforms and weather, not people, embody the heroic.'[26] The extreme harshness of her Wyoming landscape combines with loneliness and boredom to reduce human beings to their base elements, which are then twisted and distorted out of shape until they appear as grotesque caricatures. Caricature is two-dimensional; it replaces complexity with simplicity and psychology with external process, and is, as

Weltzien rightly observes, the aesthetic price for Proulx's foregrounding of landscape. It is the process of caricature that helps to establish the narrative tone of the *Wyoming Stories*, which is not premised on sympathy, pathos or even understanding, but rather on a voyeuristic mockery that distances us from the plight of her characters. Not that Proulx seems concerned by the potential limitations; she has long argued that her characters are simply a means to carry the story forward, while the complexities of human behaviour are perhaps best reported from a distance rather than pondered upon in the present.

> Characters are made to carry a particular story; that is their work. The only reason one shapes a character to look as he or she does, behave and speak in a certain way, suffer particular events, is to move the story forward in a particular direction. I do not indulge characters nor give them their heads and "see where they go," and I don't understand writers who drift downriver in company with unformed characters.[27]

In many ways Proulx's characters are the western descendants of the gallery of grotesques making up Sherwood Anderson's *Winesburg, Ohio* (1919). His caricatures explore the way in which character is distorted through alienation and loneliness. Wash Williams and Wing Biddlebaum are typical: the former is an obese and filthy misogynist who, as the local telegraph operator, is responsible for connecting people; the second is an ex-schoolteacher, whose paedophilia is blamed upon the difficulty of controlling his sensitive, roaming hands. Both would not look out of place in Proulx's Wyoming, which, as one of her characters observes, is inhabited by 'twist-face losers' who prove that the state's 'gene pool was small and the rivulets that once fed it had dried up' ('A Lonely Coast', *CR*, 221). Proulx's aesthetic intentions are signalled clearly through the cruel Dickensian names she gives her characters – Pake Bitts, Chay Slump, Dirt Sheets – which jerk the realist rug from beneath the reader's feet in a self-conscious parody of the West. Her characters, as Weltzien has observed, 'cannot wriggle out from under their cruel names', and, we might add, the cruelly compressed descriptions which perform the function of development: there is Ottaline Touhey, 'the size of a hundred-gallon propane tank' and expert in bull's scrotal circumference ('The Bunchgrass Edge of the World', *CR*, 136); slovenly, alcoholic Car Scrope, 'held together with dozens of steel pins, metal plates and lag screws', who presides over the downfall of the Coffeepot Ranch ('A Pair of Spurs', *CR*, 171); Harp Daft, bachelor telegraph operator, 'his face and neck ... a visor of scars, moles, wens, boils and acne', who keeps his female neighbours under telescopic surveillance ('Them Old Cowboy Songs', *FJW*, 52). Stripped to their base elements amidst the harsh Wyoming landscape, these characters reveal a mixture of inbreeding, petty squabbles, insatiable libido and fragile impotence that leaves the reader appalled.

Throughout her *Wyoming Stories* Proulx's characters are continually crushed by a landscape that prevents them from becoming architects of their own destiny. There are no heroes, only survivors: as Old Red observes at the end of 'The Bunchgrass Edge of the World' (*CR*): 'The main thing in life was staying power. That was it: stand around long enough you'd get to sit down' (162). It is a philosophy that brings into question Turner's myth of western conquest while simultaneously celebrating other western qualities of independence, self-reliance and stoicism. Yet, if occasionally Proulx's ambitions seem more appropriate to a classical tragedy than modern-day Wyoming, her continual mix of sublime landscape with contemporary squalor reminds us of the atavistic link that connects Wyoming's brutal past to its semi-urban present. Interestingly, Proulx's only first person narration in the collection – 'A Lonely Coast' (*CR*) – is both her least traditional, following, as it does, the grim lives of Wyoming's trailer community, and the only one in which a character appears to intuit the connection between landscape and fate.

Proulx's title is perplexing for the reader used to conceiving of Wyoming as a landlocked desert-land, but through it she evokes the 'sagebrush ocean' that met the first pioneers and also the ancient seas that once covered the state. It is this vanished sea that provides the story's central metaphor in addition to an overwhelming geological context and a catalyst for epistemological speculation. It is a trope employed by Montanan writer Rick Bass in his novella *Where the Sea Used to Be* (1998), published the year before Proulx's story. His story concerns the character of Wallis Featherstone, an oil speculator who can 'see' the ancient beach (and therefore the oil) beneath the contours of the contemporary landscape. The story is really concerned with instability, the landscape providing a geological reminder that the economic and emotional upheavals that are explored elsewhere in the narrative are a function of an environment in continual flux. To this end, Bass offers a preface with a quotation from Darwin which reminds us that there is nothing 'so unstable as the level of the crust of this earth'.[28] In such a state of instability, Bass appears to be asking, what chance has mankind of finding stable relationships?

This is the question bothering the unnamed narrator of Proulx's 'A Lonely Coast' (*CR*), as she tries to make sense of the death of her best friend during a coke-fuelled road rage shoot-out. Significantly, she lays blame not with the individuals involved, or even their drug-addled state, but with the landscape:

> You come down a grade and all at once the shining town lies below you, slung out like all western towns, and with the curved bulk of mountain

behind it. The lights trail away to the east in a brief and stubby cluster of yellow that butts hard up against the dark. And if you've ever been to the lonely coast you've seen how the shore rock drops off into the black water and how the light on the point is final. Beyond are the old rollers coming on for millions of years. It is like that here at night but instead of the rollers it's wind. But the water was here once. You think about the sea that covered this place hundreds of millions of years ago, the slow evaporation, mud turned to stone. There's nothing calm in those thoughts. It isn't finished, it can still tear apart. Nothing is finished. You take your chances. (225-6)

Once again this is a real Wyoming landscape elevated through the descriptive agency of Proulx's first person narrator to the hyperreal. Proulx has chosen her location with care. When Beth Loffreda took this route to visit the hometown of Matthew Shepard before the publication of her book on his brutal homophobic murder, she recalls it as a unique landscape. When you look beyond the plastic bags caught in the wire fence that borders the road, you become immediately aware of a geography in which dinosaur hunters 'still dig up remnants of cruel past worlds' and where it is clear that '"nature" isn't the social construction, people are'.[29] The link between the cruelty of the landscape and the brutality of the crime is implicit. In Proulx's passage, once again the reader is addressed directly and invited not only to an appreciation of the present scene, but also the narrator's comparison with a particularly bleak coastline she visited with her partner on one of their few vacations. Proulx has stated that 'I always place my characters against the idea of *mass*', and here it is in the bulk of the mountain, which gives the darkness a physical dimension.[30] The lights appear fragile rather than welcoming: a curiously organic 'yellow cluster', the 'stubby' growth of which is distorted by the darkness. Like the lighthouse on the lonely coast, they become a metaphor for the human condition; consciousness reduced to a pinprick of 'brief' illumination in a bleakly indifferent universe. With the introduction of the coastal comparison, Proulx works out the symbolic significance of her title: if the landscape is not finished then neither are people, leaving them little opportunity to determine their own lives. It is a bleak vision leading to suicidal thoughts, and therefore only to be contemplated when coked and smoked.[31]

Such moments of bleak enlightenment are rare in Proulx's fiction. In general her characters are too busy trying to survive for reflection, and when they do the landscape presents a source of bemusement rather than existential crisis. In 'What Kind of Furniture would Jesus Pick?' (*BD*) Proulx once again employs the metaphor of the sea to draw out the sense of isolation suffered by her Wyomingites, while also foregrounding the inevitability of change. These two features are effectively drawn out by the story's mock-heroic opening:

> SAILING THE SAGEBRUSH OCEAN, A TRAVELLER DISCOVERS isolated coves with trophy houses protected by electronic gates, or slanted trailers on waste ground, teetering rock formations and tilted cliffs, log houses unchanged from the nineteenth century except for the television dish. (61)

This time the reader is nowhere to be found in the composition, unless he elides with the narrator to become the ambiguous 'traveller' (a term which has connotations of psychological as well as a geographical change). Once again the narrator's voice is that of the insider describing the scene from the view of an outsider: which is entirely appropriate for a narrative concerned with how outsiders view Wyoming in general and the story's central character, Gilbert Wolfscale, in particular. The tone is portentous, but then mockingly undermined. For what is revealed through the windshield are two Wests: the mythical West of rock outcrops and log cabins, and the contemporary West, which appears – like the satellite TV dish – bolted on. Whether over the *longue durée* or the short term, the landscape is changing: change to which the story's central character is resistant. Gilbert is a man 'unmoored' as the landscape around him fills up with outsiders and the ground beneath him, which his family have farmed for generations, seems to want to 'scrape off its human ticks' (68). The real source of his bemusement, however, is his visceral need to claim ownership of such a hostile landscape: 'His feeling for the ranch was the strongest emotion that had ever moved him' (72). He both possesses and is possessed by the ranch: ownership has become an end in itself detached from economic and social context, for, as the narrative makes clear, Gilbert's possessive gaze is frozen in his boyhood. He is intoxicated by the vision of his ranch as 'timeless and unchanging in its beauty', which is not the treeless, trampled and desiccated reality. It is the legacy of ownership that blinds him to the actual landscape.

Unfortunately, in Proulx's Wyoming Gilbert's blindness is far from unusual. For all her characters work with the land, they never seem to see it, imagining instead a mythologized space detached from actual geography. This gives rise to one of the most important plot themes explored within the trilogy: the way in which the contemporary westerner is undone by their failure to acknowledge the unforgiving landscape beneath the cultural construction. It is central to both the collection's curtain raiser, 'The Half-Skinned Steer' (*CR*) (which concerns an old rancher's return to his 'place'), and one of the trilogy's final stories, 'Testimony of a Donkey' (*FJW*), which, appropriately enough, focuses on Wyoming's new thrill-seeking adventurers. These stories establish that in Wyoming you are 'on strange ground' and not in a landscape that can be approached in the same way as other places. But there again, it never was. This is the contention Proulx sets out to explore in 'The Sagebrush Kid' (*FJW*) – a contemporary fairy tale in which the spirit of Wyoming is transformed into a man-eating sage brush.

'The Sagebrush Kid'

'The Sagebrush Kid' typifies many features of Proulx's fiction. Her narrative scope is enormous (tracking the alterations to the Wyoming landscape over a period of 150 years) and comprises of a series of compressed fragments dominated by characters chiselled out of one-sentence descriptions. The story, like so many in *Fine Just the Way It Is*, emerged during Proulx's work on the collaborative history *Red Desert: History of a Place* (2006). The research for a number of her own contributions mentions the business manoeuvres of Ben Holladay (self-styled stagecoach king) during his operation of the Red Desert segment of the overland stage between 1860 and 1867, before he sold out to Wells Fargo. One incident that draws her special attention is his manipulation of the theft of copper wire by a Sioux war party from a telegraph station around Deer Creek in 1862. He exaggerates the Indian threat in a series of letters to his biggest customer, the US postal service, with the aim of allowing him to move his route to a more lucrative line. With a fiction writer's grasp of a good story, Proulx quotes extensively from the journal of Oscar Collister, telegraph operator at the station when the incident occurred. His journal entries make clear the extent of Holladay's fraud, and also record a curious allergic reaction suffered by members of the raiding party, which Proulx quotes in full:

> Some little time after this an important member of the village that the wire-stealing party belonged to, came into Deer Creek with a report that a mysterious disease had appeared in the village and had caused several deaths.... . The medicine man ordered that the wire in the camp be buried, and this was done. The disease soon subsided and the belief was universally pronounced among them that the "talking wire" was guarded by the Great Spirit, who avenged the theft and use of it.[32]

Proulx's employment of both these incidents at the beginning of her story is instructive. It immediately introduces the blurred relationship between 'fiction' and 'reality' when applied to the West, in the process preparing us for the fairy tale solution to the 'inexplicable vanishings' that took place along Holladay's route. Holladay himself takes advantage of this blurring by conjuring up the savage Wild West for nervous eastern shareholders. Collister is alive to Holladay's fraud, but his own account is presented in a curious document – *The Life of Oscar Collister, Wyoming Pioneer, as told by himself to Mrs Chas. Ellis of Difficult* – a framing structure which simultaneously promotes verisimilitude while highlighting its composite composition. For there is an artificiality about the account – the Sioux are charmingly childlike and the reference to 'talking wires' seems to be dime novel 'Indian speak' – which makes us question whose voice are we hearing: 'The important member of the village'; Collister, his idle hours at the telegraph spent reading dime Westerns; or an over-eager editor offering up Indian stereotypes for his eastern audience?

Significantly, the historical accounts upon which Proulx constructs her narrative seem to have been included to question rather than strengthen our notions of authenticity. And authenticity has always been a vital component in the presentation of the West. From the earliest pioneer accounts (generally sourced from diaries), through the adventures of Wild Bill Hickok and Billy the Kid, what mattered most to eastern consumers is that the stories were 'real'. No one understood and exploited this fact better than Bill Cody, who, as was seen in the Introduction, was the master of presenting fiction based on fact constructed on artefact. In many ways Proulx's story of 'The Sagebrush Kid' acts as a warning of the dangers of such historical reductionism. From the outset the narrator self-consciously adopts the register of historical analysis, contextualizing past events against modern equivalents, and dispensing with landscape description and character development in favour of reportage. However, because the 'historical record' offered by Collister and Holladay is of such dubious quality, Proulx underscores her narrative with a tone of gentle mockery: it is not just the characters and events that are absurd, it's the historians who record and interpret their actions. Her West, like Cody's, combines historical and fictional characters (Holladay shares dramatic space with the Fur family); with geographically real and fictional locations (the fictional Sandy Skull is located within the same geography as Rawlins); their historical authenticity validated by close attention to detail (Holladay ran Red Rupert mud wagons as opposed to the more luxurious black Concord coaches). Collister's 'medicine man' is fleshed out into the character of R. Singh, whose questionable authenticity rests on the intimidating precision of his initial, combined with the existence of documents which, according to the narrator, are too tangential to bother quoting.

The blurring of 'fiction' and 'reality' is put to the test when the narrator presents what purports to be the 'real' account of the various disappearances at the isolated staging station. We are told of stagecoaches burned by fires lit by their frozen occupants, crockery smashed to pieces in a 'whoop-up shooting contest', and a rifle buried while its owner was in the privy. But the account is delivered in such mocking tones that it seems that it is the credulous reader rather than the characters who are the object of mirth (82). But that's rather the point: in the West notions of what is 'real' are bent out of shape by isolation within a landscape so surreal that the normal rules of rationality do not apply. This is the world that Proulx records in her *Red Desert* essays, in which she quotes from the diaries of overland pioneers and cavalry officers whose landscape descriptions seem to prove the contention that 'reality's never been of much use out here'. There are pioneer parties dwarfed by a landscape which leaves them hallucinating; soldiers so cold that they freeze to their saddles; and winds so strong that cattle and horses are blown away.[33] The disappearance of livestock, horses and the occasional soldier and pioneer along Holladay's route is the starting point of Proulx's story. For how can you explain to an eastern audience that in such a country both people and cattle simply disappeared down sink holes, fell off cliffs and were eaten by marauding lions? In search of more plausible explanations, the Indians, as Holladay was well aware, could always be scapegoated. Proulx's stationmaster, Bill Fur, invokes cunning Indians to placate an emigrant party who have lost their oxen: 'They'll bresh out the tracks with a sage branch so's you'd never know but that they growed wings and flapped south' (85). Indeed, so successful was Holladay in his exaggeration of the perceived Indian threat – *perceived* is the important word here – around the Deer Creek Station in the summer of 1863, that Carroll H. Potter was tasked with securing the region with his Sixth Infantry unit. His announcement of success was followed almost immediately by the mysterious disappearance of 60 horses from the Rock Creek area.[34] The stage was set for a more surreal explanation for the 'mysterious vanishings', an explanation in keeping with the sublime landscape.

Enter 'The Sagebrush Kid', a composite of two of the West's most enduring symbols: Wyoming's eternal sagebrush and Billy the Kid. What better symbol for the western landscape could there be than a plant perfectly adapted to its brutality, and 'the Kid', a blend of fact and fiction making up an archetypal western hero? The source for Proulx's story, however, is not western at all, but a Czech fairy tale, *Otesanek*, by K. J. Erben, which was turned into the surrealist film *Little Otik* by Jan Svankmajer in 2000. In the story, the husband of a young childless couple digs up a root which has an uncanny resemblance to the human form. His wife takes it to be a baby, which she clothes and feeds. As it grows it develops a voracious appetite and is responsible for a number of mysterious disappearances – including the family cat, the postman and the father himself. On one level Proulx's narrative is simply a grim updating of this story, in which the grotesque product of all consuming desire comes back to consume its mother. Proulx transforms Deer Creek – with its connotations of pastoral abundance – into the more sinister Sandy Skull (a name more appropriate for the buried horror to follow), and creates in the characters of the stationmaster and his wife, Bill and Mizpah Fur, two Anderson-like grotesques. It is quite clear from the vignettes that Proulx constructs around the disappearance of each victim that sensitivity to symbolism should not blind the reader to the tension we feel on behalf of the unwary: this is, first and foremost, a dark fairy tale. And yet this is also a story that only gains true significance when contextualized within the landscape of the West.

Proulx's version of the story is delivered in the same mock-historical register with which she deals with Holladay's petitioning of the United States postal service. Indeed, there is an attention to 'historical' detail worthy of Bill Cody. We learn, for example, that Mizpah suckled her baby piglet with a nipple-fitted bottle that 'once contained Wilfee's Equine Liniment & Spanish Pain Destroyer' (83); we know the menus served up to gas workers from the kitchens of Mrs Quirt (89); and we are told that the notebook used by the Kid's last victim was the same as those 'used by Ernest Hemingway and Bruce Chatwin' (91). Proulx is not seeking verisimilitude through such incongruous detail, rather she is holding up a distorting lens to the familiar and transforming it into the grotesque. The technique is familiar to fairy tales and among practitioners of magic realism, but when applied to the West it becomes an indictment of Cody's historical methodology: if the details are right, so is the story.

However, the full implication of Proulx's title only becomes clear through the narration of the compressed history of the region. As the years pass, the landscape changes: the stagecoach trail gives way to the Union Pacific trans-continental railroad; it is crossed by the coast-to-coast Lincoln Highway; finally it is hollowed out by methane gas prospectors. The one constant remains the giant sagebrush, which appears in certain lights to be holding 'its arms up against the red sky' in an attitude of surrender (91). Meanwhile, it works its way through a menu of careless pioneers, deserting soldiers, methane miners, and picnickers looking for shade. As such it becomes emblematic of Proulx's West: a West built on the fiction of savage Indians ruthlessly manipulated for commercial gain; on the optimism and blood of lonely and disillusioned pioneers; and on countless brutal cowboy sagas. Its arms aloft, it suggests both a landscape and mythology surrendering to the incursions of the contemporary world. The wilderness that awed and destroyed the first emigrant parties can now be crossed in hours rather than days, its sublimity reduced to picture-postcard kitsch. As contemporary, sophisticated consumers of a commodified West, we can now enjoy the landscape as a tourist destination while consigning its dangers to a romanticized past. This is certainly true of one of the Kid's last victims, a delivery driver who is so engrossed in the western novel *Ambush on the Pecos Trail* (a conflation of two Bradfield Scott cowboy novels) that he fails to see the real danger of the landscape around him (88). But this, Proulx's narrative makes clear, is to misread the geography, which remains dangerous to the unwary. For, although Wyoming may appear to have surrendered to modernity, it will eat up everything that the modern world has to throw at it – literally!

The danger of the Wyoming landscape is a theme that underpins the trilogy, its importance signalled in the collection's curtain raiser, 'The Half-Skinned Steer' (*CR*). In this powerful frame narrative the man-eating sagebrush is replaced by the menacing eye of an eviscerated steer as a symbol of Wyoming's resistant landscape. It is another surreal and bloody version of a traditional folk tale. This time it is the Icelandic story of 'Porgeir's Bull', which concerns a grotesque, skinned creature that emerges from the woods to terrorize local villagers at night. Proulx's story, more than any other in the collection, emerged directly from her relationship with the landscape. It was the product of an invitation from the Nature Conservancy to visit one of its preserves and then contribute a story to *Off the Beaten Path* (1998). The resulting story was included in *The Best American Short Stories of the Century* (2000).

'The Half-Skinned Steer'

The story follows 83-year-old Mero Corn as he returns from the East after an absence of 60 years to the family ranch in Wyoming to bury his brother, Rollo. Narrated entirely from the perspective of Mero, the journey becomes a psychological exploration of his reasons for leaving Wyoming and his relationship with his father's girlfriend. Elegantly interwoven into this account is his memory of his own sexual awakening, his repressed desire for the girlfriend, and her narration of the story of 'The Half-Skinned Steer'. The story concerns a lazy rancher, nicknamed Tin Head because of a galvanic plate in his skull, who takes a lunch break from skinning a steer and returns to find that it has disappeared. He spots the animal in the distance and believes that the 'red eyes glaring at him' curse his family and lead to its decline. With this story ringing in his head, Mero arrives close to the ranch in a snowstorm, but gets lost and breaks down on a small road. As he attempts to complete the journey by foot, he is caught by the storm. In his death he sees the steer's red eye, which suggests that he, like Tin Head, is being punished for failing to respect the landscape.

Mero Corn is a victim of his own delusions. When we meet him at the beginning of the story he is a confident easterner: a vegetarian who keeps fit on an Exercycle and makes his money from boilers, air duct cleaning and smart investments. When he gets the call summoning him to his brother's funeral, he resolves to drive; despite his age, the distance, and the winter season, he believes that Wyoming holds no surprises for a man brought up in the West but grown successful in the East. His Cadillac, which he replaces at whim ('he could do that if he liked, buy cars like packs of cigarettes' (29)) is a symbol of his success, but it is, as he will find to his cost, useless in Wyoming's harsh landscape. His confidence is also signalled by his belief that the map of Wyoming that he carries in his head still matches the actual geography. As he crosses the state line he exultantly observes: 'Nothing had changed, not a goddamn thing, the empty pale place and its roaring wind, the distant antelope as tiny as mice, landforms shaped true to the past' (31). It is a landscape of the imagination rather than reality: the wildlife seems to have emerged from a child's toy box while the 'landforms shaped true to the past' evoke a nostalgic link to glacial carving and careful agricultural husbandry rather than mineral extraction. Because everything has changed: ranches that were once flourishing – like the deserted Farrier place – have fallen apart, and the ranch to which he is returning has become an Australian themed ranch – 'Down Under Wyoming' (35).

Through the introduction of this comical ranch, Proulx is making a serious point concerning the degree to which all landscapes are a product of cultural expectation. Just as Mero's construction of the landscape is predicated on a combination of boyhood memory and the myth of the West, our own conception of the authentic West is built on a belief in the 'naturalness' of the cattle ranch. Through her introduction of an exotic species, Proulx is reminding us, as Milane Duncan Frantz has observed, that cattle are just as artificial as emus in the West; the absurdity of the latter simply fits outside our imaginative geography.[35] Furthermore, Proulx is also using the emu to interrogate the notion of 'wild' and 'domesticated' when attached to certain animal breeds, and by extension the whole landscape. This confusion proves fatal to Rollo, who is clawed to death by an emu because he fails to recognize the wild creature beneath the absurd animal of his own advertising. His gory death not only summons his brother, but foreshadows Mero's own tragedy. This comes when his carefully constructed memory of the West (a domesticated vision transformed into postcard kitsch) comes into contact with the storm-ridden reality.

Mero's journey is not simply geographical, it is also a psychological exploration of his reasons for leaving his father's ranch some 60 years earlier.[36] Indeed, for Frantz it is his move East that has allowed him to embrace the introspection and self-awareness that are alien to the anti-psychological stance of the mythic cowboy.[37] Consequently, this is the most introspective of Proulx's stories. Apart from Louise's brief telephone call, we hear no other voice but that of Mero, who remains the focalizing agent throughout. This includes the powerful voice of the girlfriend, which is mediated through Mero. She, he is at pains to emphasize, 'was a total liar', with a storyteller's hypnotic power to draw you in so that 'she could make you smell the smoke from an unlit fire' (32, 35). Why Mero is so keen to discredit her storytelling has much to do with the sexual confusion of his younger self, and his fear of what she may have been saying to his father. For, although he congratulates himself on his sexual prowess – 'How many women were out there! He had married three or four of them and sampled plenty' – his departure was hastened by sexual confusion heightened by the girlfriend's story (33). It is a bewilderment that can be traced back to his early childhood where it emerges from a confused understanding of his landscape. When a visiting anthropologist shows him some Native American stone carvings of female genitalia, he mistakes them for horseshoes. As a result of his embarrassment, not only does Mero subsequently confuse the homophones 'cymbal' and 'symbol' (leading to a strange connection between sex and marching bands), but also from this point on 'no fleshy examples ever conquered his belief in the subterranean stony structure of female genitalia' (27). Thus, from his earliest age, sex is associated with both horses and the cold, dark and mysterious.[38]

Later, taking his cue from the ranch around him, this confused belief develops into the idea that the sexualized woman is animalistic, exemplified by his father's girlfriend, who he continually associates with a horse: 'If you admired horses you'd go for her with her arched neck and horsy buttocks, so high and haunchy you'd want to clap her on the rear' (22). She exists only in Mero's memory, and remains anonymous because she only gains significance in relation to the father and is only understood by patriarchal definitions of what is wild and erotic. After she tells the story of 'The Half-Skinned Steer' he dreams 'of horse breeding or hoarse breathing, whether the act of sex or bloody, cut-throat gasps he didn't know' (24). Sex, horses and cattle slaughter now become inextricably intertwined in his imagination, and as he begins to suspect a growing relationship between her and Rollo, he increasingly identifies himself with the steer. The full significance of Proulx's transformation of the bull of the original Icelandic tale to a steer (a castrated bull) becomes a symbol of Mero's castration complex. This symbolism, as

Bénédicte Mellion has argued, is reinforced through the inter-textual interpretation of his name, which is a truncated version of Merope, the adoptive mother of Oedipus. And Sophocles offers the literary and psychoanalytical Urtext when it comes to exploring a son's displaced erotic feelings for his mother.[39]

Once in the East, he reasons 'that it had been time for him to find his own territory and his own woman' – disturbingly Darwinian conclusions which are the product not of careful introspection but from what he had 'learned from television nature programs' (33). This, we suspect, is how Mero likes 'wild nature': he can imagine the girlfriend 'down on all fours, entered from behind and whinnying like a mare', but he shies away from the actual sexualized woman (27). He prefers his wildness – landscape or sexual – mediated through the small screen, whether a television or windshield. Sexual confusion, however, is only part of Mero's reason for leaving his father's ranch; it is also quite clear that he is not cut out for the harshness of Wyoming. But there again, as the father argues, it takes a special kind of man to run cattle where they habitually 'fell off cliffs, disappeared into sink holes' or were eaten by 'marauding lions' – an addition which forces a double-take (19). On such 'strange ground' it is possible to believe in wily Indians, a man-eating sagebrush, or the curse of a red-eyed steer (19). Certainly, the father felt inadequate to the task, breaking the cardinal rule of ranching country by giving up the 'place' to become a postman, forever wracked by guilt as he fumbled 'bills into his neighbors' mailboxes' (19). Even the young Mero and Rollo recognize his 'defection from the work of the ranch' and plan to 'pull the place taut' when given the opportunity; a plan, like so many in the collection, that never materializes (19, 20). The girlfriend seems to intuit this weakness in both father and sons, for encoded in her story is a warning that they do not possess the qualities needed to ranch in such a harsh landscape.

Tin Head is a failed rancher who blames his misfortune on the curse of the steer. However, as Ellen Boyd has noted, the girlfriend stresses that he has always been blighted, a feature she elaborates through a series of grotesque fairy tale images: 'Chickens changed colour overnight, calves was born with three legs, his kids was piebald ... Tin Head never finished nothing he started, quit halfway through a job every time' – even when skinning a steer (25).[40] While Mero, who lacks imagination throughout, dismisses the grotesquery of the chickens – 'she was a total liar' – he misses the more salient observation that Tin Head's misfortune derived from his half-hearted approach to his work (32). It is a feature that the girlfriend reinforces throughout the narrative through her repeated use of 'half' to describe Tin Head's actions: 'his pants was half-buttoned so his wienie hung out', he eats only 'half' his meal before returning to skinning the steer (25, 35). In effect, the steer becomes a personified condemnation of Tin Head's half-hearted approach to ranching in a landscape that requires full commitment. Thus, though he sees himself as cursed – 'he knows he is done for and all of his kids and their kids is done for' – the only thing that passes through the generations is his lack of commitment (38). And this is the moral of the story for Rollo and Mero: either commit or get out now.

Mero, for the environmental and psycho-sexual reasons suggested, escaped, leaving the ranch and perhaps even the girlfriend to Rollo. Mero's absence and also the stewardship of the ranch do not concern Proulx; she is only interested in exploring the motives for his return. It is clearly not pity or respect, but rather a desire to 'see his brother dropped in a red Wyoming hole' combined with a curiosity as to whether he had 'thrown a saddle on [the girlfriend] and ridden off into the sunset' (22, 24). Both images, like the eyes of the steer, are blood red – and together they form a web of literary allusion which gives the reader a sense of the forces compelling Mero towards his meeting with the steer. Blood oozes through the narrative: his brother, Rollo, is not just killed, he is brutally disembowelled – laid open 'from belly to breakfast', much like the steer, whose skinning is related in brutal detail: 'he ties up the back legs, hoists it up and sticks it, shoves the tub under to catch the blood' (21, 32). From this point on, the ranch in Mero's imagination is not steeped in nostalgia, but teetering on tubs of 'dark, coagulated fluid' – blood (29). The steer's blood-red eye is transformed into the red tail-lights of the cars on the interstate which lead him to Wyoming; blood can be seen in the dark fluids that drip out of his written-off Cadillac; it is visible in the reflection of the tail-lights, 'like a fresh bloodstain', in the snow which illuminate his death (37).

The web of blood imagery is complemented by the narrative pathetic fallacy, which reinforces the draw of the land while foreshadowing the dramatic denouement. Proulx uses the image of the 'compelled upstroke' of the 'rope of lightning' surrounded by verbs that suggest the violent, involuntary tug of a cord – 'jerk', 'pulled' – to create a sense of the powerful deterministic forces prompting his decision to return (22). During the journey the sky is described as 'curdled', connoting an unpalatable mixture, and it is also anthropomorphized into a moody giant, which is 'hulked sullen'. It squeezes down on the earth, leaving too little room for the sun, which 'bulged against the horizon' (34, 30). The most pervasive element is the Wyoming wind, which even punishes the snowflakes as it sends them 'writhing across the asphalt' of the road in front of him, transforming it into a 'rushing river of cold whiteout foam' (33).

In such conditions it is little wonder that the map in his head does not match the landscape before him.[41] As he acknowledges: 'The map of the ranch in his memory was not as bright now, but scuffed and obliterated as though trodden. The remembered gates collapsed, fences wavered, while the badland features swelled into massive prominence' (39). The trouble with maps, both real and imaginary, is that they are representations of a world held in stasis, while the landscape exists in a state of permanent alteration; a fact signified by the well-trodden path. Such scuffing should act as a source of comfort, a sign of civilization, but here it distorts because it shows change. Gates, which once parcelled the landscape into individual ranches, have now collapsed, allowing the 'badlands' to swell to their previous dimensions. Yet even in death, Mero is unable to see the landscape in front of him:

> The violent country showed itself, the cliffs rearing at the moon, the snow smoking off the prairie like steam, the white flank of the ranch slashed with fence cuts, the sagebrush glittering and along the creek black tangles of willow bunched like dead hair. (40)

Seen through his eyes it is the anthropomorphized 'violent country' (a description which sounds like the title of a John Wayne Western), which conforms to cowboy cliché rather than geography. The prairie 'smokes' and the surrounding cliffs appear to be rearing like a horse to the moon in a typical cowboy pose. In death, we are told that Mero finally understands that the steer's red-eyed stare had always been on him; a moment of seeming elucidation which only clarifies his self-delusion. For, although the steer is not to be confused with the world of Mero's Exercycle and Cadillac (it remains on the other side of the fence with the wild country), its interpretative significance remains elastic. On one level Mero's final moments 'in the howling, wintry light' provide the anagnorisis of the Oedipus narrative suggested by his name, according to which he recognizes the combination of sexual impotence and laziness that drove him from the ranch (41). On another level, the steer, like the Sagebrush Kid, is a reminder that though it, like the ranch and the wider Wyoming landscape may have been eviscerated, its 'flanks' slashed and left for dead, all three survive and will put paid to the 'cattleman gone wrong' (30).

'Testimony of a Donkey'

There is no man-eating sagebrush or red-eyed steer in 'Testimony of a Donkey' – there isn't even a donkey: there is just the crushing landscape. The story focuses on the outdoor adventurers who have transformed the principles of the Turner thesis, in which the individual develops through struggle with a hostile environment, into a lifestyle choice. The central characters, Caitlin and Marc, meet in Idaho and are drawn together through their love of hiking: 'The real focus of their lives was neither work nor clutching love, but wilderness travel ... The rough country was their emotional centre' (155). They are, however, very different characters: Caitlin has only been out of the state twice, but is in a state of rebellion against her parochialism; she has become a vegetarian and indulges in a kitsch spirituality. Marc, by contrast, is 'a man more at home in Europe than the American West', who combines an appreciation for music with sophisticated cooking and a tendency towards the aphorism (151). To some extent, the East/West tension explored in Mero is taken to breaking point through Proulx's characterization of Marc. This tension explodes the evening before one of their expeditions during an argument over a head of lettuce; this elicits the catalogue of irritations to which all relationships are prone (the historical testimony of the title). When Marc packs his bags and takes a plane to Greece, Caitlin hikes the planned trail alone as a demonstration of her independence. Unfortunately, while recklessly scrambling up a cliff she becomes trapped by a rock and the second half of the narrative records her slow death.

Like 'The Half-Skinned Steer', this is a story concerned with the relationship between landscape, maps and memory, in which navigating a difficult landscape becomes a metaphor for the challenges of living a life. Proulx foregrounds her intentions through the rare addition of an epigraph: 'Traveller, there is no path. Paths are made by walking' – a statement which prepares the reader for a moral fable that challenges the glibness of Caitlin's belief that 'the rough country' was the emotional centre of her relationship with Marc. Paths, of course, are a common literary metaphor, which take on a new power when applied to the expansive West. The poet Gary Snyder discusses their metaphoric possibilities and importance in his essay 'On the Path, Off the Trail' (*The Practice of the Wild*, 1990), in which he addresses the relationship between freedom and responsibility, and discipline and spontaneity. Using a conflation of Buddhist and Native American teaching, he argues that while the freedom of the wilderness may be enticing, there is no path because there is no destination. His conclusion could be directed at Caitlin: 'We need paths and trails and will always be maintaining them. You must first be on the path, before you can turn and walk into the wild.'[42]

The Caitlin we meet at the beginning of the story is young, rebellious and lost, seeking a closer communion with the rural West, but reluctant to follow the paths previously trodden. There is, we are warned, an element of artifice in her rebellion, as if it has been scripted by TV. This is made obvious through her beauty salon highlights, which mimic '1930s movie stars', and also her transformation of a discarded TV into an oriental shrine to whichever juju god takes her fancy (153). There is also an element of teenage fantasy in those exotic elements of Marc's biography that she finds attractive, particularly the Basque ancestor whose project of using composite photographs to find the face of 'the Universal Upright Man' is an endearingly eccentric precursor to her own search (155). In Marc she believes that she has found 'Mr Right' – his 'arched Iberian nose' and 'Mephistophelian aura' suggesting a composite picture of all Caitlin's bohemian desires: just the sort of boy to wreak havoc with her parents' parochialism (153).

Mephistophelian Marc does indeed appear to be the right partner, his suitability made apparent through his attitude to the Wyoming landscape. On their first hike together he takes her to a walking region called the 'Seven Devils', but chooses the 'Dice Roll trail', a path she has previously rejected because she considered it for tourists (152). This typifies their natures: Marc's apparent spontaneity is carefully controlled; he may choose trails that suggest devilish danger, but his preparations are meticulous. His bohemianism is fastidious: he is an adventurous skier but refuses to ski off-piste for fear of avalanche; he buys two tickets for Athens on the spur of the moment, but it is to put out fires (156, 162). He enjoys a spiritual communion with the landscape, but, unlike Mero, he never confuses the landscape before him for an imaginative ideal. Caitlin is made of flammable stuff: she can happily decorate the inside of their hired trailer in a lurid, fake bohemianism regardless of the consequences; she skis in storms; she can reject a path because it appears too conventional; and later, of course, she will hike the Jade trail, alone. Marc is what Caitlin needs; they may share 'lapsarian atavistic tastes', but he offers a means of taming the confusion. Thus, as they stand overlooking the 'the chaos of Hell's Canyon', it is clear that on an allegorical level he is enabling her to journey above, rather than through, such torment (152).

For all their talk of the wild country, however, they remain outsiders unwilling to commit to either the landscape or each other. They are essentially isolated but in harmony, and it takes very little to destroy their relationship: something as small as a head of lettuce. Their argument is the emotional centre of the story and is contextualized against their preparations for the illegal walk of the Jade trail. Marc relishes the breach of the rules, but his preparations are minutely controlled. This leads to Caitlin's irritation, which, since she remains the scene's focalizing agent, we experience through a number of present-tense observations concerning culinary matters. As the initial verbal jabs give way to more fundamental criticisms, the reader is withdrawn from the immediate exchange in favour of narrative reportage. The effect is to emphasize the universality of the argument while also drawing a deeper allegorical significance out of the relationship. Marc accuses Caitlin of being an 'American bitch' living in a 'constipated place of white, narrow-minded Republicans with the same right-wing opinions', resistant to decent food, good conversation and diversity (161). Through his 'Testimony of the Donkey' he unearths a damning indictment of the Turner thesis. The struggle endured during the push West was supposed to transform Europeans into Americans – hardy, self-sufficient, freedom-loving democrats at one with the landscape; it has instead produced rapacious individualists with a narrow-minded contempt for the land and those who do not share their vision. Caitlin represents Manifest Destiny gone wrong; a lost, little girl whose pioneer spirit has re-emerged as pseudo-spiritual recklessness.

This recklessness emerges most clearly in her decision to walk the Jade trail alone following Marc's departure. She is determined to prove her independence, not simply from Marc, but from the modern world: she leaves her cell phone and GPS behind in order to heighten her senses; she does not even have a map. She is trail blazing here as she has been in life, rejecting the irritatingly cautious conventions of her parents, landlord and Marc, preferring instead to rely on her own combustible intuitions. In this way, her journey, like that of Mero, becomes less geographical and more psychological. Initially, as she records her visual intoxication, it appears that Caitlin, like Gretel Ehrlich, will find spiritual succour in her surroundings:

> This perfection of colour and place, too rare and too much to absorb, induced a great sadness; she did not know why and thought it might be rooted in a primordial sense of the spiritual ... The solitude provoked existential thoughts, and she regretted the argument with Marc which fell steadily toward the importance of a fuzz of dust. (167)

Proulx, however, defies the pastoral morality tale; Caitlin will be denied the 'solace of open spaces' because it is too solipsistic. Throughout the narrative we are warned of the partiality of Caitlin's view of the landscape. We are continually invited to view through her eyes – to see her surroundings as in turn 'cruel' and 'blessed' in accordance with her mood. When we are not looking through her eyes, it is those of the absent Marc, who offers a conditioning influence on so much of what Caitlin wants to see. Thus Caitlin, like Mero, never sees what is in front of her, only an idealized version mediated through her lover. And it is this distorted vision that leads to her entrapment at the climax of the story.

Proulx's moral in this story seems clear: Wyoming's beauty may dazzle, but it also swallows up the unwary. There are no fairy tale monsters, just a cliff and a boulder that reclaims its victim in slow motion. The scene is clearly inspired by the cliff facing Proulx's living room at Bird Cloud, upon which she has found a number of scrawled names: the lowest one being JOHNSON (the name Caitlin gives to the Jay that follows her), the highest proving indecipherable – an unknown language, possibly Finnish.[43] In the story, Proulx incorporates a similarly indecipherable name to warn us of Caitlin's hubris. She romanticizes it as some important explorer, a famous name that vindicates her own sense of accomplishment and individuality. She is therefore disappointed to find the daubed name of 'some old Mexican sheepherder' – a name that, like Marc, reminds her of her ordinariness (169).

Her death, however, is far from ordinary. From the outset, Proulx has emphasized that Caitlin's journey has been less geographical than chronological as she passes through ancient forests and glacial lakes to learn the superficiality of her relationship with the 'the rough country'. It is a spiritual journey in which the individual is stripped of their modernity, their dignity and eventually their humanity as they are reclaimed by the Wyoming landscape. Proulx has explored similar territory before, most notably in her short story 'The Wer-Trout' (*Heart Songs*). Human relationships with the landscape are once again introduced through a monster, this time an absurd parody of the werewolf. In this Proulxian deconstruction of the familiar buddy narrative, the ironically named Rivers (an alcoholic urban incomer with an interest in Chinese philosophy), and his neighbour, Sauvage, escape for a weekend's fishing away from the troubled relationships with their wives. Proulx's use of a semi-anthropomorphized river as a metaphor for self-discovery has echoes of Conrad's *Heart of Darkness*. As they journey towards the spring of their pain and consequently a degree of self-understanding, Sauvage reveals himself to be shallow rather than savage, preferring to remain in the safe waters. Rivers, by contrast, wants to uncover the heart of his failings; an answer he finds in the bog-land source which draws him on like a whiskey bottle.[44]

Caitlin's trek offers a similar voyage of self-discovery, filling her with a 'primordial sense of the spiritual' (167). Although the landscape is empty, it is maliciously alive in a brutal struggle for existence: her pathway is 'choked' and her arms 'clawed' by broken branches, and the rock which is to be her prison warder emits a 'stony rasp as though clearing its throat' when she first steps on it (164, 169). She, like those named on the wall above her, has awakened the slumbering Wyoming landscape, which will now reclaim her. Her slow death (it takes over five pages!) mixes the realism of her limited perception (combined with continual bodily diagnosis) with more lyrical passages that reflect her disintegrating mind. Time ceases to have objective reality and 'writhed' and 'fluttered' in accordance with her suffering. Language also ceases to have meaning, her final 'Maaaa' approximates a primal wail rather than her presumed call to either Marc or her mother (174, 176). Oddly, however, we do not feel pity. Caitlin's suffering shares more with the classical figure of Niobe, whose hubris was punished by her transformation into stone, or Prometheus, who was tormented on a rock and brought to greater knowledge of the world around him. The lesson that Caitlin learns, albeit too late, comes from the lichen that covers the stone that imprisons her (167). According to Marc, lichens were the world's first plants and they 'were still devouring the mountains', converting rock to soil and enabling life (167). Caitlin becomes part of this process, 'her hands and arms' turning slowly 'to black and grey leather, a kind of lichen' (175). Essentially, the lesson taught by the rock with the 'malevolent personality' is similar to that given by the 'Sagebrush Kid' and the 'Half-Skinned Steer': Mankind, for all his fencing, mining and drilling, cannot alter the landscape; instead, the landscape will reclaim man (171).

In Proulx's fiction, landscape description re-emerges as significant in the development of plot and character. This is no mean feat in a contemporary world in which people's experience of the natural environment is limited to television documentaries, car journeys and organic food stores. It is a problem amplified in the West, where landscape features have stopped referring to a particular geography and become part of a visual grammar designed to evoke an entire cultural legacy. Proulx's *Annales*-inspired solution is to offer a new notion of landscape, which deliberately foregrounds its position as cultural product. Landscape is transformed from something static and 'out there' to a palimpsest revealing a legacy of human interaction. Such a conception demands a less selective, but more dynamic view of landscape that blurs the distinctions between beauty and squalor, in the process reminding the reader that their environment is the product of cultural expectation. Proulx's characters, for all they work with the land, are unable to differentiate between the authentic and the artificial: that is their tragedy. Through the agency of a carnivorous sagebrush, a half-skinned steer and a malevolent rock, Proulx sets out to remind the reader that beneath the postcard kitsch and trailer park grime, Wyoming remains 'dangerous ground' for the unwary.

2

Pioneers

In a virtuoso performance worthy of Bill Cody, Frederick Jackson Turner's delivery of his 'Frontier Thesis' ended with the intriguing concept of its closure. Around 1890, he argued, census data suggested that there was no new land to be discovered, thus bringing the curtain down on the first epoch of American history. The West, defined in terms of a process of struggle rather than a geographical location, was closed, giving rise to a generation of historians determined to capture its essence for perpetuity while warning of the spectre of Malthusian overcrowding. More pressingly, they questioned where immigrants could learn the essential American qualities of hardiness and self-reliance if not through the experience of frontier pioneering. Where, demanded Theodore Roosevelt in the most Darwinian of his works, *The Winning of the West* (1889), was the young American to escape the emasculation of the East and re-create himself through struggle? He need not have worried: not only do the facts question Turner's rather arbitrary date of closure (there were more homesteads established after 1900 than before[1]), but the concept of both the 'frontier' and by association the 'pioneer' had, like so many products of the West, long ceased to reflect any relation between an actual geography and a real population, if, indeed, they ever had.

Proulx, like the many historians following Turner, is alive to the conceptual elasticity attached to both terms. Her thoughts are revealed in the essay 'Traversing the Desert' in which she discusses the westward migration over this most inhospitable terrain. Although the pioneers who followed the Cherokee trail may be long gone, their legacy is written into the landscape, not by graves, which are unmarked, but by their wheel ruts.[2] It is movement that is their monument; a process that transforms the day-trippers who now follow this route into modern-day pioneers: tourists become travellers. It recalls Stegner's notion of the West as 'not a place but a way, a trail to the Promised Land', its routes marked not by 'settlements' but by 'way stations'.[3] What changes for Proulx in the pioneer experience is the means of transport.

Proulx's essay divides pioneers into four groups: those who packed their lives into a prairie schooner and moved West pursuing the agrarian dream of free land; railroad pioneers who travelled West inspired by railroad advertising; automotive pioneers travelling in ramshackle trucks (Proulx argues 'the invention and manufacture of the automobile and paved highways provided the national psyche with a surrogate frontier'[4]); and interstate pioneers in search of a pastoral dream. This broad classification forms the basis of her presentation of pioneers in the *Wyoming Stories*: 'Them Old Cowboy Songs' (*FJW*) records the experiences of Rose and Archie McLaverty, homesteading emigrants brought West by the railroad companies' promise of cheap, fruitful land; 'The Great Divide' (*FJW*) introduces the automobile pioneers, Hi Alcorn and his wife, who buy into the pioneer dream packaged by unscrupulous real-estate agents; in 'Man Crawling Out of Trees' (*BD*) we meet Eugenie and Mitchell Fair, who have escaped the crime and grime of the city and have retired West in search of clean air and cowboy dreams. Schooner pioneers are absent from the *Wyoming Stories*, their biographies recorded in compressed histories rather than forming the focus of individual tales. Proulx does write about them at length in 'The Goat Gland Operation' (*Accordion Crimes*), which, for reasons of context, will also be discussed in detail.

These stories appear in different volumes covering a decade of Proulx's writing career; they concern characters of different social backgrounds and ages struggling in a variety of historical periods, but they are united in her determination to give voice to the female experience. For Proulx, pioneering is a male activity engaged in by naïve young men dragging their reluctant and largely silent wives into a dream of western nostalgia. This is, of course, far from unusual, but lies at the heart of the western literary narrative from Cather and Rolvaag onwards. It is a trope clearly exemplified by Stegner's notion of the *Big Rock Candy Mountain* (1943), the illusive location 'where life was effortless and rich and unrestricted and full of adventure and action, where something could be had for nothing'. Unfortunately, locating it becomes a very masculine quest for Bo Mason, to which his wife, Elsa, is a reluctant accomplice.[5] Proulx's work builds on such gender tension, her approach reflecting the re-evaluation of the female pioneer experience that formed an important part of the general overhaul of western history taking place in the mid-1980s (outlined in the Introduction). Of central importance is the deconstruction of the archetypes of 'the prairie madonna' and the 'soiled dove'. The latter, epitomized by Calamity Jane and Belle Starr, need not detain us; she does not appear in Proulx's fiction until the advent of her late twentieth-century trailer-trash sister, Joanna Skiles ('A Lonely Coast' (CR)). The prairie madonna, however, immortalized in statues off the highway in Oklahoma, Kansas and Nevada, offers an interesting starting point for Proulx's critique. Historian Teresa Jordan makes clear her attributes:

> She made great pies, babies, and floursack curtains ... She rose in the middle of the night to punch down her bread. She kept immaculate house under impossible conditions – floors of raw dirt or unfinished wood; windows little more than holes in the wall blocked by shutters that swung insecurely shut on rawhide hinges.[6]

She may have had a baby on the hip, but she had a shotgun in the hand ready to ward off savage Indians. And yet, despite her hardiness and capacity for violence, she was also regarded as a 'gentle tamer', both of the landscape and masculine excess. She brought table manners, family values, sobriety and a dose of Christianity to the Wild West. Essentially the process of civilizing and feminizing became synonymous.

Concomitant with, and in opposition to, the image of the prairie madonna is that of the 'suffering angel', wrenched tearfully from the sophistication of the East to the barbarous West, condemned to a life of isolation and drudgery. She is a woman cut off from female companionship and abused by a patriarchy unhindered by the social constraints apparent in the communities from which they had departed. Overworked and over-birthed she is driven insane by the sheer physical drudgery. As Patricia Limerick notes:

> Of all the possible candidates, the long-suffering white female pioneer seemed to be the closest thing to an authentic innocent victim. Torn from family and civilisation, overworked and lonely, disoriented by an unfamiliar landscape, frontierswomen could seem to be tragic martyrs to their husbands' wilful ambitions.[7]

The feisty madonna – at home with a hoe, shotgun or broom; the suffering angel – isolated by landscape and patriarchy: these are the positions occupied by women in pioneer fiction such as Willa Cather's *My Antonia* (1918), Ruth Suckow's *Country People* (1924), Dorothy Scarborough's *The Wind* (1925), and Ole Rolvaag's *Giants in the Earth* (1927).

Much of the historical re-evaluation that began in the 1980s sought to establish the truth behind these contrasting archetypes by giving voice to the female experience. However, locating such a voice in a western space usually filled with the heroic exploits of men recorded admiringly by male historians – what Susan Armitage has termed 'Hisland' – proved problematic.[8] Official documentation was replaced by letters and diaries as the New Historians attempted to construct a coherent account of women's experience; a methodology which, according to some feminist critics, simply reinforces a gender binary of Male/Public, Female/Private, while excluding those who were not writing.⁹ Methodological debates aside, one simple question dominated this revisionary period: did the move West leave women more or less emancipated than their eastern counterparts? The West is full of contradictions: it exudes the testosterone of male conquest and yet was the first American region to accept female suffrage, and Wyoming – home of the cowboy – was the first state to grant equal rights to women on 12 October 1869. (It is probable that there was little progressive ideology behind this move: Wyoming was resource rich, but lacked the essential resource to take advantage: people. Extending suffrage was a cheap way of attracting the necessary workforce.¹⁰) Something of this schizophrenia is to be found in early feminist criticism: when Julie Roy Jeffrey set out to research her ground-breaking study *Frontier Women* (1979), she felt confident that she would 'find that pioneer women used the frontier as a means of liberating themselves from stereotypes and behaviors which [they] found constricting and sexist'. Unfortunately, she records, 'I discovered that they did not.'¹¹ Jeffrey's findings would have been no surprise to historian David Potter whose research reveals the truth behind the frontier aphorism that the West 'is all right for men and dogs, but it's hell for women and horses'.¹² He argues that it was the urban rather than the western space that provided women with economic and social opportunity and therefore female emancipation began where the frontier ended.¹³

The opposing viewpoint is ably articulated by Page Smith who observed that: 'When Eastern ladies were fainting at a coarse word or a vulgar sight their Western sisters fought off Indians, ran cattle, made homes and raised children in the wilderness. It was in the West, in consequence, that women had the greatest status.'¹⁴ Katherine Harris paints a picture of female pioneers as vigorous participants in the frontier experience, their roles not simply confined to mother and housekeeper, but also provider of cash crops and participants in local educational and church matters. The western emphasis on the role of helpmate, particularly because men were often forced to take jobs outside the homestead in order to secure a stable income, gave women a greater share of responsibility and decision making in the family.¹⁵ These more optimistic findings were reinforced by Paula Nelson's *After the West Was Won* (1986) and Harriet Sigerman's aptly titled *Land of Many Hands* (1997), which used as evidence of greater emancipation the large number of women pioneers who sought to claim their own rights following the Homestead Act of 1862.

A compromise between these two positions is to be found in Sandra L. Myres' *Westering Women and the Frontier Experience, 1800–1915* (1982). She argues that during the process of settlement gender roles became fluid as harsh conditions forced women into traditionally masculine roles. This led to a sense of self-sufficiency that never quite disappeared. However, as frontier conditions gave way to more settled communities, the men moved into the marketplace and women were confined to home, not by a vicious patriarchy, but by the much more sophisticated and restrictive 'Cult of True Womanhood'. Women's behaviour became the focus of control by an unlikely alliance of fashionable Ladies Magazines (which transformed clothing into fashion and manners into etiquette); the church (which extolled virtues of temperance, chastity and loyalty); and medical practitioners (whose discourse constantly sought to define the 'feminine nature' as a softer version of its male equivalent). The new woman must be modest, accomplished, submissive, educated and genteel, just like urban Europeans. The clash of ideology left many pioneer women in a compromising position: to ignore such dictates risked being branded a slovenly housekeeper by curtain-twitching neighbours, but to give in meant an impractical battle against dirt.[16] Elizabeth Jameson points to the telling case of the pioneer woman, Beulah Pryor, who carried out heavy manual labour in order to afford a corset, which she then wore while carrying out heavy manual labour. The resulting hysterectomy offers an ironic commentary on the dangers of women following masculinized versions of femininity on the frontier.[17]

Myres' work is not without its critics; its title, as Peggy Pascoe has noted, is illustrative of a mind-set unable to escape Turner's linearity of western movement. Defining women in the West, she argues, will never come of age until historians and writers stop seeing the frontier as a 'geographical freeway' and start seeing women pioneers at a 'cultural crossroads'.[18] More recent research, therefore, has moved away from its reliance on the correspondence of literate white women to different ethnic groupings from a variety of social classes. Proulx's West, however, is not at a cultural crossroads; indeed, she conceives of the pioneer experience in terms of the trails that Pascoe is so keen to erase. As a consequence her female pioneers – especially those represented in 'Them Old Cowboy Songs' and 'The Great Divide' – reflect the confused individuals portrayed by Myres. They are both reluctant prisoners of their husbands' ambitions, and keen participants in the pioneer project; they are fiercely proud of their right to self-determination, but tormented by the need to conform to visions of feminine behaviour. They are, in essence, deeply conflicted.

Before discussing these stories, however, I would like to turn to another feature of the female pioneer experience that was undergoing revision in the early 1980s: the metaphorical relationship between women and landscape. Gender, according to Louise Westling, is central to understanding American literary attitudes to landscape; attitudes which are at once misogynistic and erotic, cloyingly sentimental and brutally exploitative.[19] The misogynistic potential is apparent in the title of Henry Nash Smith's seminal *Virgin Land: The American West as Myth and Symbol* (1950) – a work that gave birth to the whole field of American studies. His rhetorical conception of a virginal country waiting to be deflowered and seeded with the components of masculine culture is a trope against which feminist scholars have been rebelling ever since. Much early work in this field was inspired by Annette Kolodny's *The Lay of the Land* (1975), in which she argues that the discovery of America allowed the dead metaphor of the feminized landscape beloved by European Romantics to be revitalized and re-enter the vocabulary of everyday discourse. At its heart is the uncomfortable tendency to see landscape as both an Earth Mother (a bountiful protector who would provide for her sons), and a 'virgin wilderness' to be 'penetrated', 'husbanded' and 'mastered' – both extremes validated by the concept of Manifest Destiny. Once the landscape is seen as female it becomes a playground for infantile male desire, which leads to the development of some unsettling metaphorical relationships, including maternal rape and incest. Once mastered, there arises a 'pastoral paradox' in which the male conqueror, through his violent act of conquest, loses both emotional and psychological contact with the very object of his desire: a distancing played out repeatedly in American fiction.[20] Although feminist scholarship has moved on a good way since Kolodny, her views remain influential generally, and decisive when considering Proulx's pioneer experience. This is particularly pertinent in her chapter 'The Goat Gland Operation' taken from *Accordion Crimes*.

'The Goat Gland Operation'

Proulx's interests in this story are signalled by the unusual title. It refers to an operation carried out by the historical figure John R. Brinkley (radio pioneer and quack), who promised to reinvigorate flagging male sexuality by introducing the testicles of a buck goat into the human scrotum. The idea was that the fertility and vigour of the foreign glands would be absorbed by the weaker host, leading to general fruitfulness. This operation provides the overarching metaphor for the story, in which a group of energetic Germans are transplanted to an impotent host (it is significant that the immigrants take over a failed settlement rather than conquer virgin territory), which they make fruitful through a combination of hard work and innovative farming techniques. Proulx, however, is interested in the dark side of their success. Firstly, she uses the fact that the buck testicles were nearly always rejected in Brinkley's experiment as a cue to explore the theme of cultural assimilation – the theme that dominates the novel as a whole. Secondly, following Kolodny, she is concerned with the correlation between the fertility of the soil and sexual fertility, and between male mastery of the virgin landscape and the exploitative relationship it fosters between men and women.

The three Germans who arrive in Iowa – the self-styled *Home of the Immigrants* – in 1893 are certainly energetic: Loats arrives on the *Vigorous*, and Messermacher arrives with a seemingly irrelevant tale about the horse that only he can break: a story that prepares us for a narrative concerned with taming (73, 71).[21] Their confidence is announced in the name they give to their settlement – Pranken (hand) – suggesting that they expect to succeed by the power of their hands. They are, however, as the linguistic choice indicates, insistently German hands, which leads to a cultural narrowness that will later become a source of mirth for their neighbours, or a 'prank' upon them. To begin with, Proulx records an immigrant narrative of bucolic bliss: the men tame the land while their children run free on the prairie with bells on their feet to prevent them getting lost. Beneath this idyll, however, Proulx sets about exploring the way in which domination of the land is transposed into sexual relations. Initially, she employs another linguistic sleight of hand in the form of the term 'maniac' to describe the fertility of the land (the crops grow '*manically*') and the sexual appetite of the third German, Beutle (he is described as a sexual 'maniac') (79, 96). This adverbial transposition exposes the casual misogyny that lies behind the land-as-female metaphor and by extension the entire pioneer narrative.

Proulx's traditional storyline has an interesting literary precedent in Ruth Suckow's *Country People* (1924). The novel, like Proulx's story, also traces a group of German immigrants through their initial settlement in Iowa, the trials of building a community and their difficulties with assimilation, particularly during the First World War. Of particular interest is Suckow's presentation of pioneering as an essentially male activity (the patriarchy encoded in the masculine names given to the farms), in which women remain largely anonymous, their lives lived in geographical and linguistic isolation on lonely homesteads. In this story the central female figure may share the name of Cather's female heroine – Alexandra – but she certainly does not run the ranch: she doesn't even get to go to town. Suckow's fiction is corroborated by a number of recent historical studies of the female German pioneer experience. Linda Pickle's study of immigrants in Nebraska – *Contented among Strangers* (1996) – was published in the same year as Proulx's story and paints a picture of a group of women who conformed to the traditions of frugality, hard work and self-sacrifice while suffering from homesickness. She records suicide, infanticide and a sense of cultural alienation exacerbated by the First World War.[22] Indeed, many of the conditions experienced by Proulx's female characters.

In Proulx's narrative, the metaphorical domination of women and landscape is further enriched by her introduction of a musical trope. Beutle is a successful farmer and superb accordionist, and he expects women to yield to the adept touch that he brings to the land and his instrument. Within the story music also becomes indicative of insularity. Because it is non-linguistic, music is an ideal measure of cultural assimilation. By any measurement, the three Germans fail; they will only play music from the Fatherland, and they will only play together (even their wives are excluded). This lack of cultural adaptation extends to their sex lives: their contempt for other cultures and their own wives means that incest becomes a means of cultural affirmation rather than crime. The female equivalent of music making in the story is sewing. While Beutle plays, his wife, Gerti, sews: this is not a picture of domestic harmony, but another rich source of Proulxian irony. As the couples age, the women become increasingly isolated while the men go into the field, the neighbouring towns and the larger cities. On such visits they are exposed to the new America: a land of labour-saving devices that would unshackle their wives from domestic drudgery. However, when Beutle is faced with a choice between a sewing machine and a wind-up phonograph, he buys the latter, giving his wife a 'God Bless Our Home' embroidery frame by way of compensation. This casual misogyny becomes more brutal when Beutle is caught having sex with a neighbour's daughter in the hen-house. Gerti's reaction, to slash her throat, suggests the only weapon at her disposal; if male conquest is measured by possession, whether of land or the female body, women's power can only be restored through denial. Her decision to sew the wound back up brings closure to Proulx's metaphorical trope. She denies Beutle the satisfaction of her death, but acknowledges that she is unable to 'sew something else up as well' – her vagina, his penis (100). Instead, she is reduced to the petty pleasure of emending his present to '*God Damn Our Adulterer*' – a detail he never notices (107, Proulx's italics).

Central to the suffering of Proulx's female pioneers is the behaviour of men. She reinforces this point late in the story through the abduction of Florella and Zena (Beutle's twin granddaughters) and their mysterious return some days later having been violated. Their disappearance is a mystery which invites an interpretation that illuminates the preoccupation of the believer: Ribbons, one of the girls who had been playing with the twins immediately before the abduction, suggests the presence of a bear, the kind of animal that has fuelled her bedtime stories; Gerti remembers a frightening black man she had once seen, an observation that substitutes racial prejudice for fairy tale. The men, however, can only conceive of the probable rape as 'revenge for Belgium' (110). To their mind the female body once again becomes equated with a geographical location and transformed into a site for male conquest. The mother blames Beutle, takes a fork to his crops and then to him. Thus Proulx symbolically brings to a close the connection between the rape of the land and of women, closure made clear linguistically through the narrative condemnation: 'Jesus Christ, the woman's a *maniac!*' (110, my italics).

Her admission to an asylum by a doctor just 'a little bored with female insanity' reinforces the cosy patriarchal conspiracy in which women who fail to comply to male codes of conduct are medicalized then confined (110). Her confinement illustrates Elaine Showalter's contention, presented in *The Female Malady* (1985), that patriarchal oppression leads women to lash out in frustration or to retreat into silence, either of which is conveniently diagnosed as a symptom of madness. But whereas Rolvaag's Beret is driven mad by the isolation of the plains, Pernilla is the victim of the behaviour of men. She is closer to Clara Vavrika in Willa Cather's *The Bohemian Girl* (1912), or Kerrin in Josephine Johnson's *Now in November* (1934), women who acquiesce to the patriarchy for an extended period before exploding in violent and suicidal rage. The irony in Proulx's story is that the female characters prefer the comforts of hospital to their pioneer lives. Truly, this is a landscape which moulds and is moulded by the *maniac*.

'Them Old Cowboy Songs'

Twelve years later, Proulx returns to the pioneer theme in 'Them Old Cowboy Songs'. The story records the fate of Archie and Rose McLaverty in their attempts to homestead in Wyoming in 1885. Their tragedy is made clear in the italicized prologue, in which Proulx addresses directly Turner's notion of endeavour and eventual conquest. This is the struggle embedded in the folksy cowboy ballads alluded to in the title; the songs that Archie sings while walking the boundary of his property to announce his ownership. While presenting a world of uncompromising harshness, they nevertheless celebrate a spirit of hardy self-reliance combined with fierce loyalties. It is the lie of these songs that Proulx sets out to expose in this story.

The story begins in 1885, a period when – due to the Homestead Act of 1862, the end of the Indian threat, and the expansion of the railroad – the slow march of settlement had turned into a stampede. By 1880 Wyoming had become a magnet for both homesteaders and the cattle industry. Most pioneers, however, did not arrive in prairie schooners to stake out a homestead on vacant land (the myth propagated by Turner), but travelled on specially chartered trains in response to advertisements circulated by the railroad companies. 'Who do you think settled the West?', Proulx asks through the character of LaVon Fronk in *That Old Ace in the Hole*, before proceeding to disabuse both Bob Dollar and, by extension, the reader of the nostalgic vision of intrepid pioneers:

> No, *not* pioneers. Business! First the traders like the Bents and St. Vrain, then the army posts a protect the traders and wagon trains, then the rayroads ... The rayroad corporations said where the towns was goin a go and that's where they went. Nothin a do with pioneers. It was all corporate goals and money and business. Then they sold lots and hoped it would all work out. (91, 92)

In Wyoming, according to Proulx, this meant 'The Union Pacific Railroad,' which cut through the centre of the Red Desert, [and] created Wyoming.'[23] For this reason, John McPhee observes, 'Out here, Uncle Sam is a gnat under a blanket compared to Uncle Pete.'[24] Federal government gave the railroad 50 per cent of the land in a 40-mile swath along its route in checkerboard fashion, one square mile in every two – a feature diagrammatically represented in Proulx's *Bird Cloud* (139).[25] This meant that 'towns grew up around construction camps and coal mines, then around refuelling and water stops', which were largely owned by the railroads.[26] Furthermore, as the railroad companies spread West they began to understand the importance of establishing a solid customer base on the margins of the tracks: the West was no longer to be conceived as a wilderness to be travelled through, but as a destination in its own right.[27] It was rebranded, shedding the sobriquet of 'The Great American Desert' (under which it had laboured in the reports of the first immigrants), to be reimagined as a garden of plenty awaiting the sacred plough and the heroic pioneer.[28]

Unfortunately, the tragedy of the pioneer experience is encapsulated by LaVon's final statement: there was too much hope and no acknowledgement of the reality of the situation. In *Bird Cloud* Proulx argues that the railroad companies were guilty of the cynical exploitation of the dream of ownership and she condemns 'the great nineteenth-century giveaway of huge chunks of public land to a handful of railroad barons in the name of patriotic progress and "opening up the country"'.[29] Typical adverts encouraged pioneers to 'Come to the Garden of the West!' while promising free travel and cheap land: 'Homeseekers! A Farm for $3 per acre! Every Farmer, Every Farmer's Son, Every Clerk, Every Mechanic, Every Labouring Man Can Secure a Home.'[30] Archie and Rose are victims of just such railroad puff. In 1885 the Union Pacific were engaged in a cost-cutting exercise and were attaching special emigrant sleeping cars to their normal trains, with flat rates and cheap baggage costs. The horror of such trains was noted by Mrs Frank Leslie, wife of the owner of the influential *Illustrated Newspaper*, who accidently strayed into one during a trip to Green River, Wyoming: 'By the dull light, we could see the poor creatures curled and huddled up in heaps for the night, with no possibility of lying down comfortably; but men, women, bundles, baskets, and babies, in one promiscuous heap.'[31]

The promise of ownership in an agrarian utopia proved irresistible for many couples. But this was not an orchard awaiting harvest, but an arid landscape in need of 'dry farming methods'. In his 1878 report for the United States Geologic Survey, John Wesley Powell stated that only 3.3 per cent of the short-grass plains of Montana and Wyoming land were irrigable, an aridity crisis exacerbated by the railroad's practice of dividing up homestead plots into a grid in defiance of natural features.[32] His report was ignored. This meant that thousands of emigrants, beguiled by the promise of cheap land, were transported into an inhospitable landscape with inadequate infrastructure, support or even farming know-how. In *This House of Sky* (1978), Doig records the disaster created by the grid system during his family's attempt to pioneer in Montana: 'My family's history is very closely tied back to that careful Jeffersonian geometric mesh of net': not only did it ignore where 'the water flowed', but 'the mesh [was] much too small', transforming it from a dream of freedom into a net of captivity.[33] William Kittredge echoes these sentiments in his observation that having completed his Great Northern Railroad in 1910, James Hill cynically sold tickets for 320-acre plots, thus condemning immigrants to near certain failure: they came, 'they built shacks, they tried to farm, most failed, most left having wasted years in dirt-eating poverty'.[34]

Even before they arrive, then, the destiny of Archie and Rose is sealed, not by the hand of fate, but by the unscrupulous railroad companies. Problems with aridity and the spectre of plagues of grasshoppers (Wyoming had been decimated by this particular instrument of 'fate' in 1874) were supplemented by land overstocked with cattle. Wyoming, as Gretel Ehrlich notes, was attracting the wrong kind of rancher: remittance men, generally British, who were paid to come West and get out of their families' hair and understood neither the cattle, the range nor the activities of wily managers.[35] The 'elegant Brit remittance man Morton Frewen' in the story is just one such black sheep; Karok – 'a foreigner from back east' – is typical in caring only for the number of cows in his herd above their condition, or provenance (61, 59). The result of such overstocking was soil depredation and a subsequent shortage of both feed and water. For homesteaders like Archie and Rose, already competing for scarce resources, the consequences were disastrous.

Proulx heightens the sense of inevitability surrounding the fate of Archie and Rose still further by timing their arrival with one of the worst winters in Wyoming's history. In her essay 'Red Desert Ranches' Proulx observes that the spring roundup of 1887 told its own story of decimation. She quotes the *Carbon County Journal*: 'The roundup is over and the cattle men have disbanded and gone home. From the most reliable sources we learn that the loss has been far greater than anyone anticipated ... it is fair to say that many men would be happy if they could gather 50 per cent.'[36] It was so bad that when the thaw came one rancher from Kaycee claimed that he could walk for twenty miles over the carcasses of dead cattle without setting foot on the ground.[37] This is the freeze that kills Archie, the inspiration seemingly coming from an article taken from the January 1889 issue of the *New York Times* found by Proulx's sister, Roberta, in 2006, when dealing with the effects of their recently deceased father. Headlined 'They Left Him to Die' it tells the story of one of Proulx's ancestors, a lumberman on the St-Maurice River called George Proulx, who fell sick and, with no conveyance available, was taken by two other workers to find medical aid in a distant town. About one hundred miles from their destination, the party ran into a severe storm and, with very little shelter available, 'the two protectors abandoned their charge on the river Bauke and left him to die'.[38] Although the newspaper article is clear in blaming those closest to the victim for his death, Proulx's story is more ambiguous. Karok, who prizes his cows above women, and his cancer above his cowboys, is selfish, but allows Archie to go; Archie's friend, Sink, remains with him to his death.

The tragedy of Archie and Rose derives not from a single act of betrayal, but a series of historical coincidences which lock them into a narrative that projects them towards catastrophe. This sense of doom begins with the epigraph and is reinforced by details such as the moths that burst into flame during their first evening meal together: the first of many deaths brought about by the pursuit of illusory illumination. It is also suggested by the songs that Archie sings as he walks the perimeter of his claim. For, despite the seemingly romantic nature of their shared enterprise, these are songs sung by men who are lonesome and nomadic. His laconic version of 'The Old North Trail' is greeted by the listeners at the 'all-male roundup nights' as 'the true history they all knew' (49). The very idea that they should be sung to celebrate land ownership, or with a wife – both equated with a domesticity with which the cowboy is at odds – is ironic. His last lyric – 'never had a nickel and I don't give a shit' – is fine for the cowboy, but not for the family man: no wonder Rose can't keep up with him and does not know the words (50). Tom Ackler is a better singing partner. An old sailor, he is no stranger to stories of remarkable sea creatures, or nostalgic sea shanties that sentimentalize a world that he is only too ready to reject. But there is a further irony here; for although Archie assumes that he is singing authentic cowboy songs – an assumption reinforced through the title of the story – the idea of an oral tradition passed through generations is a stubborn myth. 'Many so-called "traditional" cowboy songs', according to historian David Fenimore, had been learned from books such as John L. Lomax's *Cowboy Songs and Other Frontier Ballads* (1910) and re-oralized.[39] Thus, like the pioneer dreams sold by the railways, Archie once again finds himself naively buying into a pre-packaged western dream.

Rose is not in harmony with her husband, nor with the mythology of the prairie madonna. Brought up on an isolated 'Jackrabbit stage station' by an alcoholic father and a mother bedridden from 'some wasting disease', Proulx paints a picture of a childhood reminiscent of the surreal stories of Sherwood Anderson (51). The station is a site of surveillance, taking an erotic voyeuristic form in the behaviour of Harp Daft (a typical Anderson grotesque), the scrofulous 'telegraph key operator' who observes the women through his telescope (52). Through the stationmaster's wife, Flora, Proulx debunks the myth of the western prostitute with a heart of gold. It is a subject she addresses in her essay 'How the West was Spun', reminding us that frontier prostitutes led harsh lives of abuse and alcohol dependency and died young.[40] While acknowledging that 'prostitution in the West connoted exploitation, abuse, poverty and abandonment', the historians Karen Jones and John Wills argue that 'it also suggested female companionship, a decorous lifestyle, the promise of monetary gain and a modicum of female agency'.[41] Flora provides an excellent example: she may have escaped the sordid destiny of the brothel by marrying a stationmaster, but she is not above offering her sexual services in order to advance her husband's career.

More important to Rose, however, is that as relatively settled and wealthy women, both Flora and her stepdaughter, Queeda, are able to follow the 'Cult of True Womanhood'. As such, they are transformed into figures of ridicule by Proulx; they adopt airs and graces and wear the latest fashions, leaving the envious Rose to admire from afar 'the beautiful dresses, the fire opal brooch, satin shoes and saucy hats so exquisitely out of place at the dusty station' (52). Their impracticality is reinforced by other behaviour observed by Rose, which emphasizes the coarseness of the women. She has seen Flora 'spit on the ground like a drover' and 'scratch her crotch on the corner of the table when she thought no one was looking'. She also notes that Queeda, 'beneath the silk skirts ... had to put up with sopping pads torn from old sheets, the crusted edges chafing her thighs and pulling at the pubic hairs' (52). The power of this combination of gossip and jealousy is important to Proulx's deconstruction of the mythology of the prairie madonna. For when Rose moves into her homestead with Archie she is preoccupied not with the success of the pioneer project but with the necessity of keeping up appearances: 'She did not want to become like a homestead woman, skunky armpits and greasy hair yanked into a bun' (53). It is a competition with fatal consequences.

Rose is not the heroic pioneer whose capacity for hard work and self-sacrifice leads to successful settlement; nor is she the suffering angel condemned to a life of drudgery and isolation. She lies somewhere between, her physical suffering supplemented by constant comparison with Queeda. She is similar to Dorothy Scarborough's Letty Mason (*The Wind* (1925)) – a reluctant pioneer as overwhelmed by the dictates of good housekeeping as by the hostile environment. Letty's pioneer experience is far from the heroic role scripted by mythology, focused as it is on her resentment at her lack of preparation and guidance for the role. The titular 'wind' is less an existential threat than a force against which Letty struggles in order to keep the house clean before the censorious eyes of her neighbours. Cleanliness becomes an end in itself, and while she acknowledges her husband's endurance, she is disgusted by his lack of cleanliness. Like Letty, Rose is obsessed with appearances. She resents the fact that while Queeda had little to do but 'primp and wash and flounce', she 'lifted heavy kettles, split kindling, baked bread, scrubbed pots and hacked the stone-filled ground for the garden' (53). This is not the pioneer experience celebrated in 'Them Old Cowboy Songs', but a mundane catalogue of complaints derived from a concept of femininity dangerously at odds with the western environment.

Despite such contradictions, Archie and Rose initially find contentment away from the surveillance and corruption of the station. True love even seems to break down the stereotype of the hard-bitten cowboy, leaving Archie struggling to articulate emotions he has never felt before: '"It's. I ain't never been. Loved. I just can't hardly *stand it* –" and he began to blubber "feel like I been shot"' (55, Proulx's italics). Like Ennis del Mar in 'Brokeback Mountain', Archie struggles to express emotions through a lexicon of cowboy terminology. However, despite these expressive limitations, there is a sincerity here that is missing in the cowboy songs that usually make up his emotional range. Archie genuinely appears to be moving towards an accommodation with another human being unmediated by his folkloric ballads. Unfortunately this ends when Rose becomes pregnant, and they shift 'out of days of clutching love and into the long haul of married life' (57). For pioneer couples, childbirth became a clear practical means of differentiating male romanticism from female pragmatism. Elizabeth Jameson's interviews with pioneer women concluded that 'the strains of childbearing and the work involved in caring for small children formed an important difference between male and female experience'. Contraception was available, and Jameson points to 'a rich and largely private world of women sharing information about it'.[42] But Proulx's Rose, isolated on her homestead, would not have been aware of such things, unlike Queeda and her mother. Archie, we may imagine, will have been equally clueless, not simply because of his touching innocence, but because birth control plays no part in the cowboy mythology around which he constructs his life.

It is now that money becomes important, and the significance of Archie's disastrous decision to buy his land outright rather than take advantage of one of the government homesteading schemes becomes apparent. Unfortunately, he remains naively obstinate in facing his responsibilities. When Rose asks him to hire somebody to dig a well, Archie promises to do it himself and transforms it into a ballad; when she suggests that he takes a job in a mine, he refuses because it does not conform to his vision of the West, and sings: 'I'm just a lonesome cowboy who loves a gal named Rose, I don't care if my hat gets wet or if I freeze my toes' (57). His song not only announces his selfishness, but also predicts the manner of his death: a cowboy's end. Faced with childbirth, Archie and Rose find themselves travelling in opposite directions, a social dislocation reinforced by the narrative splitting into two and the narrator's observation that 'for the first time [Rose] recognized that they were not two cleaving halves of one person but two separate people, and that because he was a man he could leave any time he wanted, and because she was a woman she could not' (61). Rose could return to the station, but that would mean dealing with local gossip. Instead, Archie signs on for Karok, an absentee rancher whose restriction on married men is a crude formalization of the all-male bunkhouse world to which Archie has subscribed.

Despite the hard nature of the work, heard through Archie's attuned ear there is a romanticism to life on the open range where the only form of boundary is imaginative and auditory: 'On the clear, dry nights coyote voices seemed to emanate from single points in straight lines, the calls crisscrossing like taut wires' (63). It is here that his cowboy songs – which tell of the warm hearth and a girl named Rose – make sense, because they describe a dream rather than the confines of reality. In such a landscape he is unable to conjure a baby, but can conceive teaching a young boy (a girl isn't even considered) cowboy skills. In this world, Rose's emotional place is taken by Sink, a cowboy bachelor who considers himself 'old enough to be [Archie's] daddy' and takes on the paternal role (67). He teaches him how to fall properly (63); he tells him 'the facts of life' concerning bunkhouse homosexuality (62); and, despite avowing that he is no 'wet nurse', he takes care of Archie when he freezes amidst the lakes. He, unlike the cowpunchers who inspired the story, lives by a cowboy code that prizes loyalty and dies with his charge (73).

Rose, by contrast, dies abandoned. The narrative, true to its aim of avoiding the sentimentality of them old cowboy songs, does not shrink from its description of the pregnancy as a 'python' that suffocates her until she is 'spiralling down in [a] plum-coloured mist' of blood, which leaves her 'glued to the bed' with 'the clotted child' next to her. And yet there is enormous pathos in the observation that as she wrapped up the 'tiny corpse' and dug a grave using the silver spoon that was 'her mother's wedding present', she felt 'the loss of the sheet as another tragedy' (65, 66). Here, observes Stephen Abell, the narrative collapses onto the symbolism of the spoon, contrasting its delicacy with the hardness of the ground, the happy expectations it signifies with her present agonized plight, and the life of comfort and wealth (the metaphorical silver spoon in the mouth), which she does not have.[43] As she lies down to die, her birthing experiences are repeated ironically in her surroundings: 'The twitching bed leg, a dank clout swooning over the edge of the dishpan, the wall itself bulging forward ... all pulsing with the rhythm of her hot pumping blood' (66). All are reminders of what she has lost: the twitching infant corpse; the swoon of motherly affection; the bulge of pregnancy; the infant heartbeat.

Rose's slow death is compounded by betrayal and cruelty. It is not simply Archie, distant and unaware of her plight, but her father who rides down to announce the family's imminent departure, but is too drunk to dismount and enter the hut. Tom Ackler discovers Rose's half-eaten body, but he is unable to understand the female tragedy of death in childbirth without contextualizing it within a typically Western narrative – that she had been 'raped and murdered and mutilated by Utes' (75). But nobody is interested in his news at the station where they are caught up in the domestic drama of the suicide of Harp Daft and his declaration of love to Flora Dorgan. This is another lonely death, which raises uncomfortable questions, not simply for Flora, but for Archie and all men who have difficulties communicating their feelings. The 'four-hundred page' pornographic love letter produced by Daft throws into sharp relief the hastily scribbled note written by Archie asking Tom to look in on Rose, or the letter that he fails to send because of the increase in postage (75, 67). Daft is a bachelor in a country 'rich in bachelors' – an example of what Sink and other cowboys who turn their backs on domesticity turn into when they retire (52). His grotesquery is simply the outward manifestation of their inward disfigurement.

It is left to Ackler to round off the story, his singing of 'when the green grass comes, and the wild rose blooms' offering an ironic contrast to the fate of Rose in the narrative that we have just read (77). Throughout the story there has been a deliberate dislocation between the life of fortitude, companionship and loyalty celebrated in 'Them Old Cowboy Songs' and the lives of those pioneers, particularly women, who died on the frontier. The story opened with P. H. Weed, the gold prospector who dies of starvation while dreaming of a lucky strike and who gives his name to the McLaverty homestead. Significantly his death introduces the theme of how the early settlers were written into the landscape, their heroic struggles transformed into 'Them Old Cowboy Songs' to be passed through the generations. However, it is his cat, Gold Dust, who remains healthy on the flesh of Rose, who provides the more suitable model for survival in a country in which the only truth seems to be that 'some lived and some died, and that's how it was' (77). It is a truth not documented in them old cowboy songs. The true monument to their deaths is the doorstep (a symbol of their failed family life) hauled upright, which significantly remains blank.

'The Great Divide'

In 'The Great Divide' Proulx fast-forwards 35 years to plot the fate of another young couple attempting to live out a pioneer dream against a background of economic turbulence. This time Proulx's narrative begins in 1920 – a boom time for immigration into Wyoming, many having been encouraged to the state following the 640-acre Homestead Act of 1916. The war had brought good times for homesteaders, cattlemen and the mines, as the government sought new sources for basic goods that allies could no longer supply (oil and corn production, for example, doubled during the war period). 'Never in the history of Wyoming', claimed the *Laramie Republican* in September 1917, 'has the entire people been more prosperous than now.'[44] With the onset of peace, many war veterans, like Proulx's Hi Alcorn, were encouraged to Wyoming by lucrative financial incentives, like the $2,000 property-tax exemption granted to them by the 1921 legislature.[45] Many were attracted to join schemes like the 'Great Divide' project outlined in the narrative. These were organized by property speculators who bought up leaseholds made available by the 1916 Act and bundled them together before selling them on at a profit.

These new homesteaders were also the first generation of automotive pioneers. A number of oil discoveries on the Muddy east of Casper and the Second Wall Creek Sand during the war years literally fuelled an enormous explosion in car ownership. This led to the development of a state highway department tasked with the opening up of previously remote parts of Wyoming to potential pioneers.[46] 'By 1927,' Proulx notes, '26 million cars stank and jarred around the country, each driver a pioneer.'[47] Pioneer is the important word here, highlighting, as it does, that once decanted from the train (with its prescriptive timetables and linear rails) into the unpredictable automobile wending its way on poorly prepared and circuitous minor roads, the newly enfranchised driver could once again imagine himself (it was always men at the wheel) doing battle with the wilderness rather than consuming it through the window of the train. Frederick Van de Water's account of his car journey West in the 1920s concluded with his family arriving in San Francisco 'thin' and 'tanned, brown as Indians', a description which he uses not to dissuade potential followers, but to emphasize the authenticity of his struggle and his family's new-found freedom.[48]

Proulx has once again chosen her dates with care. The year 1919 proved disastrous for farmers, as they suffered drought, a harsh winter and coincidental economic deflation. The prominent Laramie Plains wool grower Frank S. King, wrote in 1922:

> The summer of 1919 was one long to be remembered; drought was universal throughout Wyoming and in the fall at least one-third of the livestock had to be shipped out of the state. ... Winter started from a month to six weeks earlier than the average and in October snow covered the State. Long cold months followed, ending with an April storm that has been unequalled since the March storm of 1878 ... on top of this calamity came the depression in prices.[49]

The drought decimated the cattle and sheep industries and exposed the fact that the 640-acre units offered for dry farming by the Act were still too small.[50] As desperate homesteaders turned to other means of income they found little comfort elsewhere: there was to be no return to the railroad as 'the Union Pacific laid off one-third of its men during the four months beginning in December, 1920', and coal mines were hit by industrial unrest and a gradual decline in employment between 1920 and 1923.[51] These industries declined further with the onset of the Great Depression. Rather like Archie and Rose before them, Hi and Helen Alcorn arrive full of hope at just the wrong time.

Proulx's frontier tale focuses on The Great Divide Homestead Colony Number One, which was set up in 1915 by the publishers and property speculators, Harry Heye Tammen and Frederick Gilmer Bonfils, and the latter's bodyguard, Volney Hoggatt. Hoggatt, like Proulx's prize-fighting Antip Bewley, was directly responsible for the administration of the scheme, encouraging homesteaders through his editorship of the magazine dedicated to dry-land farming called *Great Divide*, published by Bonfils' *Denver Post* newspaper. The colony was initially very successful; in 1916 a train full of immigrants arrived with '15 carloads of household goods and stock and one coach containing sixty men, women, and children'. By the time of Hi and Helen's first visit to the Great Divide picnic, plots had been set out, water wells drilled and Hoggatt was looking to expand to Carbon, Wyoming. Proulx's inspiration for the scene was a photograph of the picnic reprinted in John Rolfe Burroughs' *Where the Old West Stayed Young* (1962). The 40 young couples in their Sunday best, children at their feet, stare earnestly at the camera, the enormous figure of Volney Hoggatt off to one side, arms akimbo, every bit the ex-fighter.[52] The pioneers presented Hoggatt with a loving cup, but there was always a whiff of corruption about the scheme: Bonfils and Tammen were both publicly horsewhipped and shot at various stages of their careers for their unscrupulous dealings. However, despite their economic opportunism and the hostile environment, the pluck and ingenuity of the pioneers allowed the colony to stagger on for 20 years, before eventual collapse in the mid-1930s.

For Proulx, however, the title also acts as a metaphor for the divisions created by frontier life: most notably the demarcation of land; the dislocation between dream and reality; class division; and, most pertinently, the disunity caused by the male/female experience. Perhaps the most obvious division is that between the ambitions of the optimistic central character, Hi Alcorn, and the reality of the economic and environmental conditions that surround him. His name suggests the pastoral abundance of the American Dream and a spiritual attachment with the Hiawatha of Longfellow's eponymous 1855 epic poem, himself a highly romanticized vision of an American Indian. Like a Hemingway hero, Hi has recently returned from the war (the industrialized slaughter of the 'western front' offering a grotesque distortion of the values of the 'western frontier'), rejecting the urban sophistication of gay 'Paree' in order to embrace the romanticized vision of the ultimate 'great divide' – the frontier (103). But quite where and how he is to live a life of rugged self-reliance when 'it seemed to him that the frontiers had all disappeared in his grandfather's time' becomes the quintessentially American problem of the narrative (104). Proulx's Hi Alcorn, like Stegner's Bo Mason, believes himself a man born too late; he finds himself 'without knowing it, searching for a purpose that his spared body might carry out', the seemingly redundant physiological clarification reminding us that the frontier dream is essentially a pitting of the male body against the wilderness (104). He is blind to the gendered aspect of his dream, preferring instead to conceive of it as a joint venture with his young bride: 'They would make their own frontier' (104). The rhetoric is compelling, but without meaning in the context of a solipsistic, masculine frontier mythology.

This gender tension is explored in the story's opening scene as Hi and Helen arrive at their new stake in a clapped-out Essex. The car places these pioneers on a timeline between the Indian travois that drags Archie to his death and the luxury car crammed with delicacies with which Mitchell Fair enters Wyoming some 80 years later. There is a deliberate contrast between its fragility and the looming, frozen landscape; indeed, Helen arrives swaddled in 'an old-fashioned buffalo robe' (similar to the one in which Archie died), which seems more redolent of 1860 than 1920 (95). Furthermore, details such as Hi's worn 'Oxfords' suggest that these early automotive pioneers were being encouraged into parts of Wyoming for which they remained unprepared. Hi's repeated insistence on the possessive plural pronoun '*our* own place' does little to disguise the fact that this is his dream (95, my italics). As the pregnant Helen shivers in the midst of the freezing wasteland she remains outwardly supportive, but her pinched expression, delicately probing comments – 'Mr Bewley ... said it would be almost a town by now' – and repertoire of grimaces articulate a dissatisfaction with the situation (95). As the narrative allows access to Helen's unspoken thoughts they focus on her husband's pronoun usage. She reminds herself that this is '*my*' rather than 'our' land, since it is her father's money that is bankrolling the venture (101, Proulx's italics). There are fence posts, but the division of a barren wasteland upon which there are neither neighbours nor competing interests is meaningless, a fact highlighted by the lack of wire between them: it takes two to string wire and make a division. Hi is on his own, the only division being with his wife.

This was not how it was meant to be when, during the 'Great Divide' picnic, Antip Bewley pointed west to show them the flower meadows and a vision of frontier living for ordinary people who 'wanted to get back to the land' (101). Just like Archie and Rose, their dream has been pre-packaged by unscrupulous speculators. It is Helen who is alive to Bewley's sinister motives. Observed through her eyes, he is every inch the menacing bodyguard: an ex-prize-fighter with 'skin the colour of raw wood', hands 'the size of hay forks', a mouth full of gold (97). However, Bewley knows that he is not selling the dream to Helen, but to Hi, which becomes clear when he introduces him to his 'special site'. It is a deal, dressed as a favour, and struck between men over a beer. The site's defining feature, the small spring, prefigures the water traps that will later be employed to catch wild horses: Hi, who will become progressively aligned with these horses, has been well and truly caught (98).

Hi's catastrophic economic mismanagement (he is unprepared for the crash in wheat prices) and the continual shortfall between dreams and reality (he envisions himself breaking horses, but is forced to buy a tractor) is skated over in a narrative more concerned with his optimism. Financial ruin causes him to cross another divide into criminality by making potato whiskey in defiance of the prohibition laws (Wyoming went dry officially on

1 July 1919 and, as Proulx writes elsewhere, many ex-ranch hands turned to horse catching and bootleg whiskey[53]). Hi chooses an Indian burial chamber for the site of his still. His casual desecration – he throws 'out the Indian corpse wrapped in deerskin and beads' – highlights a rather more sinister aspect of frontier politics: the lumping together of all those who lived beyond the 'great divide' into people unworthy of consideration. Furthermore, the replacement of the corpse with a still offers a straightforward metaphor through which the Native Americans are destroyed by whiskey. Ironically, Hi, or Hiawatha, has more in common with the displaced corpse than he realizes: he too is invested with the spirit of the wild; he too shows himself spectacularly unsuccessful in adapting to modernity (105).

A short period of imprisonment is followed by an offer to engage in work commensurate with Hi's pioneer dream: horse catching. Trapping horses, Proulx notes in her essay 'Horse Bands of the Red Desert', boomed during the Depression years when miners and ranchers supplemented their income through a means which also had a nostalgic link to their western past.[54] Hi is reborn as a cowboy: the evocative smell of coffee, the campfire chat and 'the keen wind, the badlands and outlaw cliffs, the smell of horses' all servicing the remoulding of his identity (117). Unfortunately, his partner, Helen's brother-in-law, Fenk Fipps, contradicts much of Hi's cowboy ideal. He is continually associated with a series of saloon cars of increasing luxury, thus advertising his domesticity at the expense of his ruggedness: cowboys drive trucks. There is also the lack of manliness, made apparent by his 'womanish voice', the result of a childhood suicide attempt prompted by a crisis of sexual identity – 'something else on the other edge of the great divide that separated men's and women's knowledge of sexual matters' (108). Finally, there is his cruelty: Fenk is another patriarch who believes that the wilderness, horses and women only respond to brutality. This is made manifest in the destination of the horses. Hi naively assumes that they are destined for ranches and rodeo stock, but, as Proulx's essay makes clear, an increasingly urban population needed canned pet food and not wild horses.[55] When Hi understands this, he is faced with a dilemma of classical proportions: he loves the freedom of the range, but is horrified by Fenk's methods. In desperation he turns to the mines and the descent into darkness.

The narrative is blunt in its estimation of Hi's sacrifice: 'The coal mines were hard for a man who'd once owned his place and worked all his life outdoors' (114). But whereas the mine is the antithesis of Hi's dream, the mining town, with its electricity, running water, 'plenty of people around, gossip and talk, a social life' offers an urban oasis for Helen (113). This is the great divide between the frontier spirit and domesticity played out in Stegner's *Big Rock Candy Mountain*. The wife of the questing Bo Mason, Elsa, yearns for some domestic stability, for a community to make something out of the land they spend their time traversing. Helen grasps at the opportunity, but we are reminded of all that Hi has given up through the fate of their son. He is so full of the freedom and fresh air of the plains that he cannot breathe in the town without an iron lung (114). Significantly, so attached is Helen to this new lifestyle that she directs her hatred for his condition towards the doctor rather than the town.

By the time that Hi finds himself back in the wild country, he is forced to acknowledge a very different landscape to the one he romanticized in the mine. Hi's perpetual disillusion is signalled by the name of the horse he is given by Fenk on their first trip out: Senator Warren was a popular and respected Wyoming politician who was indicted for corruption in 1905. Although Hi rejoices in 'the broken country', he recognizes that 'there were fences where no fences had ever been' (117). The fence post has become a symbol of corporate exclusion rather than individual liberty. It is therefore fitting that Hi should be killed trying to avoid one. His death, like that of Archie McLaverty, is drawn from a historical account. This time it is Bill Logan Junior's description of the death of Alec Logan after becoming entangled with a fence post, which Proulx unearthed during her research for 'Horse Bands of the Red Desert'. In her story Proulx remains true to the facts of this account, particularly Logan's gallows humour, while also drawing out a symbolic significance.[56] Hi is killed lasso in hand while pursuing a horse that has escaped his trap; symbolically the horse embodies a wild spirit as potent as the pursuing Hi. His rope, like his conception of the West, is out of date, and only serves to trip him up. Fenk would never have attempted a manoeuvre as romantic as lassoing a horse: he would simply have shot it.

The story ends, however, with Helen, who is so moved to anger by the sight of Fenk on her doorstep that language is replaced by a primordial cry of rage (120). But for what, we may ask, does she have to reproach Fenk? It is not for the specific accident, for which she is yet to learn the details. Proulx appears to be striving for that rather more primal moment peculiar to the tragic form when a character expresses their despair at the workings of the universe. Fenk's crime is not simply that he is cruel – Helen is inured to this – but that he flourishes while Hi is sacrificed. This is the ultimate 'great divide', which undermines any notion that fairness lies at the heart of the frontier dream.

'Man Crawling Out of Trees'

In this story Proulx brings the pioneer experience up to date, yet her interest remains the impact of the move West upon the dynamics of married life. Not only have we fast-forwarded 60 years, our pioneers have evolved from a young couple whose husband, Archie McLaverty, was too young to make a claim, to an old couple whose claim is constructed upon a conflict of interests. They are part of Jack Lessinger's 'fifth great migration' – wealthy retirees fleeing rampant consumerism, pollution and crime in favour of a pastoral dream, clean air and traditional values. These pioneers are not, like their forebears, seeking economic opportunity, but rather, as the title of William Kittredge's essay on the migratory phenomenon makes clear, they are searching for 'The Last Safe Place'.[57] It is just such a 'refuge' that Mitchell is seeking, dragging his reluctant kitchen-designer wife, Eugenie, in tow. And though Mitchell cites sensible arguments for moving West – low crime and low property taxes – it is clear that he is really driven by his memory of a childhood summer spent 'exploring Yellowstone trails on horseback' and 'singing around a campfire' (106). In the West he hopes to return to a happy childhood: a last refuge from his unhappy marriage.

As with the previous stories, women are presented as wary accomplices to an essentially male enterprise, a power dynamic dramatized once again in an opening scene. They could fly, but a retired couple with time on their hands have nothing better to do but drive, their journey, in the process, becoming a parody of pioneer migration. The infinite time-span suggested by the landscape is telescoped into the cramped domestic interior of Mitchell's ironically named *Infiniti*. The car covers in an hour 'the same ground that would have taken the old oxcart emigrants, trailing a wake of graves, almost a week' (95). Mitchell refers to them 'cutting prairie ... thinking it sounded Western', while in the backseat they have the luxuries – 'truffled walnut oil, jars of French cornichons' that they are unable to buy in Wyoming (95, 99). They want the beautiful landscape and the simple life suggested by western phrasing, but they remain blind to the hardship suggested by the image of the 'wake of graves'. The road becomes a spatial representation of time, which allows the narrator to fill in details of their meeting, marriage, affairs, daughter's birth and working lives through a series of detailed flashbacks. Arrival in Wyoming brings us up to date, but by this stage the narrative has established Mitchell and Eugenie as a loveless, bickering, old couple who have become used to burying the reality of their relationship in cosmetic acquiescence while leading separate lives: symbolically, when the car engine starts to make noises, Mitchell turns up the radio (99).

In this story, Proulx's pioneers are undone by neither the weather nor economic downturn, but by those submerged marital problems which the loneliness of their new lives brings to the surface. In this way the notion of a 'man crawling out of trees' becomes a metaphor that suggests both desperation and enlightenment. In truth, they should never have been married, a fact signalled by the two striking images that reveal their thoughts on their wedding day: Mitchell's vision of his wife 'naked and down on all fours, looking beseechingly at the farmer, who was coming at her with a milking machine' offers a strangely eroticized image of marriage and the bovine nature of parenthood. For her part, Eugenie reads in his countenance the fear of a man in the process of being ritually strangled before being preserved in a bog – a damning indictment of marriage and mid-life (102). And yet initially they are happy in their Brooklyn house, the 'sycamore tree' outside their window (trees are important in this story) representing their Eden 'before the snake entered the garden' (103). The snake is adultery; the result is the ironically named Honor, whose paternity remains a secret to Mitchell. (If Mitchell had had his wits about him he should have suspected that something was amiss when Eugenie insisted on naming her in honour of Honore de Balzac's *Le Père Goriot*, a novel concerned with a father's betrayal by his daughter.) Eugenie's discovery of her pregnancy is heralded as that instant 'when the woodsman's arms reach the apogee of the swing and the axe begins its irrevocable descent, the moment at which, for the tree, everything changes' (104). It is a moment of tragic potentialities, when the outward appearance remains preserved, but we, like the woodsman, are aware of massive, impending change.

Their life in Wyoming, therefore, is lived in the shadow of the falling axe, which metaphorically connotes both destruction and enlightenment. Initially the downward stroke is delayed by their talent for repression and simulation: they embrace their new lives with vigour: 'They outfitted themselves at a Western Wear store' and Mitchell buys a 'twenty-year-old pickup' and 'took to driving around with his elbow out of the window' (107). Unfortunately, Eugenie never progresses beyond the cosmetic. Early in her relationship with Mitchell, Anthony Magagna has observed, she professed a love of classical music, but it is only later that he discovers she means 'some syrupy string ensemble that played popular medleys' (102). A similar superficiality marks her work as an interior designer in which she creates rural kitchens for urban dwellings: dream spaces in which nobody cooks. Like Kaylee Felts, she has learned that the cosmetic appeal of the western fantasy can be divorced from practicality. It is fitting, therefore, that once in Wyoming Eugenie wants 'to be near the Tetons, Yellowstone Park, and the national forests' – all those regions that conform to culturally constructed expectations of a western landscape (107).[58]

It is precisely because her conception of the West is so superficial that she is the first to register the shortfall between myth and reality and to see their new home as a rustic outpost where 'every few months something inexplicably rural happened' and 'everything seemed to end in blood' (110). Furthermore, it is she who perceives their role as permanent outsiders, and begins to sense that people in the local store are talking about them. The narrative has prepared the ground for this theme by making the catalyst for the move West Mitchell's convalescence after a kidney transplant. As with 'The Goat Gland Operation', the notion of transplantation (with its concomitant ideas of acceptance and rejection, natural versus artificial) becomes an important metaphor in the story, complicated further by the uncomfortable questions it raises concerning the paternity of Honor. Initially, it is the idea of acceptance that is thrown into focus, as the transplanted Fairs find themselves rejected by their host community. The woman in the post office claims: 'They'll accept you up to the fence, but they'll never let you open the gate' (115). The local community is symbolized by Elenora Figg (from whose land the Fairs' ranch has been cut), 'an elderly widow rancher of the classic Republican, conservative, art-hating, right-wing, outspoken, flint-faced type', who immediately dismisses the Fairs as effete easterners (110). Despite her insight, Eugenie is incapable of conceiving of the locals as anything other than violent western stereotypes. In her final argument with Mitchell she ridicules his desire to stay in Wyoming, suggesting that to fit in he will need 'an ATV and a gun and a knife' (122). Her local mistrust is addressed most clearly by her reaction to the men she encounters in the woods: the first, a bow hunter, terrifies Eugenie; his blacked-up face, wolfish eyes and bow and arrow transform him into a modern version of the ancient hunters stalking the landscape of Mitchell's imagination (113). This situation is reversed, however, when she is confronted by the injured skier – the ostensible 'man crawling out of trees'. It is her city-trained eyes that interpret his distorted grimace as the expression of a madman, forcing her, according to Mitchell, to break 'the cardinal rule of the country – that you give aid and help to a stranger, even your bitterest enemy when he is down' (122).[59]

In comparison to his wife's superficiality, Mitchell seems to possess a much deeper understanding of their new home. He knows the cardinal rule and he is horrified when local teenagers chase a pronghorn until it dies. More profoundly, he is affected by what he considers the authentic, elemental Wyoming landscape, not the tourist spots. However, his architectural training means that he is attuned to the contemplation of the basic structure of the landscape rather than its functioning as a lived space. This sense is reinforced by his habit of driving through it while listening to classical music. In his description of desert driving in *America* (1986),

Baudrillard notes: 'Speed creates pure objects. It is itself a pure object, since it cancels out the ground and territorial reference points … [it] is the triumph of the surface and pure objectivity over the profundity of desire.'[60] Proulx makes a similar claim in 'Dangerous Ground', in which she argues that 'from inside the automobile, the landscape [is] transformed into a swiftly moving mass of soft color … the framed but vague windshield view, replac[ing] the particular and the specific'.[61] Driving becomes a means of reintroducing epistemological doubt into ordinary lives, a process heightened by Mitchell's appreciation of music: 'He experienced the most intense pleasure in being alone, in swallowing the landscape in great chunks, drowning in the heavy surf of sound, the transmutation of geology into music' (119).

Kittredge has long extolled the pleasures of desert driving listening to Vivaldi: it 'leaves a taste as clean as the air across the mountain pastures, and it doesn't encourage you to think'.[62] Paul Auster picks up this sense of the dissolution of the self in his novel *The Music of Chance* (1990), in which he describes driving while listening to baroque music as a means of re-ordering the world according to strict musical principles (a contemporary harmonization with the music of the spheres). In Proulx's version, music becomes a way of reinforcing Mitchell's romanticism. Insulated behind his windscreen, he is able to collapse geological time into musical time, harmonizing the world of dinosaurs with the landscape before him; a spiritual experience that highlights human insignificance while paradoxically emphasizing the uniqueness of the insight. And yet his musical experience of the land is coloured by romance, by the sense that the West is – or should be – an untouched wilderness, a pure space apart from human influence. We are told that 'he wished for a celestial eraser to remove the fences, the crude houses', anything that does not 'harmonize' with his conception of a western landscape (106). He continually ignores the West as a real location, selectively ignoring the industrial realities of modern Wyoming. When, for example, he notices 'a filthy yellow haze lying over the Wind River range' he rejects the explanation of a local storekeeper, that it is pollution from a methane gas project, preferring instead to dismiss his protestations as the judgement of a crank (119–20).

Despite Mitchell's more promising interaction with the environment, it is clear that his relationship with his new home is just as superficial as that of his wife: both have fantasy images of the West which limits their ability to experience it as a real place. This narrowness of vision is cleverly interwoven into the final argument during which Eugenie brings down the axe by revealing the paternity of Honor. It is now that Mitchell is transformed into the man 'wallowing through the deep snow and trees towards the open' – figuratively edging from the dark towards clarity (122). Unfortunately, as

Benjamin Markowitz has noted, both have failed to learn the lessons offered by exposure to the Wyoming landscape. Honor does not care about the DNA test; her relationship with Mitchell is more important than with her genetic father; the artificial matters as much as the natural.[63] Eugenie fares little better. Our last glimpse is of her flying over Wyoming and looking down on its vast emptiness. There is a moment when she finally acknowledges the existential possibilities offered by the landscape, but such thoughts are quickly buried beneath the cosmetic – 'a cowboy kitchen for urban bachelors' – a new range entirely appropriate for Mitchell (124).

Proulx's pioneers are men travelling in hope, symbols of a masculine dream of conquest. But what happens when there is no more movement, when the land is settled and they stand still? These are the concerns articulated by the generation of historians that followed Turner's closure of the frontier. What happens when they become the fixed point in a world of change and codes of masculinity are marked by a lexical shift towards concepts of 'possession' and 'ownership', rather than 'endeavour' and 'exploration'? What happens when the fabled qualities of 'independence' and 'grit' are perceived as the less celebrated characteristics of 'loneliness' and 'awkwardness'? What happens, in a word, when 'pioneers' turn into 'ranchers' and the values of the nineteenth century linger on into the twentieth? These are the themes that Proulx explores through her ranchers, men caught between the contemporary West of agribusiness, extractive industries and lecturing environmentalists, and that of their ancestral imagination – defined by archetypes of the courageous pioneer. They are men betrayed by a contemporary world that does not share their values; by wives who now refuse to 'stand by their man'; and ultimately by inherited values dangerously at odds with the real world. It is their plight that we turn to next.

3

Ranchers

There is a war being fought in the New West and the ranchers, as they were in the second half of the nineteenth century, are at its centre. They see themselves as custodians of the authentic West, descendants of plucky pioneers who overcame Indians to carve out ranches on the free range. They consider themselves model American citizens representing the virtues of self-reliance and straight talking while fulfilling the American Dream of making the emptiness profitable. But now they find themselves betrayed: they are regulated by federal bodies such as the Forest Service and Bureau of Land Management (college boys who don't know one end of a cow from the other) and given permits to graze land which they had previously, through the blood of their ancestors, owned. The Indians may have left, but now the threats come from corporate ranchers looking for tax breaks; suitcase ranchers seeking western nostalgia; urban retirees looking for the security of a 'ranchette'; and mining companies in search of the next big strike. They are confronted by environmentalists who complain that they are destroying the land they love, and nutritionists telling the world that beef is bad. Many disgruntled ranchers, without a trace of irony, refer to this new battle as 'Manifest Destiny II', arguing that they, like the Indians, are now being demonized prior to their removal by pushy easterners.[1] As one Montana rancher quipped: 'I have become, for all practical purposes, an Indian.'[2]

Disputing this seductive narrative is a formidable range of western commentators who argue that pioneer nostalgia masks a mind-set of entitlement and conquest which is at the root of much of the environmental devastation caused by ranching activities. Kittredge argues in his aptly entitled 'Owning It All' that the myth of pioneer blood sacrifice (which conveniently ignores the genocide of the Indians) gave ranchers a childish sense that the land was theirs for sole use.[3] Conquest and profit, not collaboration and husbandry, were the primary motivating factors behind opening up the range. To the rancher, according to this narrative, the West was and is just a giant feedlot in which overstocking is rampant and, because 'you can't eat scenery', diversity unwelcome. At its starkest, argues Edward Abbey, a rancher is a welfare parasite who has populated the West with 'bawling, stinking, fly-covered, shit-smeared, disease-spreading brutes' and who:

> strings barbed wire all over the range; drills wells and bulldozes stock ponds; drives off elk and antelope and bighorn sheep; poisons coyotes and prairie dogs; shoots eagles, bears, and cougars on sight; supplants the native grasses with tumbleweed, snakeweed, povertyweed, cowshit, anthills, mud, dust, and flies. And then leans back and grins at the TV cameras and talks about how much he loves the American West.[4]

This is the ranching legacy with which we are living today; a catalogue of devastation that has led Patricia Limerick to make the following observation: 'I hated westerns because they always smashed up the saloon, and broke the mirrors and bottles and then rode out of town. I'm still back in the saloon saying, "Hey, wait a minute. Somebody has to clean up this mess."'[5]

A number of commentators have encouraged strong measures: faced with the intransigence of the Wyoming Stock-Growers Association an exasperated Bernard DeVoto used his column in *Harper's* to speculate whether 'it would be simpler, less expensive, and more hopeful to shoot cattlemen'.[6] Edward Abbey has long been the voice of direct action – an iconoclast, according to Earth First's founder, Dave Foreman, who enjoys 'pissing on overblown egos'.[7] His novel *The Monkey Wrench Gang* (1975) is an eco-terrorist rallying cry in which the characters cut fences, slash tractor tyres and poison cattle with diapers with the aim of removing the rancher and returning the range to a 'natural state'. (Proulx, as we shall see, explores Abbey's politics in her own eco-terrorist creation, Wade Walls ('The Governors of Wyoming', *CR*).) A more generous tradition, however, sees ranchers as victims of their own history and an essential part of the solution. Despite the uncompromising bluntness suggested by the title of Sharman Apt Russell's *Kill the Cowboy* (1993), she argues that the West is experiencing an erosion of both landscape and a traditional way of life, which has left many, who have ranched the land for generations, in a state of turmoil. Reflecting on her home in the Mimbres valley, she observes the bitterness of the older ranchers:

> Their community is dissolving as more ranchers fail to make a living and as more sons and daughters turn the family ranch into a subdivision. Their sense of place in society is threatened. They have always felt proud of what they did and of who they were. They have, in fact, even felt righteous. Now, suddenly, they are the bad guys.[8]

Threatened by outside concerns, some ranchers are finding security in an imaginary West; it may offer solace, but it is also a prison, because it prescribes codes of conduct that are largely fictional and thereby impossible to live by. This sense of helplessness and confusion is aptly illustrated by an interview with a Texas rancher that appeared in the *New Yorker* under the title 'The Last Cowboy'. In his gloss on the interview, historian Richard White noted the following:

> He viewed his actual modern West of absentee ranchers and agribusinesses as a declension from a truer but vanished West. His true West, however, was an imagined West, and he knew it from Westerns: real cattlemen were John Wayne in *Chisum*, or Chill Wills in *The Rounders*. His own sense of himself, and how he acted, were informed not just by the West he lived in but also by a powerful cultural image of the West he *should* have lived in.⁹

Examples of this confusion abound across a West in which ranchers are facing down their economic woes with the intransigence of the gunslinger. Rather than political lobbying, Wyoming ranchers responded to congressmen who pressed for increases in federal grazing fees by issuing Wanted Posters under the title 'Hole in the Head Gang'. When Charlie McCarty, who runs a ranch in Catron County, New Mexico, describes his struggle with federal agencies, he does so within the context of his grandfather's struggle with Geronimo's Apaches: 'They're coming after us with every gun they got.' And when Patty Kluver, a 60-year-old Montana rancher, was visited by a helicopter sent to survey the damage to her water supply caused by a nearby mine, she dealt with it as her ancestors would have dealt with rustlers: with a volley of gunshots.¹⁰

These are the kind of small independent ranchers that Proulx brings to life in her fiction; old men caught between the contemporary West and that of their ancestral imagination. They are narrow-minded, misogynistic and resistant to change, but Proulx describes them with enormous tenderness. Gilbert Wolfscale is a typical example:

> He was a model of rancher stubbornness, savagely possessive of his property. He did everything in an odd, deliberate way, Gilbert Wolfscale's way, and never retreated once he had taken a position. Neighbours said he was self-reliant, but there was a way they said it that meant something else. (65)

This is Gilbert seen through the eyes of the contemptuous newcomers; men and women who revel in the quality of 'stubborn self-reliance' when applied to historical or imaginary characters, but see Gilbert as lonely and obstructive. Their sniggering contempt is completely at odds with his straight talking. However, our pity is motivated not simply by their disdain, but by his inability to live up to his own vision of his ranching legacy.

'What Kind of Furniture would Jesus Pick?'

Gilbert lives in the shadow of his western past. He is dwarfed by the original 'chock-and-log fence' with which his grandfather set out his original claim; it, rather like the ruins of a Roman aqueduct seen by barbarians, forces Gilbert to confront the inadequacy and loneliness of his present life. For this is a fence constructed by a ranching community with a shared vision of the future (64). The pieces of bone he uses to maintain tension in his own more modest barbed-wire fence paradoxically summon up the ghosts of his ancestors while foreshadowing the ranch's death. Gilbert both possesses and is possessed by the ranch: ownership has become an end in itself detached from economic and social context, leaving Gilbert, for much of the narrative, a bemused analyst of his own feelings. He wonders whether he was drunk 'with the elixir of ownership' or suffering from 'a strangling love tattooed on his heart' – a formulation that emphasizes the suffocating pain of a legacy separated from reality. For, as the narrative makes clear, Gilbert is intoxicated by the vision of his ranch as 'timeless and unchanging in its beauty', which is not the trampled and desiccated landscape that actually lies before him (72).

Gilbert is not, however, a stubborn romantic. Instead, his attempts to adapt to global economic trends have all ended in failure. His diversification into turkey farming failed because consumers demanded 'Safeway turkeys with breasts like Las Vegas strippers' (64). As a result he finds himself in a 'downward ranching spiral of too much work, not enough money, drought', while besieged on all sides by environmentalists and suitcase ranchers. Their threat is not their hostility, but the seductiveness of their appeal. His response is to retreat into the archetype of the stubborn rancher who inhabits the West of his imagination, a character implied by the combination of 'wolf' and 'snake' in his surname. He dismisses the suitcase ranchers as 'rich pricks ... lower than a snake's ass in a wagon track' – a humorously observed image, which, because of the detail of the 'wagon track', could have rolled off the tongue of Gilbert's grandfather (68). His dealings with the environmental lobby are similarly theatrical. When faced with a single female campaigner concerned with river-bank erosion, he stands on his porch, legs apart, chin thrust forward in a parody of western stubbornness, and delivers a suitably laconic putdown: 'I heard all that shit. But I'll tell you what. I let cows graze where they want and drink where they will. Been doin this for a while. Guess I know somethin about it' (69). Indeed Gilbert does, but the narrative's success here lies not simply in the way it guides our sympathies towards the aggressive rancher rather than the vulnerable environmentalist (she is presented as a 'busybody' straight out of agricultural school), but in the way in which it presents Gilbert as a confused performer in his own pantomime.

Gilbert's bemusement with the contemporary world is not simply economic and environmental, it also dominates his emotional life. Reviewing the story in *The Observer*, Geraldine Bedell noted that Gilbert is 'like a lot of men in this book: physically tough, emotionally lost, bewildered by the complexity and deviousness of women, trying to hang on to what they know'.[11] What Gilbert knows is that women should be more compliant than those of his experience. The woman of his ranching imagination is exemplified by his grandfather's wife; she was plucked from the local whorehouse in order to provide a free workforce for the ranch prior to her apotheosis into the grand matriarch of popular tradition. Accordingly, Gilbert was supposed to marry the sister of his best friend Sedley (their incestuous relationship simply confirming her suitability for the isolation of ranch life), but she had different ideas and married a Montana ranch hand. The woman he marries out of revenge is entirely unsuitable. We hear nothing of their married life together or its disintegration; this would have the combined effect of taking the narrative focus away from Gilbert's inner turmoil, while simultaneously presenting him in an unfavourable light. Instead we are presented with a list of complaints revealed in a telephone conversation with her mother: 'No telephone, no electricity, no neighbors, his mother always naggin, and the work! He wore me down. "Do this, do that," bullyin ways' (70). The list is all too credible, yet the medium of complaint seems to trivialize the sentiments into conniving gossip, which has the effect of making us feel sorry for straight-talking Gilbert rather than his estranged wife. This sense of duplicity is echoed in her future indictment for embezzlement, which once again leaves Gilbert bemused by the deviousness of women.

Gilbert does not miss his wife, and his own domestic relations – living with his mother and visiting whorehouses – offer a contemporary approximation of the domestic setup enjoyed by his grandfather. He does, however, rue the loss of his sons, who seem to have 'escaped the scorching obsession of land ownership' (72). Writing in the *Independent*, Clive Sinclair noted that Gilbert's sons play out 'the tragedy of Wyoming in microcosm', according to which 'the sons and daughters of ranchers are, with a few exceptions, a bunch of sad-sacks in dead-end jobs'.[12] This aptly describes Monty and Rod: as youths they seldom visit the ranch and Gilbert is nonplussed by their expectation to be paid for ranch work that he did for his own father for free (71). When he meets the adult Rod over a drive-through KFC, the narrative clearly marks out the gulf between them to the detriment of the latter. Rod's thinning hair, 'pale, indoor complexion' and aftershave, combined with his preference for junk food and a dead-end job in a video store – where 'you had to tell them whatever you did or were going to do and they could say no' – contrasts with Gilbert's rugged self-reliance (82). It is over this meal that

Gilbert learns euphemistically that his other son is gay and that, unbeknown to him, his youngest grandchild has had cancer. In the ranching community of his imagination, members of the family talked to one another; no wonder that Gilbert 'couldn't tell the size of things' (84, 86).

His last betrayal comes from the land he loves, as drought settles on Wyoming 'like a lamprey eel sucking at the region's vitals' (80). The drought acts as a reminder that no matter how strong the western narrative of conquest, the land is not his and will not bend to his will. Previous generations had dealt with drought through stock ponds and deep wells, but now it is as if 'the country wanted to go to sand dunes and rattlesnakes, wanted to scrape off its human ticks' (68). This situation is exacerbated when a company drilling for methane poisons the local ground water. He had always voted Republican, but now finds himself in a peculiar alliance with 'ecological conservationists' fighting for compensation. This new world seems misaligned to Gilbert, whose image of himself as a western man of action fits uneasily into a world of meetings and petitions. Yet here is the clearest indication as to why Proulx believes that we should sympathize with Gilbert: for in this New West 'ranchers were the best defense against developers chopping up the land, that ranches and ranchers kept the old west alive' (80).[13]

An unusual subplot employed by Proulx to explore Gilbert's sense of confusion and betrayal is his failure, due to a growth in the nose, to participate in the Vietnam War. One of the most powerful legacies of Turner's frontier myth was the emergence of rhetoric of civilizing conquest which has been recycled repeatedly as part of US foreign policy.[14] This is particularly true of the Vietnam conflict, which, as Richard Slotkin has observed, was pre-packaged using the tropes and symbols derived from Western movies. The politicians sold it as a war of liberation over a new frontier; the participants employed a set of ready-made metaphors taken from their cowboy heroes (scouts were called 'Kit Carsons', and the jungle, 'Indian Territory'); and it was consumed at home through an interpretative grid which broke down the political complexity into a struggle between the good guys and bad guys.[15] In essence, Vietnam, like the conquest of the West, is one of the defining experiences in the moulding of American masculinity and identity, and Gilbert missed both. We find it odd that Gilbert feels so ostracized from his fellow ranchers that he buys CDs of battlefield sounds to experience Vietnam vicariously, but Proulx is reminding us that his vision of the mythical West is constructed in an equally synthetic manner through Hollywood Westerns and Zane Grey novels. Essentially, he is the product of cultural construction rather than a notional ranching heritage.

No wonder, as he sits stranded before the cavalcade of Western history at the story's denouement (in which the local community consciously performs in an ersatz version of their past while also acknowledging their present and future), he should appear confused (see Introduction). He senses that there is 'something seriously wrong' – there is no rancher represented (86). He is very much alive, but like the Vietnam veterans he admires, denied public sympathy. Like the cowboy and the Indian, he needs to pass into history before he can be resurrected through the lens of nostalgia. Hence his bitterness as his imagination drifts to a possible answer to the question posed by the title of the story: he would become a simple carpenter and 'He wouldn't get hisself tangled up with no ranch' (86). Through the agency of Christ, Gilbert imagines a Wyoming before the complexities that plague the contemporary West. And yet it is a vision of an untouched western wilderness that is as false as the story he tells himself concerning his ranching forefathers. Both Wests only exist in his fantasy.

'A Pair of Spurs'

Car Scrope is a rancher in Gilbert's mould: he is desperate to leave (he only inherited the ranch following his brother's suicide), but acknowledges that 'ownership' is as essential to his life as oxygen. His parents had obviously expected great things of their boys – their names 'Car' and 'Train' suggest both modernity and movement. However, the latter dies young and by the time we meet Car he is so broken by a life of rodeo and ranching that 'he was now held together with dozens of steel pins, metal plates and lag screws', while living off a diet of junk food, whiskey and pornography (171). Like Gilbert, he is betrayed by everybody, his consequent decline foreshadowed in the mad, piss-drenched hermit stumbled upon by Inez Muddyman in her youth: 'He used to be a pretty good rancher,' her father claims, 'but his wife died' (184).

Proulx's interest in this story is the death of a certain kind of West, its demise signalled through the narrative sub-headings – 'the coffee pot', 'the spur maker', 'the wolf' and 'Texas boys' – which, like the notion of the West itself, are not what they seem. To this end Proulx abandons her more familiar social realism and constructs a thematic vein of magic realism assembled around the ultimate western symbol: a pair of spurs. The spur maker himself, Harold Batts, defies our expectations: he is not a gnarled, old rancher, but an ex-metallurgical engineer with a hippy ponytail and a herbal tea habit who has moved to Wyoming 'to live a simple life in a simple place' (174). Pink-slipped from his factory work, he has become obsessed with endings, whether cataloguing Wyoming's road-killed animals, or preaching the end of the world through his membership of the Final Daze religious cult (174). His spurs, which incorporate the 'Hale-Bopp' comet (an augury of doomsday), are made from metal smelted from the 'scavenged scrap from abandoned ranches'. Therefore, they are a fitting symbol for the death of a vision of the old West; a vision shared by all those who wear them (175).

Scrope never owns them: he is obsessed by them, and the form this obsession takes is sexual. Proulx once again invokes the relationship between the taming of the landscape and the exploitation of women. Scrope may be held together with bits of metal, but he has mastered the land and is able to adapt to the worst excesses of the weather and hold the winter ice melt behind his scrupulously maintained earth dams. Within the story, the water becomes analogous to Scrope's sexuality: a wild element that is constantly threatening to burst into the domesticated. What the spurs release, through a magnetic relation to the metal in his body, is the controlled wildness in Scrope: 'The rank animal was out of him and in the open' (185). It returns him to his cowboy youth, when he was part of a trio (comprising fellow ranchers John Wrench and Sutton Muddyman), who 'rode' both women and horses, and exchanged them 'often still swimming with the other's spermy juice' (173). In the sexual economy of the old West, partners precede wives in terms of affection, which is why Scrope is more perplexed by his wife's decision to file for divorce than by her sleeping with Wrench (who is no respecter of boundaries), and why Muddyman is indifferent to Scrope's sexual advances towards his wife. His pursuit of both Inez and Mrs Freeze (we are left to imagine the consequence had Haul Smith made it to his meeting to discuss boundaries with Scrope!) offers a grotesquely distorted vision of the sexualized cowboy. It is therefore apt that he should end the story sitting on a mud bank staring manically into the floodwater in search of the spurs. His defences, both earthen and sexual, have been overwhelmed by this lost symbol of the West.

The first owner of the spurs is Inez Muddyman. She was 'raised, as she said, on a horse from breakfast to bed' – but she and her husband have now taken to Dude ranching (171). This is a selling of a sanitized version of the West to tourists, which offers the excitement of the western experience without the attendant risks. For tax purposes, as Muddyman complains, they are classed as 'entertainment ranches'. However, this narrative, like those discussed in the chapter on 'Landscape', sets out to remind us that beneath the sanitized appearance, such environments are still full of risk (181). This is made plain through the fate of one of the ranch hands, Cody Joe, whose name evokes the ultimate cowboy showman. In his youth Cody Joe was the archetypal tourist cowboy, until a 'thousand-pound hay bale tipped off a stack onto him and his horse' (181). Unfortunately, Inez fails to appreciate the implications of the accident: a lifetime of selling a storybook West to eastern tourists has left her distanced from her ranch instincts, and therefore incapable of dealing with the non-domesticated elements still at work, whether these are the wolf, the predatory sexual behaviour of Scrope, or the floodwater. Thus, as Frantz notes, when one of a trio of city lawyers phones to tell Inez that they are lost and are scared of a wolf (she is certain of its identity having watched hours of footage during a court case involving urban wolves (190)), Inez at once uses her knowledge of the land to identify where they are, but also to dismiss the idea of the wolf. Indeed, Inez is so certain that the animal is not a wolf that when she does encounter it, while wearing the pair of spurs, she reverts to her cowboy youth and tries to rope it like a rodeo calf. Through the magic of the spurs, Proulx reminds us that Inez's knowledge of the 'natural' is just as much a construction as that of the Dude ranchers – who correctly identified the wolf through the medium of television.[16]

The death of Inez finds the spurs passing not to her husband, who buys a one-way ticket to Oregon, but to Mrs Freeze, the female foreman of Scrope's ranch. Freeze (her name suggesting coldness and frigidity) allows Proulx to explore a very different kind of rancher: the female cowboy. She is not a 'Calamity Jane' or 'Belle Star figure', but nor is she a 'cowgirl' in the traditional Western sense: she is not young and pretty and squeezed into tight jeans and stacked boots. Freeze is a female cowboy, and as such far from unusual in contemporary Wyoming. As she informs the incredulous Texan cowboy, Haul Smith: 'You ain't spent much time in Wyomin. Half the hands is women nowadays and not paid near as good as the men' (198). She is right: not only do Teresa Jordan's interviews for her study *Cowgirls: Women of the American West* attest to the existence of a sizeable number of active female cowboys, but women now have an increasing representation in the Wyoming Stock-Growers Association (including, in Mary Mead, the first ever female vice president).[17] Their increasing participation in ranch affairs, however, has come at a price. Women working in this highly masculine field have been forced to abandon their female identity and become default men. Proulx gives us a snapshot of such a figure in the story 'The Colors of Horses' (*Accordion Crimes*), in the grotesque figure of the ranch hand Eunice Brown – a sobering corrective to the sirens presented in Tom Robbins' *Even Cowgirls Get the Blues* (1976). She has 'a mad preacher's face' and a mouth misshapen by a cattle brand, but is liked by her employer because she 'was as strong as a man, worked cheaper, and was a better cowboy because she didn't drink' – though in reality a pint of whiskey nestled between her breasts.[18] Mrs Freeze offers a moderate version: a 'crusty old whipcord who looked like a man, dressed like a man, talked like a man and swore like a man, but carried a bosom shelf, an irritation to her as it got in the way of her roping' (169).

This, however, changes when she becomes the owner of the spurs and is viewed through the prism of the old West. Scrope has always respected her as a cowboy – 'what the old girl didn't know about stock could be written on a cigarette paper with room left over for Bible verses' – but when wearing the spurs she becomes a female to be 'ploughed' like all others (181-2). When, due to Scrope's continual harassment, she seeks work with Haul Smith, Proulx brings her face to face with another expression of the old West. Smith himself has been imported into Wyoming by the new owner of the 'Galaxy Ranch' because he constitutes what a real cowboy should look like. Unfortunately, seen through his eyes, Freeze does not conform to expectation, and he claims that some of his 'Texas cowboys' might find it difficult working with a woman. It is therefore ironic that all he wants from her is the spurs, for in reclaiming them he is salvaging his patriarchal vision of the West. The irony is amplified further when he asks her to oversee a project for reintroducing bison to the Galaxy Ranch, a request that aligns her not only with an animal that is not part of his western vision, but with one that has been wiped out.

Through the collapse of the Boxhandle Ranch and its reinvention under various owners, Proulx takes an opportunity to explore new kinds of western authenticity. The first is the millionaire suitcase rancher, Frank Fane, who has made his money playing a Jupiterean warlord in a science fiction television series and has moved West with a dream of returning bison to the landscape. He is a fictionalization of real-life moguls like Ted Turner, husband of Jane Fonda, who, having made millions selling commercials during old John Wayne and Randolph Scott movies, bought the 130,000-acre Flying D Ranch near Bozeman. To the horror of the local cowboys, he sold off the cows and reintroduced bison, claiming that as an indigenous species they do less damage and 'are better looking than cows'.[19] Clearly, in his mind, such reintroduction programmes are so environmentally and morally irreproachable that they can be announced with flippancy. To some extent, it is the truth of this contention that Proulx sets out to investigate through the activities of Fane. Although he stresses the ecological argument in favour of reintroducing bison, Proulx cleverly undermines his claims by suggesting that what he really wants to re-create is a generic western space that conforms to the one of his Hollywood-inspired imagination. He wants to create a film set every bit as inauthentic and artificial as those that back his science fiction series. Ironically, some of the Texas cowboys he imports to re-create his vision are so dissatisfied by the 'authenticity' of his plans that they leave in order to pursue their own version of the West by joining a re-enactment of a historic trail ride.[20]

What constitutes the authentic West is thrown into sharper relief when the Galaxy Ranch passes on to a breakfast food mogul 'who said he wanted nothing more than to let the new ranch "revert to a state of nature"' (204–5). Regrettably, his ecological concern is as destructive as Fane's. Not only does it presuppose a mythical state of nature (which discounts Native American land management), but it implies that it will be brought about by non-intervention. In this story, lack of intervention does not lead to the restoration of natural balance, but to the terrible flood caused by Scrope's failure to maintain his melt-water dams. The flood is presented on a biblical scale of which Harold Batts would have approved and washes away both the Coffeepot and the pair of spurs. They lodge 'under a sunken steel beam of the old railroad trestle, the spurs seeking sister metal' of another vision of the West – the age of the iron horse (204). The last owner is Haul Smith, whose bar-room swagger and macho pool play suggest his self-conscious cowboy performance; a personal vision that grows grotesquely out of proportion when he wears the spurs. His death, while crossing the flooded Bad Girl Creek, mirrors that of Inez before him. His vision of the cowboy has dulled his ranching instincts so that he fails to see the dangers of the river in front of him, which he tries to ford in imitation of John Wayne. The redoubtable Mrs Freeze would have ridden downstream to the bridge.

Landscapes of a new West

What constitutes the 'authentic' West is a question that dominates contemporary ecological debate. Teasing out Proulx's attitude on the subject can be difficult. The gentle mockery of range restoration projects in 'A Pair of Spurs' would suggest scepticism, yet elsewhere in her fiction, and, indeed her private life, she is much more positive – as her sowing of wild grasses around her Bird Cloud Ranch attests. Her most positive endorsement of restoration schemes (such as the 'Buffalo Commons' policy first advocated by geographers Deborah and Frank Popper in 1987) is to be found in the novel *That Old Ace in the Hole*. The novel appears to be a western morality tale in which the white-hatted eco-cowboys struggle against the black-hatted industrialized hog farmers for the soul of Bob Dollar. The former are represented by Ace Crouch, a local rancher who wants to run bison (a local variation on the 'Buffalo Commons' idea) on land brought back from the hog farms. This is not just a practical attempt to limit the spread of agribusiness, but a moral campaign to allow ranchers to determine the region's future. As Ace notes: 'You think it's just a place. It's more than that. It's people's lives, it's the history of the country' (333). It is also, through Proulx's inclusion of Brother Mesquite (cassock over blue jeans with cowboy boots), a spiritual crusade. He challenges the Christian orthodoxy that man was given dominion over the land and animals – the dogma that condoned Manifest Destiny – offering instead a 'moral geography' predicated upon the symbiosis of animal and landscape. We have much to learn, he argues, from the evolution of bison within the landscape: 'The two grew up together, they *belong* together in this place, this landscape' (274, Proulx's italics). It is the cow, and by extension man, that is the interloper, which is why they require so much work and yet still remain out of place.

The book's 'happy ending', which envisions Bob finding both friends and a meaning to his otherwise unfocused life by joining the scheme, suggests Proulx is sympathetic to its aims. And yet, as critics Matthew Cella and Elizabeth Abele have noted, Proulx's carefully crafted ending is perhaps less rosy than it appears. The plan to return the plains to a 'state of nature' dismisses the existence of the farming practices of Native Americans, who Ace dismisses with the casual: 'They didn't *live* here. They were nomadic ... No, the first people tried a *live* here was those old farmers and ranchers' (Proulx's italics, 111). Racist implications aside, Ace's position is ironic because 'the plan calls for and relies on a strategy of land use that echoes the one employed by the nomadic and semi-nomadic tribes of the pre-contact Plains'.[21] Furthermore, Ace's 'white hat' is not perfectly gleaming: Abele draws attention to the fact that he initially made his money installing windmills, which for decades have sucked up the Ogallala aquifer leading to present-day problems with aridity. He also inherited a fortune from his former partner who made his money in the environmentally suspect oil business. Furthermore, the project depends on the sale of luxury homes to people who 'want a live where they can see bison and watch the prairie come back' (356).[22] And the trouble with yuppie incomers, as Proulx makes clear through the character of La Von Fronk, is that their demands destroy the local infrastructure: '"They want organic grocery stores. ... They want likker stores. They want *restaurants*." She gave the last word a tone that equated it with "leper colonies"' (99, Proulx's italics).

The ambiguities surrounding back-to-nature programmes presented in *That Old Ace* are transformed into a much more strident critique of the Buffalo Plains concept in 'The Governors of Wyoming' (*CR*). In this story the battle for the New West is waged by eco-terrorist Wade Walls, who is the only voice Proulx gives to the Deep Green lobby. He is a follower of Edward Abbey, at times appearing like a figure stepping out of the pages of the *Monkey Wrench Gang:* 'These subsidised ranchers', he rails, Abbey style, 'and their gas-bag cows destroying public range, riparian habitat, wiping out rare plants ... and for what? A pitiful three per cent of the state's gross income. So a few can live a nineteenth-century lifestyle' (241). What he wants is similar to Ace:

> I want it to be like it was, all the fences and cows gone. I want the native grasses to come back, the wildflowers ... I want the ranchers and feedlot operators and processors and meat distributors to go down the greased pole straight to hell. If I ran the west I'd sweep them all away, leave the wind and the grasses to the hands of the gods. Let it be the empty place. (243)

The aims are shared, but Walls advocates direct action: cutting fences, poisoning cattle with diapers, leaving threatening calling cards. Ironically, he sees himself as Shane (his personal soundtrack 'would be a huffed and spitty harmonica'), the mysterious force for good living on his wits and taking on the big ranch outfits (235). But to the ranchers he is a terrorist. Proulx brings out this irony of labelling through the decoration of the 'cowboy room' he stays in when in Wyoming. On the wall hangs 'a digital reproduction of a chromolithograph showing a rustler caught in the act': Walls is the anti-cowboy, but does that make him the rustler, the man who defies cowboy conventions (240)? Proulx's narrative goes out of its way to make him an unappealing character. His name suggests both slow moving and blinkered, and he is described as 'slump shouldered' with the face of 'a grouper fish'. He is a vegan vegetarian, with a homemade hemp suit and a non-leather briefcase, but continually drinks bottled water in an arid region. In addition, he is a casual misogynist, referring to women as girls and expecting them to cook for him. Furthermore, his motives for terrorist action, like those of his partner, Shy Hemp (see the chapter on 'Indians'), are far removed from ecological concerns. Walls is motivated by class envy and revenge for the death of his father – Mr Walasiewicz – who was an assembly-line butcher killed by 'some malignant infection' (272). However, most damning of all in cowboy country is the revelation that Walls is a coward: when Shy is shot, Walls runs away, leaving him, like the titular governors of Wyoming, to meet his public.

Perhaps, considering Proulx's attitude to the environment discussed in the chapter on 'Landscape', her scepticism towards Deep Green environmentalism is unsurprising. Advocates may dream of nature before the interference of man, but are caught in the paradox of being unable, by definition, to visualize such a space. Furthermore, there is an ironic arrogance in their self-appointment as spokesperson for nature. Indeed, cultural geographer John Brinckerhoff Jackson argues that the 'state of nature' lobbyists are a cultural elite determined to serve its own anti-technological, anti-urban, anti-people sense of nostalgia by transforming the landscape into something to be looked at rather than lived in.[23] For Proulx such projects can only be understood metaphorically, because they deny the landscape as a dynamic, lived space. Thus, though the New West may see the reintroduction of buffalo herds, the pump jacks and trailer parks that announce the presence of a population going about its business will remain. In the pursuit of blinkered ideology, men like Wade Walls must not be allowed to *Close* the *Range*.

One group for whom the range has remained forever closed, whose role in the mythical West remains undocumented, whose presence on ranches has been all but invisible, is the female rancher. It is their plight that forms the focus of 'Tits-Up in a Ditch' and 'The Bunchgrass Edge of the World' – to which we turn now.

'Tits-Up in a Ditch'

Verl Lister, like Gilbert and Car, is a rancher at sea in the contemporary world, defending his dilapidated ranch and his resistance to change with the plaintive appeal: 'Wyomin is fine just the way it is' (189). The implication of this statement is what Proulx sets out to explore in the collection as a whole and this story in particular, and her conclusions are ambiguous at best. For, while we are invited to feel some sympathy for the bemused Verl in his battles with his neighbours, ill-health, and a wayward daughter, the narrative tone is less generous than that extended to Gilbert. This is largely because in Verl the stoical resistance of the cowboy has been transformed into the listlessness anticipated by his surname. The tale he tells of a cow landing tits up in a ditch reveals both his inertia and fatalism; he dismisses the event as bad luck, but does nothing to re-wire the fence to prevent it happening again (189). Proulx throws this listlessness into sharp relief by giving a voice to those outsiders who were held up as figures of ridicule in Gilbert's world, especially those belonging to women. One such is Californian Carol Match, whose feisty independence of spirit is signalled by her 'tiny blue skirt', 'robust breasts' and determination to catalogue Wyoming's shortcomings from greater ethnic diversity to road safety (189). Her criticism not only upsets the cosy patriarchy which allows inertia to masquerade as the voice of tradition, but it also highlights a crisis of cultural identity among a generation of western men for whom the 'pioneer spirit of freedom' has been reduced to the right not to wear a seat belt (189).

Carol's husband is millionaire Wyatt Match, a suitcase rancher in the tradition of Frank Fane. Having made his fortune from the absurdly un-rugged 'Cowboy Slim' weight-loss mail-order programme, he is determined, as his name suggests, to re-create the 'romantic heritage of the nineteenth-century ranch', proof that 'Wyoming was *fine just the way it was*' (183, 184, Proulx's italics). Ironically, he dismisses the only authentic rancher around, Verl, as a 'trash rancher', because he refuses to fit into this mythologizing of the landscape (181). Beneath the cowboy nostalgia, however, Wyatt understands that Wyoming is 'fine just the way it is' because women run the ranch, leaving men to indulge their cowboy fantasies. When he divorces in order to marry Carol Shovel (the surname suggesting a gold digger), he keeps on his first wife as ranch manager: 'She was a good worker and he wasn't going to let her go' (185). The same is true of Lister's ranch, which is run by his wife, Bonita; a situation made explicit through a passage within the text which wavers between the voices of the narrator, a horrified granddaughter, and, we speculate, Proulx's own:

> On the ranches the wives held everything together – cooking for big crowds, nursing the sick and injured, cleaning, raising children and driving them to rodeo practice, keeping the books and paying the bills ... and often riding with the men at branding and shipping times ... and were treated with little more regard than the beef they helped to produce. (205)

Bonita's limited horizons are both literal and metaphorical: she is seldom depicted anywhere but at the kitchen sink using implements – 'an ancient peeler', the 'chipped and rusted enamel colander' – that belonged to Verl's great-grandmother, thus reminding us of the perpetuation of female bondage (187). Not for her the time-saving microwave oven owned by Mrs Crashbee, wife of the enlightened priest; in Verl's kitchen they'll be sticking with the good old kitchen stove, since that's the way things have always been. Her bondage is maintained by the religious puritanism espoused by TV evangelist, Jim Bakker, who commends 'thankless work as the right and the good way' (180). Proulx exposes this fraud through the coincidental birth of Bonita's bastard granddaughter and the exposure of Bakker as a sexual hypocrite on the same day: April 1st. Men seem to be having a laugh at Bonita's expense.

This is the hypocrisy and exploitation against which her daughter and granddaughter rebel. Young Dakotah is named after Verl's 'homesteading great-grandmother', who buries her husband and then, despite public disapproval, hastily claims the ranch deed. Proulx is offering us a glimpse of a type of woman whose toughness extends not simply to her dealings with the environment, but also to her determination to transform the move west into a liberating experience. She is part of a sizeable minority of female ranch owners air-brushed out of the western narrative (see 'Pioneers'). Verl treasures an old photograph of her proudly displaying the deed, but he fails to grasp its implications: Dakotah is no mere appendage to her husband's dream of ownership – whether of land, cattle or a wife – but an individual with her own ambitions. Though the country has changed beyond recognition, her spirit of independence has passed down to her namesake: Dakotah. And where Verl's shattered body and flaccid acceptance of fate exhibits the limitations of the male western narrative in the contemporary world, Dakotah's pioneer spirit emerges in a form of independence that Verl, if he knew the word, would have branded 'feminism'.

From an early age Dakotah seems to understand and resent the limitations placed on ranch daughters in contemporary ranching society. Proulx, always better at presenting individual psychology through vignette rather than introspection, illustrates this resentment through a childhood scene in which the young Dakotah reproves a stranger (whom we later learn was possibly her father) for only throwing to his son, not his daughter, during a game of Frisbee (206). Ranch sons, she learns quickly, are heirs to both the ranch and western tradition. The neglect that she experienced during her own upbringing is transformed into conscientious care for her bastard son, little Verl: 'Among the privileges of western malehood from which the baby benefitted were open dams of affection in Bonita and Verl' (203). If Dakotah wants affection, the narrative makes clear, she needs to marry. Unfortunately, like her grandmother and mother, she is in the thrall of the western myth and ends up choosing a cowboy. Sash Hicks may have the glamour of Billy the Kid, but for Proulx it is the childish simplicity of his expectations of marriage, implied by both 'Hicks' and 'Kid', that are worthy of comment. He sees marriage as an opportunity to replace a dutiful mother with 'a biddable handmaiden who would look to his comforts' (195). Unfortunately, Dakotah, as she makes abundantly clear, is the wrong choice: 'I been bossed around since I was a kid. I didn't agree to be your maid' (200).

His departure leaves Dakotah literally dreaming of the freedom of single motherhood, the contemporary equivalent of her grandmother's pioneer isolation. However, as the narrative proceeds to demonstrate, her grandmother's freedom is a pipe dream in contemporary Wyoming. To begin with, she is fired from her waitressing job for being pregnant. The interview with her outwardly liberal boss, Mr Castle, takes place in an airless room beneath 'a huge tinted photograph of his wife and triplet daughters' – an environment that foregrounds his suffocatingly, narrow-minded conception of what constitutes a family unit (202). The photograph is tinted, blemishes and irregularities cosmetically removed, a process that applies to both Castle himself, and his notion of moral behaviour. There will be no storming of this 'castle' of conservative values. Furthermore, her attempts to contact Sash are met by his mother, who believes him the innocent victim of a woman who wants to 'squeeze money out a him' (203). Verl rejects the idea of welfare as a matter of western pride, dismissing it as a 'pantywaist' solution that leaves her 'suck[ing] on the taxpayer's tit' (204). The message seems clear: the frontier that offered her grandmother so much freedom has been appropriated by a patriarchy that condemns the single mother while defending the errant father.

The only solution available to Dakotah is to strike out for a new frontier where a liberated identity can be forged through struggle with a new environment: in this narrative this space is occupied by Iraq. From the moment the smoke cleared following the collapse of the twin towers it was clear from the rhetoric of George W. Bush, the last in a line of cowboy presidents, that the campaign in the Middle East was to be conceived of in frontier terms. As with Vietnam, western rhetoric was appropriated to galvanize a national response. Jones and Wills draw attention to the fact that alongside his infamous 'Wanted Dead or Alive' address, Bush issued a rousing 'bring 'em on' challenge to the Islamic terrorists at a press conference situated in front of a picture of Theodore Roosevelt on horseback. The Iraqi Defence Minister, Ali Ahamkhani, observed that 'Bush thinks he is still living in the age of cowboys, and that the world is like Texas with him as its sheriff.'[24] And this, as Proulx has observed, is the problem when cowboy rhetoric is used to endorse foreign incursions: 'The west has come to symbolize the policies and character of a country increasingly hated in the larger world, cutting fences and forcing its cows through. Thus has the heroic myth circled back to bite its creator on the ass.'[25]

In this story, however, Proulx's target is not rhetorical misappropriation, but the relation between this new frontier and female emancipation. The fact that Dakotah is able to enlist at all suggests more equality; that she becomes a Military Police officer suggests that she is going to play sheriff and set the rules on this new frontier. Unfortunately, despite her early optimism she finds that the army 'was still a man's army and that women were decidedly inferior in all ways' (206). Her treatment, however, pales into insignificance beside the oppression suffered by the Muslim women: 'Never had the world seemed so vile and her own problems so mean and dirty' (213). In this oppressively male world, Dakotah finds a soul mate in another woman, Marnie Jellson. When a friend's letter arrives informing them that 'two lesbian women' have set up shop in their home town without comment, it seems that the narrative is preparing us for a happy ending in a more enlightened Wyoming (212). But Proulx resists such an ending, not least because the message that female happiness comes with the absence of men is unsatisfactory. Instead, Proulx's climatic end blows apart the bodies and the dreams of Dakotah, Marnie and, we later learn, Sash. Their disintegration offers an ironic parody of the Turner thesis, in which individuals are broken down and rebuilt as Americans. For when these particular pieces are reassembled it does not produce free, self-reliant individuals, but an exaggerated version of the cripple and handmaiden relationship endured by Verl and Bonita.

There is, however, one more emotional atrocity that Proulx has in store for Dakotah: the death of her son, little Verl, in a farming accident. His death not only vindicates Bonita's sense of righteous suffering, but allows Proulx to draw out parallels between the old and new frontiers. On Dakotah's journey home she drives along a stretch of road referred to locally as the 'Sixteen Mile'. It is a name that has always puzzled her, but as she acknowledges the similarity between the blood-stained deserts of Iraq and the 'hammered red landscape in which ranch buildings appeared dark and sorrowful', she realizes that every ranch had lost a boy, not to war, or even a glorious shoot-out, but to tractor rollovers, 'rodeo smash-ups', and the fatal combination of 'liquor and acceleration' that comes from too much testosterone and boredom. This, she understands, is the 'waiting darkness that surrounded ranch boys' in a land where, like Iraq, 'it didn't pay to love' (218–21). In such an environment the 'grief counseling' offered to Dakotah seems ridiculously inadequate, and is rejected in favour of the metaphorical cowboy lasso: a sure means of numbing the pain (221). The full implication of Proulx's title now becomes clear: ranchers are 'tits-up in a ditch' struggling to escape from the mud that threatens to suck them down. Verl Lister's apparent listlessness now takes on the character of a survival strategy: the land has taught him that the secret of successful ranching is not innovation but endurance. This is the lesson that Dakotah has now learned. Thus, when Sash's mother reminds her of her wifely duty to look after the shattered remains of her husband, she now feels 'her own hooves slip and the beginning descent into the dark, watery mud' (221).

Dakotah's dreams of emancipation founder on the cold reality of Wyoming ranch life. The empty West, which offered Dakotah's grandmother a degree of self-determination, has now been colonized and reordered to suit men. Clearly, if women are to emerge from a male western legacy, then there needs to be a change to a gender-neutral narrative form, which is what Proulx offers in 'The Bunchgrass Edge of the World'.

'The Bunchgrass Edge of the World'

In this story Proulx transports the reader from a recognizable Wyoming landscape, with named urban centres, to a marginal space at the edge of the world to explore how it might be feminized. This is a story concerned with reinterpretation, which is made absolutely clear by the opening paragraph's insistence on the way that we view the land: 'The country appeared as empty ground ... Nothing much but weather and distance, the distance punctuated once in a while by ranch gates' (131). The country may appear 'empty' but it has still been divided up into ranches, the ownership of which will be passed through a patriarchal line. 'In this vague region' it is clear that Proulx will be abandoning realism for fairy tale to explore how the usual male hegemony can be challenged and subverted at the margins of civilized society.

Old Red, the patriarch, has a largely symbolic role, his very existence conjuring up the harshness of the 'Red Wall' landscape and the endurance required to ranch it. He is an older and tougher version of Verl, believing that successful ranching derives from 'staying power': 'Stand around long enough you'd get to sit down' (162). Throughout the narrative, he encapsulates the spirit of the old West: his entirely negative commentary offering a homegrown fatalism which at once privileges the strength of the cowboy while mocking the vanity of human attempts to alter the overpowering landscape. He is not, however, ranch-born and raised, but a convert whose vision of the old West is constructed on a combination of John Wayne movies and Zane Grey novels. This is the vision of the West that he wants to pass through the generations. Therefore it is ironic that despite the sexless nature of his cowboy heroes, he is another Proulxian character who elides conquest of the land with sexual conquest. During one particular battle for succession he reminds Aladdin, as he clutches his crotch, that 'I made this ranch and I made you' (134). It is a sexual energy that seems to have diminished little, as Aladdin's wife, Wauneta, is forced to warn her daughters against playing on his lap. Like Gilbert and Scrope he is deserted by his wife and five children, with only Aladdin, 'the giant of the litter', remaining (132). The term 'litter' tells us everything we need to know about Red's attitude towards domesticity and the inheritance of the ranch.

Aladdin's marriage to Wauneta is touched by magic, as the wheat seeds thrown at the ceremony grow into the romantic image of the 'wedding wheat' that surrounds the house. And yet by evoking the bunchgrass (or wheatgrass) of the title, it serves to define the limits of Wauneta's world, just as the natural prairie grass delimits the ranch. Aladdin does not inherit the ranch, but he 'wrenched' it from Old Red when he was 26 (133). In contrast to Red, he offers a vision of the future of ranching: he wears the essential cowboy boots and hat, but has never sat on a horse. In a symbolic gesture, he trades the symbols of a heroic western past – a couple of bulls, a saddle, and an 1860 Colt .44 – for a Piper Cub light aircraft: the future of the West (135). However, despite embracing technological change, his vision is still limited by gender stereotypes: he perceives his aeroplane and tractors as females, to be driven hard and discarded when of little use. This narrow-mindedness extends to his own children: while Tyler, the heir-apparent, plays with plastic cattle and sleeps in the bunkhouse, the girls learn to bake cakes. Even in the aeronautical age the patriarchy remains intact.

The problem for Aladdin is that shared by all Proulx's ranchers: none of the younger generation wants to inherit the ranch. Both Shan and Tyler escape to Las Vegas, a highly stylized environment which trades on its superficiality and lack of connection with the 'real' world. But in Proulx's West, 'reality' has never been much use, and Las Vegas is not an aberration, but an exaggeration of the plight of numberless towns in which the locals are forced to perform the role of walk-on minstrels. Shan has simply traded one home, surreal in its emptiness, for a version of the hyperreal. Her decision to become a vegetarian and a bodybuilder indicates her desperation to remove herself even further from cowboy culture in terms of both diet and the acceptable patriarchal view of the female form. Indeed, by using her body to blur the distinction between the masculine and feminine she foreshadows Ottaline's later blurring of gender roles. Tyler, despite being inducted into cowboy tradition, leaves the ranch only to return on Ottaline's wedding day, when the narrator's carefully crafted description captures his lack of empathy:

> Tyler inspected the ranch, looking it over with a displeased eye. Everything was smaller and shabbier. Why had he wanted this? He had a cell phone and sat on his horse talking to someone far away. Wauneta told Shan she intended to come out to Las Vegas and visit one of these days. (159)

There is, as Frantz has noted, an implication of measured criticism in the term 'inspected', which is emphasized by the displeased eye. Even as he sits astride a horse, he is not communing with the land, but communicating with an anonymous listener far away. The punctuation allows Wauneta's promise of temporary escape to mix with Tyler's imagined conversation, thus underlining her sense of entrapment.[26]

This leaves Ottaline: she dreams of getting away, of 'wearing red sandals with cork soles', but is a prisoner of both the ranch and her own body. She is 'distinguished by a physique approaching the size of a hundred-gallon propane tank', which fails to fit into cowboy visions of femininity (136). She is nagged by Wauneta for her size and dismissed from the traditionally feminine realm of the house for being too clumsy. She therefore swaps her XXL skirts for trousers and becomes Aladdin's unpaid and unconventional 'cowgirl'. Ottaline's story traces her transformation from lonely runt of the litter to ranch owner, a narrative which has more in common with Cinderella than the traditional cowboy fiction read by Old Red. Before Proulx waves her magic wand, however, her focus is on the existential crisis experienced by women living on isolated ranches. Ottaline, like her pioneer ancestors, is forbidden to drive or ride to town (because she will damage the suspension), leaving the only contact with the outside world to come from listening to conversations on the police scanner. Ironically, these meaningless fragments represent an external reality that stands in contrast to the coherent voice of Aladdin's junked John Deere: the voice of Ottaline's interior life.

Proulx's venture into fairy tale reveals not only Ottaline's existential barrenness, but also her awareness that she is playing a part in two familiar narratives. At one point Ottaline says to the John Deere: 'Are you like an enchanted thing? A damn story where some girl lets a warty old toad sleep in her shoe and in the mornin the toad's a good-lookin dude makin omelettes?' (150). Essentially, she understands that in both fairy tale and western narratives women remain the passive recipients of male attentions. This changes in Proulx's unorthodox love story when Ottaline decides to rebuild the tractor; a decision which flies in the face of the pessimism of her father and even the tractor itself: 'It's men that fixes tractors, not no woman' (153). On one level the rebuilding of a machine condemned as useless symbolically suggests the salvaging of Ottaline's otherwise expendable person. It is a bonding exercise that brings together father and daughter in a traditionally masculine activity, a role subversion challenged further by their attribution of different genders to the tractor. For Aladdin, all machinery is female, an updated western horse to be mastered; for Ottaline, the tractor is a male to be dominated sexually with her can of 'penetrating oil'. She even uses the words of one of the cowboys who had seduced her in her youth: 'I was you I'd lay back and enjoy it' (154). The story seems to suggest that, as they were for the first pioneers, the presupposed gender roles are meaningless at the bunchgrass edge of the world.

Working on the tractor enables Ottaline to find a voice, but she is still not in a position to wrench the ranch from Aladdin. That only comes from marriage to Flyby Amendinger, whose name suggests that he is the flighty answer to her prayers. The marriage, however, is not a celebration of male dominance, for Flyby is attracted by her ranching knowledge over her 'upholstered' good looks. Rather, as Frantz has observed, in marriage Ottaline becomes a rancher who has a husband and not a rancher's wife, the position occupied by her mother.[27] The changing dispensation is symbolized by Flyby's cutting the wedding wheat while Ottaline plays with the bolts of the stripped-down John Deere: Ottaline has figuratively dismantled the traditional gender roles so that her horizon will not be confined to her mother's wheatgrass. Old Red fears that Ottaline's grim reaper has come for him, but his scything of the wheat prefigures the death of the only real obstruction to Ottaline's inheritance: Aladdin. Ironically, it is Wauneta who articulates the fatal wish during Aladdin's staged 'fly by' – 'YOU GET DOWN HERE!' The John Deere, which throughout has given a voice to women, plays the part of Aladdin's magic lamp by granting it (161). In the recriminations that follow, it is Old Red who understands that for all Aladdin's technological innovations, it is Ottaline, the unconventional 'cowgirl', who offers a direct challenge to the male hegemony that he represents.

There is a war being fought for the legacy of the West, and Proulx's small independent ranchers are in the middle of it. They are the men – 'men' is important here – who built the West, but they now find themselves suffocating beneath the weight of their own narrative myth. They are victims of fluctuating markets, nutritionist health scares, and environmental politics. They see themselves as stoical, but to big business they are obstinate. To Proulx they are the bemused spectators of the demise of a certain vision of the West, a vision that has been spectacularly appropriated by incoming corporate and suitcase ranchers. The New West has become a simulacrum, a space in which myth and reality have become so blurred that there is no sense of the original to which contemporary signs may refer: a point Proulx makes clear through the interpretative elasticity she accords to the ultimate western symbol – 'a pair of spurs'. Significantly, though the myth is amenable to different interpretations, it remains insistently male. Though her ranchers acknowledge their failure, they still believe that Wyoming's 'fine just the way it is', and that innovation is to be measured in terms of machinery, rather than radically different power structures. For Proulx's ranch daughters, the only way to experience the emancipation enjoyed by the first female pioneers is to either renounce their femininity and become proxy cowboys, or to find their own frontier. Tellingly, the only successful female rancher is Ottaline Touhey, a character whose story is only possible at the 'bunchgrass edge of the world', where fairy tales unfold.

4

Cowboys

> I grew up a-dreaming of being a cowboy,
> Loving the cowboy ways.
> Pursuing the life of my high ridin' heroes,
> I burned up my childhood days.

So sang Willie Nelson in the soundtrack to the 1979 film *The Electric Horseman*. The song's title – *My Heroes Have Always been Cowboys* – and lyrical content (in which the narrator contrasts his boyhood aspirations with his adult life spent on the road – a mockery of a cowboy riding the range) capture the juvenility underlying America's love affair with the cowboy. It is perhaps unsurprising that when Proulx moved to Wyoming – home of Shane and the Virginian – she should set about exploring the myth. Her opinions are made clear in the opening paragraph of her essay 'How the West was Spun':

> The heroic myth of the American west is much more powerful than its historical past. To this day, the great false beliefs about cowboys prevail: that they were – and are – brave, generous, unselfish men; that the west was 'won' by noble white American pioneers and staunch American soldiers fighting red Indian foe; that frontier justice was rough but fair.[1]

As the essay title implies, the cowboy is a tribute to the power of marketing. Initially he became the popular hero of the dime novel market, when, following the carnage of the Civil War, publishers were seeking a new figure to re-establish values of decency and loyalty. This popularity was reinforced by Turner's closure of the Frontier in 1893, which forced historians, Theodore Roosevelt among them, to look nostalgically westwards for a potent symbol of American hardiness and self-reliance. But why publishers, historians and the public at large should alight on a cowhand to embody such values requires some explanation. On the face of it there were better qualified contenders: the trappers and mountain-men (who lived in isolation in a hostile environment); the scouts (who really fought the 'Red Indian' menace); or the pioneers, ranchers and homesteaders (who actually settled the land and tilled the soil); but instead the model became 'a hired hand with a borrowed horse, a mean streak and syphilis', usually caught off the prostitute for whom he pimped during the winter months.[2]

To some extent the cowboy's popularity rests with his visual appeal to the earliest recorders of the West, the painters George Catlin, Charles Russell and Will James. They grasped the narrative potency of the ten-gallon hat, chaps, and spurs set in binary opposition to the war bonnet, peace pipe and bow of the Indian. So strong was the symbolism that a single canvas could evoke the whole history of the western plains. Cody was quick to understand the theatrical potential, raising the curtain on Buck Taylor, 'King of Cowboys', just as Turner was lowering his. With his easily identifiable visual signifiers (gun, spurs), entourage of archetypes (sheriffs, gunslingers) and easily choreographed activities (shoot-outs, cattle drives), he quickly became a star with mythological appeal. And as Taylor became the 'fictional hero' of Prentiss Ingraham's dime novels of the same title, interiority emerged, which transformed the cowboy from icon and performer to an archetype of a certain kind of western masculinity. Theodore Roosevelt seized upon the political potentialities, representing him as the guardian of a new set of common-sense values that he considered American. In *Ranch Life and the Hunting-Trail* (1888) (a text illustrated by Remington) he announces in his faux-cowboy voice that:

> A cowboy will not submit tamely to an insult, and is ever ready to avenge his own wrongs; nor has he an overwrought fear of shedding blood. He possesses, in fact, few of the emasculated, milk-and-water moralities admired by the pseudo-philanthropists; but he does possess, to a very high degree, the stern, manly qualities that are invaluable to a nation.[3]

Essentially the cowboy becomes the repository of those stern, masculine qualities that built America and which are, alarmingly, contrasted with the 'emasculated', probably European, philanthropic moralities. In the world of Roosevelt's cowboys, kindness ceases to be a virtue, and is replaced by a rough, intuitive morality. He is a white (there is a wholesale ethnic cleansing of the mixed racial composition of working cowpunchers), rugged and handsome loner with a personalized code of honour; a man of action and few words, a free agent (sometimes an outlaw in the case of Jesse James), who employs his gunslinging skills (his opponent would always draw first) for the good of the community (to which he remains at best ambivalent), before riding off into the sunset.

These cowboys, as Owen Wister has observed, have left cows behind and have become knights of the plains, their lineage stretching 'from the tournament at Camelot to the round-up at Abilene'.⁴ They are the cowboy-knights, immortalized in countless dime novels and Hollywood Westerns, mythical figures whose participation in the founding of the nation has come to define it. It is a relentlessly male narrative in which women are equated with domesticity, family responsibilities, the need to earn a living, and, by extension, the urban: all that is antithetical to the freedom of the cowboy. According to this misogynistic narrative, the only acceptable woman, apart from the symbol of virtue kidnapped by 'Red Indians' to galvanize the cowboy into action, was the frontier prostitute (the hard woman with a heart of gold), whose transience fitted the cowboys' itinerant lifestyle. Hence, the only real emotional attachment for the cowboy was to his horse and his 'pardner' – the death of either precipitating a display of manly emotions combined with a justification for vengeance.

The cowboy has become a symbolic figure dislocated from historical precedent, who represents a version of masculinity which, if it ever did exist, is so distorted as to be impossible to achieve. This distortion is particularly apparent when considering sexuality. William Dale Jennings observes that for all his macho posturing it is as if 'Hollywood would have us believe that erectile tissue was completely missing in the metabolism of the West.'[5] Perhaps not missing, but redirected through suggestive metaphors into the mastering of the virgin landscape, the breaking of horses and prowess with a Colt 45. For all their swagger, Shane and the Virginian make poor role models when it comes to relationships with women, while the masculinity of Zane Grey's cowboys is largely defined by the size of their weapon. David Fenimore guides us to a scene when Grey's most famous creation, Lassiter, hangs up his guns in a form of ritual emasculation, only to put them back on again with the observation: 'Where would any man be on this border without guns? … It's the difference between a man and somethin' not a man.'[6] Such sexual childishness would be amusing if the impact of such role models was not so damaging. William Savage Jr has noted that:

> The cowboy hero is symptomatic of a good deal of American confusion over sexuality in general and sex roles in particular, and he deserves study from that perspective no less than, say Hugh Hefner. Each in his own way has been responsible for promoting male fantasies on a vast scale, and each has misrepresented "womanhood" by means of distortion that does not even begin to approach subtlety.[7]

Cue Annie Proulx: for her *Wyoming Stories* are concerned with precisely this Hefner-like distortion of male sexuality. It is literal in the outward disfigurement and sexual exhibitionism of Rasmussen Tinsley in 'People in Hell' (*CR*), but internalized in the bestial sexual attitudes of the rodeo rider

Diamond Felts in 'The Mud Below' (*CR*). In 'Brokeback Mountain' (*CR*) the internal distortion derives not from the homosexuality of the central characters, but from their attempts to reconcile their sexuality with their perception of themselves as cowboys.

An interesting prologue to these stories is Proulx's shortest short story '55 Miles to the Gas Pump' (*CR*), a Gothic Western based on the story of Blue Beard. In the first sentence of this two-sentence narrative, a drunken rancher Croom, dressed in typical cowboy attire, is depicted attempting to commit suicide by throwing himself into a canyon. It appears to be a heroic gesture from which his horse is spared. However, he does not die, but rather floats back to the surface like a cork. This mysterious event precedes the discovery by his wife of 'the corpses of Mr Croom's paramours' in a locked attic. Some are 'desiccated as jerky', others wrapped in newspaper, still others painted blue, but all show the 'marks of boot heels' and of being 'used hard' (279–80). Through this extraordinary story Proulx seems to be suggesting that the isolation and much-vaunted rugged independence of the cowboy from social norms does not necessarily stimulate the heightened sense of morality suggested by commentators such as Roosevelt. Indeed, a model of masculinity which privileges horses over women, and treats the sexualized woman as a horse to be 'ridden hard', is more likely to bring deviance. This is the conclusion to which we are guided by the narrator's laconic observation: 'When you live a long way out, you make your own fun' (280). Essentially, Croom is a grotesque distortion of cowboy mythology, a mythology which, as his miraculous levitation demonstrates, will not die.[8]

'People in Hell Just Want a Drink of Water'

Proulx's story offers a grotesque reinterpretation of *Shane*. The cattle baron Fletchers are replaced by the Dunmire family, a ranching family of father and six sons who have been running stock and their neighbourhood for two generations; the Starrett family are transformed into the Tinsleys: greenhorn homesteaders, with a dreamy conception of both farming and the landscape. The Dunmires are also presented as an antidote to the Cartwrights of *Bonanza*. There were no women on the *Bonanza* range, just a patriarch and his sons, their different physiognomies (deliberately tailored to appeal to a range of female tastes) explained away by three different mothers. And yet there is not an absence of the feminine: these are cowboys whose masculinity is coupled with innate sensitivity in addition to good table manners. Not so the Dunmires; their femininity stops at their curiously female names. Their measure of a man is his ability to endure hardship and they have an arrogant contempt for art and intellect (112). Ice Dunmire raises sons to fill his labour needs: they receive cowboy regalia for Christmas presents and a handshake each birthday and grow up hard with a shared contempt for those who do not, like themselves, find pleasure in kicking 'the frost out of a horse in early morning' (110). This includes women. Even their mother is conceived of as livestock for producing cowboys 'as fast as the woman could stand to make them' (109). And when, after years of being 'ridden hard and put away dirty', she runs off with a tinker, they can only conceptualize her behaviour in accordance with the only other women of whom they have knowledge: prostitutes (109).

Attention within the narrative settles on the eldest boy, Jaxon, a model of human adaptation in this hostile environment. In his youth he had been a bronc-buster, the epitome of cowboy masculinity, but was so badly torn up inside that he was reduced to riding 'easy horses broke by other men' (110). By the time we join the narrative he keeps the ranch books and sells Morning Glory windmills, jobs which compromise his cowboy credentials but demonstrate his adaptability. For in this arid wasteland he has quite clearly seen which way the wind is blowing and traded his horse (an out-of-date consumer of water) for a car and windmill trailer (a means of providing water). In harnessing the wind he is able to transform the 'endlessly repeated flood of morning light' into a glory rather than a burden, bringing people in hell their drink of water (107–8). He also brings more. For despite the plaid suit, he maintains the swagger of a cowboy, bringing to the bored ranch housewives a little sexual glamour. As he says to his appreciative younger brother: 'Some of them women can't hardly wait until I get out a the truck' (111). Significantly, in his choice of women he maintains the rhetoric of the broken rodeo cowboy: he refuses the 'bad' women of the brothel and will only 'ride' the women broken by another man.

By contrast, the Tinsleys are ill-adapted urban outsiders. Horm has no feeling for the land; he stakes their claim on dry, infertile land and fails in a number of farming ventures before settling on the water-intensive crops, water melons and tomatoes. His wife is a grotesque parody of the prairie angel archetype, her frailty emphasized by her lack of name. She is so disconcerted by the Wyoming landscape that upon first entering it she impulsively throws her baby daughter into a river while crossing it; an act which underlines her nervous disposition while symbolically reminding us that the West is no place for young women (113). As a consequence, their young son, Rasmussen, is brought up smothered by his mother's guilt and paranoia. He grows up a reader and mathematician, 'indifferent to stock' and desperate to escape the land the Dunmires both cherish and represent.

That he does escape and is horribly disfigured in a near-fatal car crash is of little concern to Proulx; she is only interested in the symbolic significance of this returning monster in relation to Jaxon Dunmire, the character he most unwittingly resembles.

Ras's return coincides with a spring of biblical harshness (Jaxon talks of prairie dogs being devoured by crickets and plagues of grasshoppers), which allows his mother to view his deformity as punishment for her earlier sin, his monstrous features 'her fault through the osmosis of guilt' (118). In other ways his deformity transforms him into the spirit of a hostile landscape. Just as spring seems to have become distorted, his own regenerative urges have been warped into a desire to ride from ranch to ranch exposing himself to women occupiers. Perhaps most importantly, as Frantz has observed, in his depiction as a horseman – 'elusive, slipping behind rocks, galloping long miles on the dry, dusty grass, sleeping in willows and nests of weeds, a half-wild man with no talk and who knew what thoughts' – it is clear that he has become a grotesque parody of Shane: the distorted spirit of cowboy masculinity. More specifically, Ras holds up the distorting mirror to Jaxon: his tame horse, Bucky, is a parody of Jaxon's bronc-busting; Ras's outward disfigurement is a contrast to the inward deformity of the emotionally stunted Jaxon; his desire to expose himself is a parody of the Dunmire's sexual machismo.[9]

When faced with this outsider, Jaxon retreats further into a cowboy mythology that does not accept deviance. Even the Sheriff's friendly warning to Horm to have Ras 'hobbled' reveals the pervasiveness of cowboy culture. Jaxon deals with the problem in the only way he knows how, through his knowledge of livestock. He justifies his actions on the grounds that women must be protected, thereby exhibiting the hypocrisy of a cowboy culture that can only conceive of women as either sexual objects or damsels in distress. However, as Milane Frantz has argued convincingly, Ras is castrated not because he is a threat to women, but because he is a threat to the standing of men, both sexually and mythologically.[10] The story ends as it began: 'The morning light flooded the rim of the world, poured through the window glass, coloured the wall and floor' (128). The message is bleak: despite the capacity for human cruelty demonstrated by this wreck of a figure, the sun continues to shine, simply illuminating man's inhumanity more clearly. The narrator's final observation ridicules our smugness while cajoling us into an acceptance that this is not a period piece, but an exploration of the legacy of cowboy culture.

As if to prove the point, Proulx brings us up to date in her story 'The Mud Below' (*CR*), which centres on the character of Diamond Felts, a vulnerable young man as disfigured on the inside by the cowboy myth as Ras is on the outside. Interestingly, as Anthony Magagna has observed, Proulx offers a cautionary tale to all would-be cowboys in her short story 'Florida Rental' (*BD*). It concerns a young ranch-fencer, June Bidstrup, who is plucked out of obscurity to feature on the cover of *Western Cowboy* magazine as the archetypal cowboy. He is subsequently lured to Hollywood to star in a Western, but, because he does not fit with the director's expectations of what a cowboy should look like, he is required to have Botox injections. They go wrong leaving him grotesquely deformed; a conclusion that enables Proulx to cleverly highlight the dangers in attempting to mould reality to myth (211).[11] 'The Mud Below' offers a similar critique of the distorting influence of western values combined with a family drama in which questions of paternity and sexual confusion help to mould a grotesque, individual identity.

'The Mud Below'

Diamond is certainly a conflicted individual: fatherless, a 'virgin at eighteen' with 'little talent for friendship or affection', demeaned by the pejorative names Half-Pint, Shorty, Sawed-Off, he is a 'rapping, tapping, nail-biting' ball of unease in search of a masculine role model (47–8). That he should choose the cowboy is not obvious. His western credentials are unpromising: Proulx's fictional Redsled may be in the West, but his local geography comprises 'the pawnshop, the Safeway, the Broken Arrow bar, Custom Cowboy, the vacuum cleaner shop' (67). Ironically, his mother, as was seen in the 'Introduction', has rejected her own ranching roots to run a store specializing in cowboy memorabilia, thus selling a commercialized vision of the West back to nostalgic tourists. Kaylee understands the gap between myth and reality and is determined that neither of her sons will succumb to the distortion that plagues so many of her customers: 'I worked like a fool to bring you boys up in town, get you out of the mud, give you a chance to make something out of yourselves' (54). Thus, the 'mud below' becomes an overarching metaphor that transforms the rodeo ride into an individual's precarious passage through life.

Mud clings to Diamond's memories of boyhood days on his uncle's ranch. He remembers the 'hoof-churned mud' and dirty chaps, which he elides with the whispered comments passed between his uncle and mother that left him marginalized (49). From an early age, mud and cowboys are intimately linked with sex and betrayal. When, therefore, much later he is invited by classmate, Leecil Bewd, for a day's ranch work, he is reluctant. The fact that

Leecil is clearly a misfit, combined with the punishing nature of the work – 'the weekend was a windy, overcast cacophony of bawling, manure-caked animals, mud, dirt, lifting, punching the needle, the stink of burning hair that he thought would never get out of his nose' – and his belief that he is surrounded by men whom he considered 'losers for no reason but that they were inarticulate and lived out on dirt road ranches' serves to reinforce the perception that cowboy life is far from the fabricated mythology sold by his mother (50). This all changes, however, when he is introduced to rodeo.

Proulx's choice of rodeo as a model of cowboy masculinity is full of irony. It is used by ranching communities as a ritualistic means of affirming and perpetuating the protocols, values and attitudes of the old West. And yet, as Diamond's experience on the Bewd ranch makes clear, it is as far removed from real ranch work as the contents of Kaylee's souvenir shop. It is a theatrical expression of an already highly stylized and suspect mythology. To anthropologist Elizabeth Atwood Lawrence, rodeo is a ritualistic re-enactment of the taming of the virgin wilderness.[12] As such it becomes amenable to various psycho-sexual interpretations in which male conquest of a feminized landscape is symbolized through the cowboy breaking of horses; an act which can be extended to male domination of women in general. Indeed, for Lawrence brutal sexuality is never far from the performance of rodeo. The riders continually associate women with animals, there to be ridden and left before they dilute the sexual male through a process of domestication. A subset within the rodeo community are the bull riders, Diamond's speciality. They are the loners among the lonely – 'a breed apart'.[13] Bull riding differs from horse rodeo in having no basis in cowboy skills; there is no ritualistic taming of the West because the bull remains a wild symbol of ultra-masculinity. This gives rise to a very different psycho-sexual symbolism in which the rider's goal is not to tame the bull, but to merge with this symbol of exaggerated masculinity. In effect, bull riding is an exclusively male domain with no vestige of the feminine.[14]

It is this exclusivity that is central to Diamond's confused reaction to his eight-second ride:

> The shock of the violent motion, the lightning shifts of balance, the feeling of power as though he were the bull and not the rider, even the fright, fulfilled some greedy physical hunger in him he hadn't known was there. The experience had been exhilarating and unbearably personal. (52)

Diamond's emotional reaction suggests that his version of the cowboy myth is rooted in a painfully personal experience. What happens to him on that windy afternoon is a symbolic re-enactment not of western conquest, but of the most important moment in his life: the departure of his father with the words, 'Not your father and never was. Now get the fuck out of the way, you little bastard' (72). The castration of the bullocks he observed in the morning is figuratively what happened to him all those years ago; on top of the bull he rediscovers a form of masculinity to equate with his father. This latter point is reinforced in the narrative through his memory of a childhood visit to a merry-go-round. He refuses to mount the little horses because he is appalled by the rear view of the 'swelled buttocks and the sinister holes where the ends of the nylon tails had been secured before vandals jerked them out'. Instead, he is lifted onto a 'glossy little black bull' by his father, who continues to reassure him with a steadying hand (53). Through the identification of a single childhood experience as the cause of a profound alteration in a child's development, Proulx is on familiar ground: we saw it in the young Mero's misinterpretation of Indian cave paintings in 'The Half-Skinned Steer' (*CR*) and in the cause of Shy Hemp's paedophilia in 'The Governors of Wyoming' (*CR*). Here, Diamond's rejection of the 'ruined horses' with their 'sinister holes' in favour of the bull would appear to suggest that for him rodeo is a misogynistic closed circuit that entirely excludes the feminine while reigniting his relationship with his father.

For this reason his mother's attempts to divert him from becoming a bull rider are bound to fail. They are based on her knowledge of the down-at-heel riders who come into her shop and her belief that 'rodeo's for ranch boys, who don't have the good opportunities you do? The stupidest ones are the bullriders' (55). Unfortunately, her appeals are delivered in her kitchen: an antiseptic world of salads, dehydrated potatoes, microwaveable supermarket pies and instant coffee – the domestic antithesis of everything the rodeo cowboy symbolizes (60). His brother, Pearl, is the embodiment of his younger self, brought up not to say 'ain't' and watch his cholesterol levels, but secretly excited by Diamond's profanity and his urge to eat eggs out of the pan. It is a domestic world that Diamond is eager to put behind him, his chapped fingers and strong body odour are a source of pride, a sign that he is the real cowboy upon which he models himself. It is on this last point that Kaylee becomes contemptuous:

> You're no more a cowboy than you are a little leather-winged bat. My grandfather was a rancher and he *hired* cowboys or what passed for them. My father gave that up for cattle sales and he hired ranch hands. My brother was never anything but a son-of-a-bee. None of them were cowboys but all of them were more cowboy than a rodeo bullrider ever will be. (Proulx's italics, 64)

This cuts straight to the heart of tension between myth and reality: Kaylee understands the theatricality that underpins rodeo. Diamond's rodeo riding is not an extension of ranch work; he attends college to learn the requisite skills to become part of the spectacle of cowboy mythology. However, though he may dress the part and engage in macho posturing, his vision of western masculinity is as synthetic as one of Kaylee's microwave ready meals.

In a last desperate attempt to dissuade him she takes Diamond to see Hondo Gunsch, a legendary rodeo star who was brain damaged in an accident and who now endlessly waxes saddles in a stables run by one of Kaylee's male friends, Kerry Moore. Once again it is a scene rich in narrative tension, pathos and sexual symbolism. The glory days of Gunsch are captured in a single photograph on a magazine cover for *Boots 'N Bronks*, August 1960: 'A saddle bronc rider straight, square and tucked on a high-twisted horse, spurs raked all the way up to the cantle, his outflung arm in front of him. His hat was gone and his mouth open in a crazy smile' (65–6). He is a personification of Wyoming's State symbol. The image contrasts vividly with the wreck of a man they meet: an image of where Diamond is heading. Diamond, however, is not interested in lessons of the future, he is still living in his sexually traumatic past. His attention is taken not by Gunsch, but by the secret messages flying between Moore and his mother, messages which once again leave him on the outside (67). In a moment he is reduced to the figure of Shorty, while Moore becomes the bull in this particular triangle, leaving Gunsch to become symbolic of Diamond's shattered attempts to assert his masculine vision.

All these warnings prove useless: Diamond glorifies rodeo – the 'rough, bruising life with its confused philosophies of striving to win and apologising when he did' – becoming in the process a latter-day cowboy (56). Some of this glamour is captured in the narrative descriptions of late nights on the road with Pake Bitts at the wheel, descriptions which become allegories of the whole western cowboy existence:

> Pake knew a hundred dirt road shortcuts, steering them through scabland and slope country, in and out of the tiger shits, over the tawny plain still grooved with pilgrim wagon ruts, into early darkness and the first storm laying down black ice, hard orange dawn, the world smoking, snaking dust devils on bare dirt ... turning into midnight motel entrances with RING OFFICE BELL signs or steering onto the black prairie for a stunned hour of sleep. (74)

It is a journey that takes us off the beaten track and along the pioneer wagon routes into the heart of western mythology. It is an ultra-masculine world which envisages cowboys tackling wild animals in a hostile natural environment, the indoors represented by dingy, transient motel rooms. This is contemporary cowboy glamour: a life lived at breakneck speed.

In his own western narrative 'only the ride gave him the indescribable rush, shot him mainline with crazy-ass elation', and the ride, whether on the bull or in the truck, is a particularly personal experience, which translates uneasily into the world beyond (73). For Diamond's version of the myth is particularly egocentric, based on the idea that cowboys are rugged, isolated individualists with no need for external ties. He therefore conceives a deep-seated contempt for all those who do foster connections, whether with wives, family or even God. His problems with domesticity are foreshadowed in the narrative by his reaction to calf-roper, Sweets Musgrove (a name suggestive of his femininity), who stops to help him when Diamond's truck breaks down. Diamond is appalled that Sweets attempts to fix the engine holding a pink-clad baby while his chain-smoking wife looks on. Indeed, when Leecil requests a knife to 'cut the sumbuck', in Diamond's mind it becomes a call for the symbolic castration that he believes has taken place already. It is more fitting for Diamond's cowboy vision that he is picked up later by a group of 'buckle bunnies' who stick so close to him that by the time he arrives at the arena he was 'in a visible mood to ride but not bulls' (57).

Diamond sees himself as the Lone Ranger, contemptuous of even his fellow rodeo riders. His lack of empathy is apparent in his aggressive sexual behaviour towards the numerous 'in-and-out girls' who keep him company in motel bedrooms, and especially the parking lot rape of the wife of another travelling companion, Myron Sasser (73). The event is narrated from Diamond's perspective and becomes a bronc-busting ride in which a tall, feisty female (who had earlier mocked his size) is tamed. Perhaps nothing shows his social marginalization more clearly than his bewilderment at her affronted reaction, and Myron's subsequent anger. Pake Bitts attempts to contextualize his behaviour within rodeo, claiming that if Diamond is guilty of anything, it is the misinterpretation of signs: 'The bull is not supposed to be your role model, he is your opponent and you have to get the best of him ... you got a quit playin the bull' (76). But this, according to Diamond, is what all cowboys do – it is part of the DNA of the West. He makes clear: 'I ride a bull, the bull's my partner' – a symbiotic symbol of potent male sexuality (76). Like Ras Tinsley before him, Diamond holds a mirror up to the cowboy community to show a distorted version of their own brutal misogyny. His parking lot rape was, as he makes clear to Myron, nothing more than what the latter had done to some 'wormy Texas buckle bunny' (71).

The rodeo community, however, is not prepared for such blistering honesty, as is evinced by their reaction to Diamond's drunken harangue on the subject of cowboys and domesticity. It is a carefully staged scene; the bar in which the assorted riders and calf-ropers meet – the 'Saddle Rack'

– teeters between authenticity and kitsch. We enter through a 'plank door, pocked with bullet holes in a range of calibers' to a bar with 'cattle brands' and 'dim photographs of long-dead bronc busters' (78). The music is country, the talk of 'babies and wives' – leaving it to Diamond to point out the glaring hypocrisy:

> You all make a big noise about family ... but none of you spend much time at home and you never wanted to or you wouldn't be in rodeo. Rodeo's the family. Ones back at the ranch don't count for shit. ... Here's to it. Nobody sends you out to do chores, treats you like a fool. ... They say we're dumb but they don't say we're cowards. Here's to big money for short rides, here's to busted spines and pulled groins, empty pockets, damn all-night driving ... (80)

As a toast it venerates a violently individualistic form of the cowboy myth while pinpointing the essential tension between the myth and domesticity. The family is best viewed bleary-eyed through the bottom of a glass while singing along to the sentimental lyrics of a Dwight Yoakam ballad.

This speech marks the beginning of Diamond's decline, as even he begins to suspect the cowboy dream and to sense that 'he was getting down the page and into the fine print of this way of living'. His dramatic decline is brought into sharp focus by his hang-up in Oklahoma, the bull ride which frames the entire story. Its symbolic significance is signalled by the announcement 'let's give thanks we're in a enclosed arena or it would be deep mud below', which clumsily elevates the ride to more existential heights (47). In the chute we are given a gentle reminder of what brought Diamond here, the steadying hand of the rodeo cowboy on his shoulder calming his nerves in a way that he is still unable to understand (46). The reader, however, recognizes it as the memory of his father's arm as it steadied him on the merry-go-round bull when he was five years old: the catalyst for his love affair with rodeo. For Diamond, rodeo has always been an intensely personal experience, yet as he prepares for this ride his thoughts are governed by the realization that his performance will be met with cynical disregard by the public: 'The watchers knew as well as he that if he burst into flames and sang an operatic aria after the whistle it would make no damn difference' (46). When he is bucked from the bull and finds himself scrambling for safety with a dislocated shoulder, their ambivalence is transformed into humorous contempt by a rodeo clown. The rodeo clown, himself a map of scars, is perhaps the clearest symbol of the surreal nature of the West: we laugh at him, yet his role is to protect cowboys lying injured in the mud.

The callousness of the public is matched by that of the local doctor who tells him to 'cowboy up' (83). The full implications of this phrase only become apparent when Diamond catches sight of himself in the mirror and sees not the mythical figure of his imagination, but a grotesque parody: 'Two black eyes, bloody nostrils, his abraded right cheek, his hair dark with sweat, bull hairs stuck to his dirty, tear-streaked face, a bruise from armpit to buttocks' (84–5). Now his inner and outer deformity coincide, and it appears that the narrative is preparing us for a moment of self-revelation in which Diamond finally acknowledges the error of his ways. Proulx, however, resists a happy ending. If he can drive, he can rodeo, and accordingly our last view of him is on the road. And yet, as he chooses this time to phone his mother and demand his paternity, the reader understands that in his mind the goring he has just received and his father's rejection are deeply connected. However, not only does he refuse to believe his mother's reassurances, but she is sharing her bed with another man; a man who Diamond can only conceive of as 'the big slob with the black hat' – his nemesis neatly attired in the colour-coded regalia of a cowboy bandit (87). Once again, Shorty is on the outside, emasculated by the presence of another man. As he ponders the histories of Hondo Gunsch and Leecil Bewd, the image of the 'ranch hand bent over a calf, slitting the scrotal sac' pops into his mind with the subsequent realization that 'the course of life's events seemed slower than the knife but not less thorough' (87). In effect, growing up in the contemporary West, continually measuring oneself against symbols of masculinity that can never be equalled, is a form of slow emasculation. Essentially, life is 'a hard, fast ride that ended up in the mud' (88).

'Brokeback Mountain'

Like 'People in Hell' and 'The Mud Below', Proulx's most famous story, 'Brokeback Mountain', is also concerned with the disastrous effects of cowboy mythology on the lives of vulnerable young men. More specifically, Proulx sets out to explore the paradox of a model of masculinity that privileges male relationships while condemning intimacy among men. It is, as has been suggested, a remarkably sexless mythology, its desires reduced to plaintive song lyrics which idealize and normalize heterosexual relationships and the comfort of the hearth while vigorously rejecting their feminizing influence. In this macho yet sexless world the subject of cowboy homosexuality has remained taboo. William Savage Jr raised the issue in the 1970s, arguing that the scarcity of women on the frontier raises the spectre of homosexuality, but then retreated, noting that 'few historians or novelists have dared to touch the subject'.[15]

One who did was Alfred Kinsey, who as early as the 1940s was talking openly about 'a type of homosexuality which was probably common among pioneers and outdoor men in general ... men who have faced the rigours of nature in the wild'. In a report remarkable for its candour, he notes that 'such a background breeds the attitude that sex is sex, irrespective of the nature of the partner'. Such 'hard-riding, hard-hitting assertive males' would be intolerant of the 'affectation' of urban homosexuals, 'but this, as far as they can see, has little to do with the question of having sexual relations with other men'. And this, he argues, is a sexual attitude found today among 'ranchmen, cattle men, prospectors etc'.[16] Kinsey's findings are significant because they break the link between homosexuality and effeminacy, allowing for relationships which do not fall into the camp stereotypes portrayed in contemporary media. These surprisingly liberal views are articulated in Proulx's writing by the tough cowboy poet, Rope Butt, who 'didn't much care for the two nancy boys who had lately come up from Dallas' to take over the old school in his home town of Wooleybucket, 'but he was willing to live and let live, for certain bunkhouse friendships were not unknown, though little talked about'.[17] They were, however, written about. Proulx notes in 'How the West Was Spun' that the evidence gleaned from letters and poetic fragments amassed by John D'Emilio and Estelle Freedman in their comprehensive study of American sexuality – *Intimate Matters* (1988) – suggests that cowboys 'were not the pure heterosexual tough guys we might think'.[18]

Such findings make uncomfortable reading for custodians of cowboy mythology, for as Vito Russo notes: 'If there is no real difference between the cowboy hero and the faggot on Forty-Second Street, then what remains of American masculinity?'[19] This, quite clearly, could never be the case, hence the desexualization of the cowboy during the twentieth century. This is particularly the case in the classic Hollywood Western, in which, though male camaraderie is central, every effort is made to avoid touching: even wrestling rarely occurs. And yet, as Gary Needham has observed, homoeroticism (a pleasure observing and being in the presence of men), if not homosexuality, has long been the cornerstone of the classic Western, which is rooted in the spectacle of male display. Westerns tend to display men's fascination in other men's guns (which are inherently phallic), which are fondled, measured, pressed into each other's faces and slotted into low-slung, leather gun belts.[20] Homoerotic moments in traditional Westerns abound: the first meeting of Victor Mature and Glenn Ford in a saloon in John Ford's *My Darling Clementine* (1946) is full of lingering glances typical of a male pick-up; Howard Hawks's *Red River* (1948) opens with a boyishly good-looking Montgomery Clift gazing at John Wayne's crotch while sucking on a piece of straw;[21] the eyes of slovenly homesteader, Joe Starrett, linger appreciatively over the glistening body of Alan Ladd's Shane as they dig up the roots of the tree in his yard. These are men brought together by a special chemistry of appreciation, the kind exemplified perhaps most clearly by *Butch Cassidy and the Sundance Kid* (1969). As Russo notes: 'Who remembers Katherine Ross?'[22]

'Brokeback Mountain' is important not simply because it explores the homosexual relationships identified by Kinsey, but also because it makes explicit the homoerotic relationships that have been implicit between screen cowboys for decades. It was, according to Larry McMurtry (who, with Diana Ossana, wrote the screenplay), a story waiting to be written: 'I was more stunned when I read "Brokeback Mountain" because I realized that it was a story that had been sitting there all my life, fifty-five years of which have been lived in the American West.'[23] It may have been sitting there, but it had quite clearly been repressed by a lifetime of presenting a particular vision of the West in such film and television classics as *Hud* (1963), *The Last Picture Show* (1971) and the *Lonesome Dove* series (1989).[24] Furthermore, perhaps McMurtry was not looking too hard: the original Wyoming cowboy story, *The Virginian*, appears very camp to modern-day eyes. William Handley has identified a deep well of homoerotic desire at work between the Virginian and his best friend Steve (the only one who uses his first name), in which the unnamed narrator freely participates. Our first sight of him is mediated through an enthralled narrator who describes him as a 'slim young giant, more beautiful than pictures', before claiming: 'Had I been the bride, I should have taken the giant, dust and all.'[25] In the only outburst of male emotion in the novel, when the Virginian is out of his mind in agony, it is Steve, not his intended, Molly, that he calls for, leaving the tending women to observe, 'it was a name unknown'. It is the love that dare not speak its name and, as Jane Tompkins has observed, we get 'the feeling that if times had been different this could have been a story about "Jeff and Steve".'[26]

Two later novels that deal with the subject of male intimacy in a manner appreciated by Proulx are Thomas Savage's *The Power of the Dog* (1967), for which she wrote an afterword when it was republished in 2001, and William Haywood Henderson's *Native* (1993), a work she described as exhibiting 'some of the most evocative and transcendently beautiful prose in contemporary American Literature'.[27] In fairness to McMurtry, so deft is Savage's handling of *The Power of the Dog*'s interior tragedy that, as Proulx makes clear in her afterword, most critics failed to recognize it.[28] Set in the early 1920s, the novel's central character, Phil Burbank, is an intelligent and cultivated rancher who presents himself as a hard-bitten cowboy: he seldom washes; eats in the bunkhouse with his cowboys; is violently misogynistic to his brother's wife, Rose; and has a hatred for what he terms, 'sissies' (typified by Rose's sensitive son – Peter). Yet beneath this tough exterior lies an emotional turmoil revealed by fleeting references to his boyhood adoration for the now-deceased character of Bronco Henry, an idealized cowboy and object of Phil's adolescent, erotic affection. This relationship exists for Phil on the symbolic level (which allows him to repress his own homosexuality, and Savage to avoid presenting contact between men), their shared sensitivity signalled by their ability to read in the shape of a distant rocky outcrop the form of a running dog. This shared perception guides us to the full implication of Savage's title, for in some sense Phil is the dog – the powerful embodiment of the western myth. However, in another sense, he, like Bronco Henry and also the only other person who can see it, his 'sissy' step-nephew Peter, is prey to a cowboy culture and Christian dogma (the title comes from Psalms: 'Deliver my soul ... from the power of the dog') that would, if they ever caught them, tear them to pieces.[29]

Henderson's *Native* centres on the 23-year-old foreman of a Wyoming ranch, Blue Parker. He values his isolation in the mountains, but also yearns for the affection of a young ranch hand, Sam. The feelings of both men are released by the arrival of Gilbert, a wandering Native American struggling to reclaim his people's ancient customs. He presents himself as a 'berdache' – a 'male squaw' – who combines both masculine and feminine attributes and is a source of spiritual and ceremonial power to his people before, as Gilbert observes archly, 'berdache became faggot'.[30] Gilbert, the ethnic outsider, can get away with his erotic behaviour, but Sam and Blue, who are both beaten up in homophobic attacks by their ranching 'friends', are forced to retreat to the high-altitude cow camp for their relationship to flourish. Here, in lyrical passages that anticipate those of 'Brokeback Mountain', the two men are transported to a realm above the homophobic concerns of the ranch (personified in the disapproving figure of ranch owner, Mr Fisher – the forerunner of Proulx's Joe Aguirre) into a landscape that both dwarfs and empowers them to consummate their intimacy. Indeed, fellow American novelist, Tom Spanbauer, observes of *Native* that 'I have never seen the American cowboy and his natural environment so intimately drawn.'[31] It becomes a verdant 'Mount Parnassus' (a classical realm in which same-sex love is not condemned), in which the spirit of the berdache is released into the open, their only constraint coming from fear of detection.[32]

Despite the work of Henderson, Savage and indeed Spanbauer's own *The Man who Fell in Love with the Moon* (1991) (which reappraises the mythology of the West through the dislocated narration of a half-Indian, bisexual transvestite prostitute called Shed), McMurtry is correct in his suggestion that Proulx brought the issue of cowboy homosexuality to a wider audience. Even then, its initial publication in the highbrow liberal arts magazine the *New Yorker* (the text positioned just a few pages after a picture of a topless Truman Capote) suggests that this is a story with which the West is still not comfortable. Its subsequent publication as a novella and in *Close Range* brought the story further mainstream, but, as Proulx herself recalls in interview, she was surprised that her original text did not cause more of a stir, particularly in the gay community.³³ What gave Proulx's story national and international prominence was Ang Lee's film version. Proulx was justifiably incredulous at the choice of Taiwanese-born Lee, whose directorial repertoire includes the martial arts extravaganza *Crouching Tiger Hidden Dragon*, the English satire of manners *Sense and Sensibility*, and the comic-strip action adventure *Hulk*, and yet his sensitive handling of the story transformed 'Brokeback Mountain' into an international phenomenon.³⁴ In doing so he brought into question exactly what we mean when we allude to the work, 'Brokeback Mountain'. For, despite Proulx's own belief in the fidelity of the film (much of the dialogue and many of the screen directions are lifted straight from the story), the change of medium combined with additional scenes and characters designed to flesh out themes means that 'Brokeback Mountain' has become an interpretative collaboration involving scriptwriters, the director, actors, critics and consumers, of which Proulx's story is just a part.³⁵ The success of the film has spawned a cultural phenomenon, leading to the establishment of numerous websites and chat rooms and the term 'Brokeback' entering common speech as a noun (it's a bit Brokeback'), adjective (I'm a Brockoholic) and even verb to describe various emotional states. The cultural impact of the Brokeback phenomena will form the final section of this chapter, the bulk of which will consist of a close reading of Proulx's text supplemented by references to both screenplay and film where appropriate.

The importance of the mountain in 'Brokeback Mountain'

Proulx's account of the genesis of the story focuses on an evening in a bar in early 1997 when she spotted an older ranch hand watching young cowboys playing pool:

> There was something in his expression, a kind of bitter longing, that made me wonder if he was a country gay. Then I began to consider what it might have been like for him – not the real person against the wall, but for any ill-informed, confused, not-sure-of-what-he-was-feeling youth growing up in homophobic rural Wyoming. A few weeks later I listened to a vicious rant of an elderly bar-café owner who was incensed that two 'homos' had come in the night before and ordered dinner. She

said that if her bar regulars had been there ... things would have gone badly for them.[36]

There is, as D. A. Miller has noted, an air of narrative artifice about this passage: the observed observer already bearing the hallmarks of a character in the making, as if Proulx has simply found what she was looking for and mapped out his tragic life.[37] It is also a passage full or irony when we consider Ennis's observation in the film: 'You ever get the feelin', I don't know, when you're in town, and someone looks at you, suspicious ... like he *knows*.'[38] Fear of discovery in this story, as in Henderson's *Native*, is crucial because the consequences are dreadful. Wyoming, Proulx notes, is notoriously homophobic, as evidenced by the homophobic murder of the student Matthew Shepard just outside Laramie in the year after the story was published.[39] Matthew, a sensitive blond-haired college boy, was strung up on a buck fence (the ultimate symbol of western settlement and division), before being bludgeoned to death by two local boys – Aaron McKinney and Russell Henderson – steeped in a distorted cowboy mythology. Wallace Stegner argues that 'the hoodlums who come to San Francisco to beat up gays' are simply the contemporary equivalent of 'the ranchers who rode out to exterminate the nesters in Wyoming's Johnson County War': the assailants may not have donned spurs and chaps, but at some level, they were enforcing a western code which they considered sanctioned by a brutal cowboy mythology.[40]

Proulx's main concern in 'Brokeback Mountain' is not the cowboys who administer frontier justice, but the inner corrosion that derives from the attempt to reconcile cowboy mythology with same-sex desire. It is therefore vital to the story that Ennis and Jack wanted to be cowboys – part of the great Western myth – and were clearly homophobic themselves, especially Ennis. Indeed, as Helene Shugart has noted, in this story desire becomes the new 'frontier of the contemporary cowboy, and it is rendered every bit as epic, vast, compelling, raw, rugged, and powerful as the physical frontier against which the archetypal cowboy was drawn'.[41] To accentuate this confusion further, she set the story in the early 1960s, thus allowing Ennis and Jack to grow up in the repressive 1950s. Meanwhile their struggle with homophobia, both internalized and external, would have been set against the universal liberation sweeping the country's cities – a time when the machismo represented by the cowboy was under attack. Thus, on every level Ennis is struggling against forces that condemn his way of life. Proulx makes it clear in the opening description of an older Ennis shuffling around his dilapidated trailer at the start of a working day. He is the shattered husk of a man, disfigured by a life of repression – the bar-room rancher fictionalized.

Proulx bookends this scene with the story's final trailer-scene in which Ennis reveals his belief in the 'open space between what he knew and what he tried to believe' – an apt description of the troubled territory covered by the story (318). For, as Neil Campbell has observed, on Brokeback Mountain Ennis enjoys the 'free range' of loving relations, which is continually challenged and 'closed' off in a world of moral surveillance around him.[42]

Such is the strength of Ennis's homophobia that one of the most difficult tasks facing Proulx in the story is making his attraction to Jack credible. She achieves this task through her use of landscape – a fact signalled, of course, by the title. Indeed, this story, perhaps more than any other, exemplifies Proulx's belief that story emerges from landscape. Reflecting on this issue, she has noted:

> In my mind isolation and altitude – the fictional Brokeback Mountain, a place both empowering and inimical – began to shape the story. The mountain had to force everything that happened to these two young men. ... In such isolated high country, away from the opprobrious comment and watchful eyes, I thought it would be plausible for the characters to get into a sexual situation.[43]

Brokeback is a fictional location within the context of a very real Wyoming, the geography of which is described during Jack and Ennis's fishing trips. Its very name is suggestive of both back-breaking labour and an individual broken under the weight of oppressive social norms. As such it acts as both a catalyst for, and later a symbol of, their relationship, which, by mutual consent, both men refuse to revisit after their initial summer herding sheep. On one level, Proulx's emphasis on the importance of the mountain is simply an acknowledgement that codes of masculinity change once men escape the urban, particularly the tyranny of 'female' domesticity. This is the crisis of maleness faced by many of Hemingway's characters, particularly during his 'men without women' phase. His *The Sun Also Rises* (1926) is of particular interest since it describes a scene in which the central protagonists escape from the female-dominated Paris salons to go fishing in the mountains. At one point Bill Gorton says to Jake Barnes (who carries a more violent version of the sexual wound that marks Jack): 'Listen. You're a hell of a good guy, and I'm fonder of you than anybody on earth. I couldn't tell you that in New York. It'd mean I was a faggot.'[44] The denial of homosexuality is implicit in the use of the conditional, yet there is also a startling realignment of masculine sexual mores brought about by companionship in the great outdoors.

Proulx's Brokeback, however, is not simply a backdrop to intimate male relationships; in her descriptions of the mountain she weaves an allusive web of mythical references to the classical realm of Arcadia, the biblical Garden of Eden, and the myth of the lonesome cowboy, which have the cumulative effect of transforming it into a region which actively promotes the flowering of male love. In this she shares more with Henderson than Hemingway, whose cowboys find release in a Wyoming transformed into Parnassus. Both are exploiting an Arcadian tradition that can be traced back to Virgil's *Eclogues* – in which he evokes a land of pastoral beauty (pastoral deriving from the Latin for shepherd) in which evenings are spent drinking, playing the pan pipes, and telling tales of heroes; it is a masculine world in which women are only present in the form of woodland nymphs and in which male love, through a form of pathetic fallacy, is both naturalized and sanctioned. Arcadia, Eric Patterson observes, re-emerges in the European artistic imagination as the ideal location for the exploration of male relationships, a feature that becomes particularly significant in the repressive nineteenth century when the pastoral elegy became the accepted means of expressing otherwise censored feelings: Shelley transformed the dead Keats into *Adonais* (1821), and Matthew Arnold turned Arthur Hugh Clough into *Thyrsis* (1866). In his *Calamus* poems, Walt Whitman removed this tradition to America, seemingly recognizing in the splendour and marginality of the untamed American landscape a freedom for male love to express itself away from social condemnation.[45]

Proulx, through her descriptions of Brokeback Mountain, with its 'great flowery meadows' and 'glassy orange' dawns, is clearly seeking to invoke this tradition (287). The fact that Jack and Ennis tend sheep rather than herd cattle further softens the rugged cowboy aesthetic. Proulx's descriptions evade the area of sexual deviance to accentuate the innocent and pastoral, reminding us of those countless Claude Lorrain landscapes of contented shepherds, nurturing and protecting their flocks. This pastoralism is accentuated in the film version through sweeping panoramas of rivers of sheep with close-ups of Ennis carrying a lamb in a saddle-bag and Jack fording a brook with a sheep on his shoulder: they are protectors and nurturers in this idyllic surrounding – heirs to the tradition of Virgil. Encoded in the Arcadian allusion, however, is the tradition that defiance entails retribution: the mountain air is both 'euphoric' and 'bitter' (291). The narrator further emphasizes the dangers of defiance through Jack's admission that the feather in his hat came from an eagle shot the summer before (286). It is the typical trophy of a rodeo rider, but, as Ginger Jones has observed, it also aligns him with mythical wanderers such as Coleridge's Ancient Mariner (whose shooting of an albatross condemns him to years of storms), and with the myth of Hercules, whose act of shooting an eagle is punished when his male lover, Hylas, disappears leaving Hercules only a *shirt* for remembrance.[46]

The relationship between pastoral pleasure and the threat of retribution is also played out in the Christian story of the expulsion from the Garden of Eden, a myth which is invoked here in the narrator's account of Jack and Ennis's descent from the mountain. There is an Old Testament resonance to the narrator's description of the way that the mountain 'boiled with demonic energy' projecting Ennis into a 'headlong, irreversible fall' (292). The connection between the American landscape and the Fall has always weighed heavily upon the imagination: though the first Puritan settlers could convince themselves that they had arrived in a new Eden, they could not blind themselves to the evil that lurked in the dark woods, made manifest by the presence of Indians and the activities of witches (a tension explored in Nathaniel Hawthorne's *The Scarlet Letter* (1850)). One particular evil to Christians is same-sex love. Thus, by invoking the Fall, the narrative prepares us for the social condemnation of Jack and Ennis, condemnation which Lee demonstrates by allowing the voiceover of Ennis's wedding vows to Alma Beers to intrude upon his emotional departure from Jack. Proulx's evocation of the Fall also allows her to turn a myth that is a celebration of heterosexual relations on its head. In their pre-lapsarian garden, Jack and Ennis eat Forbidden Fruit and gain knowledge about themselves, which they do not repress but transform into love.

Proulx's classical and biblical allusions provide a mythical context for the flowering of homosexual relations and its subsequent doom. This mythologizing gives context to her dissection of the most pertinent myth of them all – that of the cowboy. Central to the tragedy of both men is their desire to be cowboys. However, like Diamond before them, they are not really cowboys at all: they are a hundred years too late, and they herd sheep not cattle. They have simply bought into the myth with their ten-gallon hats and pearl-buttoned yoked shirts. This theatrical element is accentuated in the film through their deployment of studied movements, gestures and poses that they consider appropriate for cowboys (particularly in the opening sequence outside Aguirre's trailer), which are underscored by a meta-narrative of country and western songs designed to remind us of the mythology guiding their performance. However, as we have seen, the cowboy myth is not without complications when interpreted by two emotionally confused Wyoming ranch hands. For Jack, its importance is captured through a single image of his time on Brokeback Mountain, when Ennis had stolen up behind him as he stood in front of the fire and held him in a silent embrace that 'satisfied some shared and sexless hunger':

> They had stood that way for a long time in front of the fire, its burning tossing ruddy chunks of light, the shadow of their bodies a single column against the rock. The minutes ticked by from the round watch in Ennis's pocket ... Ennis's breath came slow and quiet, he hummed,

rocked a little in the sparklight and Jack leaned against the steady heartbeat ... until Ennis, dredging up a rusty but still useable phrase from the childhood time before his mother died, said, "Time to hit the hay, cowboy. I got a go. Come on, you're sleepin on your feet like a horse," and gave Jack a shake, a push, and went off in the darkness. Jack heard his spurs tremble as he mounted, the words "see you tomorrow," and the horse's shuddering snort, grind of hoof on stone. (310–11)

Henderson employs precisely the same pose in *Native*, the lack of eye contact implicit in the wraparound hug allowing it to become the springboard for an eight-page exploration of Blue's internalized homophobia: 'What would it take to turn around and hold him?' he asks in one breath, while supplying the answer in another: 'If anyone were to drive up the road and see – but why would anyone approach? I could be dead. Or gone.' Significantly, Blue never turns round.[47] Jack, like Blue, never turns round, for to do so would be to acknowledge the presence of another man and shatter the illusion. In Proulx's version, the illusion is not simply sexual, but an exploration of their boyhood dreams. Passion is replaced by a 'shared sexless hunger', with an anonymous Ennis fulfilling the role of both mother and lover allowing Jack to return to a childhood dream of being a cowboy. It is a dream forged in the glimmering of the campfire, fanned by the breathless rendition of traditional tunes, the neighing of horses and the tremble of spurs. Through Ennis's observation, 'you're sleepin on your feet like a horse', the narrator artfully extends the myth that a cowboy's best friend is his horse. It is a moment of perfect reciprocity symbolized by their merging together into a single shadow. However, the shadows also present dark foreshadowing of their doom, the symbolism augmented by the presence of the pocket watch given to Jack by Joe Aguirre back in the trailer when hiring them. Now in Ennis's pocket, it acts as a reminder of the world outside Brokeback Mountain, where time is work-time. On Brokeback Mountain, time is measured by their humming, gentle rocking, and the steady heartbeat that counts off their time of happiness together.

For Jack and Ennis cowboy dreams are rooted in childhood fantasy. Like Diamond Felts, both men exist in a state of arrested development, their childhoods scarred by death and cruel fathers. Cowboy dreams were among the few things that sustained them. Ennis recalls how his emotionally inarticulate father justified his violent child-rearing philosophy with the aphoristic, 'Nothin like hurtin somebody to make him hear good' – and 'hurtin' is what men do throughout the story (300). In one particular example, Ennis recounts how as a child he was taken as a warning to see the mutilated body of a suspected homosexual. In the film version the impact of this scene is increased because we are shown the body as seen through the eyes of Ennis before, according to Ossana/McMurtry's screen direction, 'WE SEE the horror wash over his nine-year-old face.'[48] The action proves spectacularly successful, since Ennis grows up as homophobic as his father. When his parents are killed, the emotionally stunted young Ennis finds security, not with his older brother and sister, but on the various ranches where he finds himself working: hence, ranch work is intimately connected for Ennis to notions of family life.

Jack too is the product of harsh parenting. In a memory as formative in the development of his sexual identity as Diamond's ride on the merry-go-round bull, he relates how as a three-year-old he was savagely beaten and urinated upon by his father for sprinkling on the bathroom floor. Significantly, it is during this event that Jack notices that his father had not been circumcised, his foreskin appearing as 'an anatomical disconformity' to the young boy while 'I seen they'd cut me different like you'd crop a ear or scorch a brand. No way to get it right with him after that' (314, 315). After what, we may ask? In Freudian terms Jack perhaps fears the castration that has already been partially achieved – a revelation that will scar him for life; or maybe it is because in that very element that identifies his sexuality he has been treated like a calf.[49] Whichever, it marks him out as different from his father, and his father has seemingly noted a 'difference' in him. Like Diamond, Jack retreats from his father's harshness into a childish world of hyper-masculinity; his bull-riding career demonstrates his desperation to impress his rodeo-riding father, while his bedroom, which remains untouched following his departure, is a shrine to a young man's desire to play at cowboys and Indians.

It is the mountain itself that allows both characters to live out these childhood fantasies. When Jack parks his pick-up, the characters seem to step back in time: it is 1963, yet there is no news of the Vietnam War, the assassination of Kennedy, or the Civil Rights movement. The only contemporary event mentioned, the sinking of the *Thresher* submarine in April 1963, simply reinforces the theme of men trapped in a claustrophobic space as they suffer a 'headlong, irreversible fall' (289, 292). On the mountain they can play at being cowboys, sitting around the fire drinking whiskey and telling stories of horses and dogs that they have owned. Jack even plays the harmonica while Ennis, like a latter-day Gene Autry, sings along! The only named song, 'The Strawberry Roan', is, as Patterson notes, a humorous cowboy song about a rider who fails in his attempts to master a bucking horse: a song that alludes to the world of Wild West virility that brings them together and looks forward to the trouble that Jack will have mastering Ennis (290).[50]

Beneath their macho posturing, however, Proulx sets out to explore the contradictions underpinning their rugged lifestyle. Cowboys may be tough on the outside, but their work demands that they are also cooks, midwives, nurturers and providers – compassionate roles aligned with the feminine. Gretel Ehrlich has coined the term 'androgynous cowboy' to describe the domestic qualities required by the squint-eyed and calloused Marlboro Man.[51] On Brokeback Mountain the narrator exposes this contradiction through the patient cataloguing of a domestic routine in which one cooks and cleans while the other commutes and guards – roles which conform to those of a stereotypical heterosexual family. Significantly, Ennis and Jack swap jobs – indicating that they feel more comfortable conforming to differently gendered roles to those randomly assigned by Joe Aguirre, with Jack preferring the more 'feminized' role (288). Lee's film version, to the consternation of some critics, spends a great deal of time establishing the camp routine in order to develop the psychological intimacy between Jack and Ennis before their first sexual encounter. Two additional scenes help in this process: when Ennis's horse is spooked by a black bear as he returns to a waiting Jack with supplies, it leads to a familiar heterosexual domestic encounter. Initially an impatient Jack is angry that his food isn't 'on the table', but when he notices the injury his mood alters and he unthinkingly takes off his bandanna and raises it to Ennis's forehead. Ossana's direction reads: 'Jack hesitates ... awkward ... hands the bandanna to Ennis', a moment of instinctive tenderness brought under control at the last minute.[52] In the very next scene, also additional, they are shooting a deer together – bonding in a safely masculine manner.

The continual reinforcement of their domestic roles, the late-night drinking and the feeling of isolation, allows their largely wordless romance to develop. And yet the leap from 'buddies' to sexual partners is profound, not least because of the impact that it has on their perception of themselves as cowboys. Significantly, the terminology that both men employ to describe their behaviour – Jack's climatic 'gun's goin *off*' and his later avowal that it was 'a one-shot thing' – suggests that they are only able to externalize their confused feelings when framed within the language of cowboy mythology (291, Proulx's italics). The narrator is complicit in these allusions, describing the motel room in which they re-forge their relationship after four years in terms that resemble a barn: 'The room stank of semen and smoke and sweat and whiskey, of old carpet and sour hay, saddle leather, shit and cheap soap' (297). Even Ennis's acknowledgement of the dangers inherent in their relationship – 'there's no reins on this one' – transforms their desire into a wild bucking horse, which, like the 'Strawberry Roan', enhances rather than compromises their shared sense of masculinity (299).

Home on the range: Cowboys and domesticity

Following their descent from Brokeback, it seems that both men are condemned to the life of wandering outcasts. They have strayed from Aguirre's injunction to 'SLEEP WITH THE SHEEP', the narrator observing wryly that when Ennis and Jack's sheep mingle with those of another flock, 'in a disquieting way everything seemed mixed' (285, 292). The denial of their homosexuality seems hollow, the narrator's apposite double negative in Ennis's statement 'I'm not no queer' indicates a confused lack of acceptance, while his visceral retching suggests that he is both lovesick and sickened by his behaviour (291, 293). It would be easy, therefore, to interpret their married lives – compressed into a couple of paragraphs in the case of Ennis and Alma – as attempts to conform to safer sexual stereotypes, which are bound to fail because of their homosexuality. But this is too simplistic. Ennis, at least, shows no inclination for other men, and furthermore, although his sex life with Alma recreates that with the 'bucking horse' Jack, their marriage is not blighted by misogyny. Indeed, Lee goes further and adds a number of scenes which have the effect of suggesting that Ennis adapts to heterosexual domesticity with relative success. He pictures the happy couple sledging ('ALMA squeals in delight; ENNIS whoops it up'), and enjoying a drive-in movie ('ENNIS arm around her, she's pregnant, just showing'). When the girls are born, domestic life is presented as difficult, but Ennis is a less cynical and more caring father figure. Indeed, both men are portrayed as better fathers in the film: Ennis remains loved by his daughters even after the divorce, and Jack is pictured teaching his son to drive a tractor – 'whoa, son, there you go. No hands!' – in a scene of typical male bonding.[53]

Undermining this domestic harmony, however, is the desire of Jack and Ennis for both each other and their cowboy ideal. Lee chooses to explore and amplify the irony of Ennis's situation through an additional scene during which he takes his family to a fourth of July picnic. During the fireworks' display he becomes so incensed by the lurid sexual commentary provided by two foul-mouthed bikers that he confronts and summarily dispatches them in a fight.[54] It is a scene worthy of *Shane*. As he stands cowboy hat on head silhouetted against the celebratory fireworks, he appears to embody all the masculine virtues of cowboy mythology: a brooding presence prepared to leap to the defence of his family with actions rather than words. It is, however, a scene full of irony, since in the very act of defending his family, Ennis demonstrates the characteristics that will undermine it. To begin with, his act of violence is presented as less a chivalric act of defence than an eruption of his inarticulate and repressed desire. It manifests itself throughout the story in scenes of fist-pounding rage and is as likely to be directed at those he cares for – Jack on their last day on the mountain, Alma when he believes she 'overstepped his line' – as those who pose a threat to his family (303). Secondly, cowboy violence in defence of the family has always been a prelude to riding off into the sunset, far away from the domesticity that threatens his mythical status. Ennis, we know, is not riding anywhere, and if he was, it would be with Jack in a relationship which offers the most overt challenge to the family unit.

Ennis's marriage fails not simply because of his repressed homosexuality, but because of the incompatibility of his domestic life with his cowboy dream. Proulx's narrative makes clear that initially Ennis is happy with family life because he is able to conceive of it as an extension of ranch work. The family bedroom at Hi-Top Ranch is described as 'full of the smell of old blood and milk and baby shit, and the sounds were of squalling and sucking and Alma's sleepy groans, all reassuring of fecundity and life's continuance to one who worked with livestock' (293). His horse, daughters and Jack – the things he cares for most – all receive the same endearment 'little darlin', indicating that Ennis is most content when viewing his life through a cowboy lens (295). Things go wrong for the del Mar family when they move above the laundry, where the tumble of domestic appliances replaces the whisper of the tumbleweed.

Signal and Riverton are presented in both story and film as intolerably bleak. Both Ossana and McMurtry acknowledge the influence of Richard Avedon's *In the American West* for their visualization of the film, a photographer praised by Proulx for his presentation of the 'stern beauty' of 'tough lives in tough places'.[55] This 'stern beauty' Rodrigo Prieto (the director of photography) and Judy Becker (production designer) sought to realize in the film. Prieto made the distinction between urban and pastoral clear through his use of two different types of film to create subtle textural effects, while Becker utilized a more muted palette in order to make the town 'feel a little grayer, a little harsher than the mountain scenes'.[56] The interior of Ennis's Riverton apartment, for example, is dingy and claustrophobic, the low lighting helping to give the impression that he is too big for the room, around which he paces like a caged animal.

Proulx's narrative also makes clear that Alma's decision to leave Ennis derives less from her suspicions concerning his sexuality than from his 'disinclination to step out and have any fun', his limited contributions to childcare, and 'his yearning for low-paid, long-houred ranch work' (302). Proulx's treatment of Alma is subtle: she knows about Ennis; the narrator tells us that she glimpsed him kissing Jack on the stairwell of their Riverton apartment before adding the platitudinous, yet tragically inflected, observation: 'She had seen what she had seen' (296). The film presents it as another moment when the camera's perspective is attributed to the surveillance of a character (the most obvious being Aguirre watching Jack and Ennis through his binoculars as they cavort on the mountain), while their reaction is relayed through their facial expression. Alma's face registers shocked confusion: the scene is so far beyond her experience that she is able to delude herself and, as Ennis will do later when Jack is killed, make use of the 'open space between what [s]he knew and what [s]he tried to believe' (318). She falls into denial, half-heartedly seeking proof of her suspicions (attaching notes to his fishing line), while ignoring the evidence of her own eyes (302). It is this space that allows her to make a go of the marriage.

Jack's descent after Brokeback is reported in fragments and allows Proulx to reinforce the paradox of their situation. Like Diamond Felts, he lives out his cowboy fantasies by rodeo, but seems to understand its theatricality: 'Ain't like it was in my daddy's time. It's guys with money go to college, trained athaletes' (298). We see nothing of him in action; his exploits – which are a catalogue of personal injury – are related in coarse detail to Ennis during their reunion in the Motel Siesta. Thus, the narrative timing deliberately contrasts Jack's ultra-masculine discourse with his sexual activity with Ennis, drawing both together in the ironic observation that he 'had been riding more than bulls' in the years away from Ennis (298). In Lee's film version, Jack's rodeo career is developed in order to explore the dangers facing the more feminized male in a western environment. Men seem to 'know' about Jack, a feature which the film dramatizes through an additional scene in which he attempts to buy a drink for a rodeo clown who had earlier saved him from a mauling. McMurtry/Ossana's screen direction notes: 'There is something, a frisson, a vibe, that gives the CLOWN an uneasy feeling.' When the clown joins a group of drinkers, he shares something that makes them all stare over at Jack, who realizes he had better leave.[57]

In both story and film, therefore, Jack's marriage to Lureen is presented as a bid for heterosexual and financial security. The fact that she is a barrel racer, the only rodeo event designed for women, seems to resolve the tension between domesticity and cowboy mythology. Yet even here, as on Brokeback Mountain, it is Jack who falls into the feminized role, worrying about his son's schooling while 'Lureen ha[s] the money and call[s] the shots' (307). As the sound of the rodeo gives way to the image of Lureen behind a desk with a calculator, we are reminded of the domestic imprisonment of both men. In Proulx's text, Jack's father-in-law (whose farming machinery business represents everything that the cowboy dream refutes) clearly senses something different in the behaviour of Jack that does not equate with his idea of what a man, and particularly a son-in-law, should be, and is willing to pay handsomely to get rid of him. In the film this marginal figure becomes the fully fledged character, L.D. – a replacement 'stud duck' for both Aguirre and John C. Twist in Jack's development. He continually undermines the younger man's role as both husband and father. When Bobby is born, it is L.D. who is pictured with the radiant mother, dismissing Jack from the reproductive process with his cooing, 'he's the spittin' image of his grandpa'.[58] As he tosses him the keys to fetch the formula milk from the car, it echoes the scene in Aguirre's trailer: like Ennis, he isn't worth the reach. Later in the film, L.D.'s contempt for Jack's effeminate behaviour is made clear in his insistence that Bobby watches the football during the Thanksgiving supper: 'You want your son to grow up to be a man don't you, daughter? (direct look at Jack) Boys should watch football.'[59]

Huntin', shootin' and fishin'

Escape from domesticity comes in the time-honoured American way: hunting and fishing trips. Significantly, Jack and Ennis do not return to Brokeback Mountain, not wishing to sully its symbolic importance by making it the venue for a few 'high-altitude fucks' (309). Instead the narrator compresses their relationship into a travelogue in which they work through a landscape – 'the Big Horns, Medicine Bows ... Owl Creeks, the Bridger-Teton Range' – which evokes the spirit of the Wild West (304). The screenplay transforms geography into mythology, referencing classic Western scenes – they ride 'like Randolph Scott and Joel McCrea in *Ride the High Country*' – to reinforce the studied theatricality of their trips.[60] Lee further emphasizes their happiness together through their contrast with largely dysfunctional heterosexual couplings: Ennis's relationship with Cassie, which develops out of an aside in Proulx's story, is half-hearted; their drunken daytime dancing in seedy bars is a parody of the single idealized moment that symbolizes his love for Jack. Lureen ages gracelessly, her big hair and heavy make-up failing to hide the hard, chain-smoking businesswoman: truly she is her father's child. Both L.D. and John C. Twist are presented as bullies who have successfully terrorized their wives into submission. Alma's second husband, Monroe, offers a glimpse of the new man, but the way he primly slices the Thanksgiving turkey with his electric carver while smiling smugly at Ennis almost makes us nostalgic for L.D.'s insistence that 'the stud duck does the carving'.[61] Most damning of all are Jack and Lureen's friends the Malones, marginal figures in Proulx's story, who once again become fully fledged characters in McMurtry's/Ossana's screenplay. In an additional scene set in a western dance, Lee shows Lashawn holding forth with vacuous chatter, while her husband and Jack escape outside. Here her husband proposes that they escape to a cabin where they can 'drink a little whiskey, fish some. Get away, you know?' Jack does *know*, and the film's message is disturbingly clear: domesticity and dominant women drive men to rediscover their masculinity in the woods, with sometimes surprising consequences.⁶²

Considering the short shrift that heterosexual relations receive in the film, it is perhaps surprising that Jack is continually attempting to replicate them in his dream of a 'little cow-and-calf operation' with Ennis. In Proulx's text we are guided to believe that Ennis's refusal derives less from the pragmatic reasons he gives – the threat of violence and his need to support his daughters – than the fact that he remains in denial about his homosexuality right to the end. Thus, the ferocity of his assault upon Jack for his euphemistic visits to Mexico during the climatic final parting is fuelled not only by jealousy, but also by the fear that an acknowledgement of Jack's sexual orientation would entail his own. As an exasperated Jack claims: 'We could a had a good life together, a fuckin real good life. You wouldn't do it Ennis, so what we got now is Brokeback Mountain' (309). Since the story concludes in the 1980s, their relationship could indeed have ended differently if they had moved to the city, Mexico, anywhere where there were no cowboys. But for Ennis this is impossible, since his relationship with Jack can only be sanctified when viewed through the prism of cowboy nostalgia. Without the elevating dream of Brokeback Mountain, he is left having to admit the truth of his own sexual nature.

Proulx recollects that when writing the end of the story she 'was occasionally close to tears. I felt guilty that their lives were so difficult, yet there was nothing I could do about it. It couldn't end any other way'. To W. C. Harris this acknowledgement simply panders to the cliché that homosexual love must end badly, and he cites as counter-examples Tom Outland and Roddy Blake in Willa Cather's *The Professor's House* (1925), and the gay relationships in rural environments in the work of Tennessee Williams and Alice Walker.⁶³ Such criticism, however, ignores Ennis's attachment to a cowboy mythology that keeps him rooted in Wyoming. Furthermore, Proulx's ending offers an opportunity to explore the complex reactions to Jack's death articulated by various characters – reactions which once again explore the 'open space between what [they] knew and what [they] tried to believe' (318). Lureen's phone conversation with Ennis sanitizes the mystery of Jack's death for both her and the world at large. Significantly, we do not hear her account directly, it is reported through the narrator from Ennis's perspective, the detail of her 'level voice' suggesting that she is parroting the account of somebody else. Even when we do hear her voice, we are guided in our response by Ennis's observation that 'she was polite but the little voice was cold as snow' – the tone of somebody who is masking a public disgrace rather than mourning a loved one (312). Ironically, her reference to Brokeback Mountain as the place 'where the bluebirds sing and there's a whiskey spring' to indicate Jack's propensity for delusion, merely underlines her own (312). The words are, as Patterson has noted, taken from the old hobo song 'Big Rock Candy Mountain', which tells of an earthly paradise where hobos are happy together. It was popularised by Burl Ives, but his version is a sanitized adaptation of an original song in which the male relationships are far more intimate. Ironically, it seems that Lureen, like Ives, is happier with a cleaner version of events.[64] For Ennis, however, Jack's death can only be interpreted as the result of homophobia, symbolized by the tire iron. It is this version that is depicted over Lureen's account in the film, thereby privileging its veracity. It is, tragically, a fulfilment of Ennis's father's warning, and therefore a justification for his former refusal to live together. The threat of violence was always present for Ennis; thus in dreams that take him back to the most idealized moments on Brokeback Mountain, the spoon handle sticking out of the can of beans that they share by the cowboy campfire 'was the kind that could be used as a tire iron' (318).

The shirts, by contrast, become a symbol of their repressed love, the memory of Hylas clasped by the heroic Hercules. They are first mentioned in the prologue: 'The shirts hanging on a nail shudder slightly', the intransitive verb 'shudder' implying both sexual excitement and fear – an apt description of their relationship (283). However, it is only when Ennis discovers them in the closet within a closet (an obvious symbol of repression) within Jack's childishly furnished bedroom that their significance is explained. In the film, the camera initially looks out towards Ennis, as if the shirts are drawing him towards the closet and a final release of his feelings for Jack. They are described as 'like two skins, one inside the other, two in one' covered in the blood of their final encounter (316). The blood is both a symbol of their parting grief, their hatred for what each has revealed about the other, and their blood brotherhood in frontier mythology. Noticeably, Jack's shirt enfolds Ennis's, a reversal of their position in the symbolic flashback scene around the campfire, suggesting that Jack has come to consider himself the protector of the emotionally vulnerable Ennis. Furthermore, it is only through the substitute of the shirts that Ennis is prepared to embrace Jack, pressing his face into the fabric while trying to summon up the memory of their embrace on Brokeback Mountain.

It is entirely appropriate that the shirts and a postcard of Brokeback Mountain should make up the shrine to Jack in Ennis's trailer, since postcards have been used throughout as a means of arranging their assignations. This ensemble is still tucked away in a closet, and when, in the story's final scene,

Ennis steps back and begins 'Jack, I swear –', his elliptical sentence allows us to speculate on his feelings (317). The phrasing echoes the marriage vows, suggesting that, given another chance, Ennis would be ready to step out of the closet and embrace his sexuality with Jack. This, however, is immediately undermined by the narrator's bathetic observation that 'Jack had never asked him to swear anything and was himself not the swearing kind' (317).

In the film version, this scene is embellished with a number of additional details, which alter our interpretation of this declaration while suggesting a happier ending. When Alma Jr turns up to ask Ennis to attend her wedding (her fiancé's gaudy Chevy Camaro is a vulgar assertion of his redneck masculinity), he offers his stock response to evade emotional commitment: 'Supposed to be on a roundup over near the Tetons.' Whereas previously he proved inflexible with Jack, her disappointment leads to a new resolution: 'I reckon they can find themselves another cowboy ... my little girl ... is getting' married.'[65] Familial duty and affection at last conquer the spirit of the cowboy, celebrated with cheap white wine left by Cassie, a reminder of his own failed heterosexual relationship. As she drives away, however, he returns to the closet that hides his shrine to Jack. Significantly, the shirts are once again reversed, with Ennis now figuratively clutching Jack, suggesting that in death he is prepared to acknowledge his love. (This was Ledger's idea, which supports Proulx's claim that he 'knew better than I how Ennis felt and thought'.[66]) In these circumstances, Roy Grundmann argues that Ennis's elliptical 'Jack, I swear' is clearly to be understood in the context of his daughter's wedding as an enactment of his own secret marriage.[67] As the camera pans, Lee constructs a final shot of multiple frames: the closet door frames his secret shrine, the trailer window frames the straight road outside. The symbolism is clear: he remains wedded to Jack in secret but is determined to travel the straight road, starting with the ultimate symbol of familial and heterosexual love, his daughter's wedding. Ennis, above all others, knows from the death of those he has loved – his parents and Jack – the dangers of deviation from the straight road.

Beyond 'Brokeback Mountain'

As was suggested at the outset, 'Brokeback Mountain' has become a cultural phenomenon detached from Proulx's original story. It is ironic that Lee's film has done more than any of her *Wyoming Stories* to draw attention to Proulx as a western writer. It has also done a great deal to draw attention to Wyoming: for all the wrong reasons, according to enraged locals. As one Sheridan rancher complained: 'They've gone and killed John Wayne with this movie. I've been doing this job all my life and I ain't never met no gay cowboy' (the irony of the double negative couldn't be scripted).[68] Unfortunately for him, according to Chuck Coons of the Wyoming tourist board, people are flocking to Wyoming in search of Brokeback Mountain (regardless that it is fictional and was represented in the film by shots of the Canadian Rockies), and the real-life Jack and Ennis, with very reluctant locals playing suitably western parts.[69] Not only this, but among those who are happy to acknowledge that 'Brokeback Mountain' is entirely fictional are readers who are dissatisfied with Proulx's ending, and who have taken it upon themselves to write 'improved' versions which fulfil their particular emotional or political agenda. 'I wish I'd never written it' Proulx explained to Susan Salter Reynolds in *The Los Angeles Times* in 2008 before adding somewhat laconically: 'They certainly don't get the message that if you can't fix it, you've got to stand it'.[70]

'Brokeback Mountain', it seems, is a story that comes shrink wrapped in irony, especially when it comes to the film. It won both critical acclaim and every award available on both sides of the Atlantic (Golden Lion at Venice; a sheaf of Baftas; Best Picture at Golden Globes), but failed to win the Oscar for Best Picture, occasioning Proulx's 'Red Carpet' rant.[71] It would be easy to suggest that the Academy was reflecting the views of a nation not quite ready for this reinterpretation of their national icon. Throughout the country the film garnered hostile reaction. While residents of one Utah town picketed the local cinema carrying placards with the ironic message 'Armies of Satan', Stephen Bennett opined on his aptly named 'Straight Talk Radio', that it was: 'A sad day in America when a movie that glorifies homosexuality, adultery, dangerous and deadly unprotected anal sex and deception is up for Best Picture of the Year.'[72] More explosively, an incandescent David Kupelian, editor of *World Net Daily*, screamed: 'Hollywood has Now Raped the Marlboro Man.'[73] Within the Academy, homophobic attitudes were not explicit, though when stalwarts such as Tony Curtis claimed that he had no intention of seeing the film, his meaning was clear.[74] However, to claim that homophobia was responsible for *Brokeback Mountain*'s failure is too simplistic. As Charles Mehler has pointed out, Hollywood's record on gay issues is not bad: as early as 1969 John Schlesinger's *Midnight Cowboy* won Best Picture, despite offering a sexually compromised vision of the contemporary cowboy; and, most revealingly, in the same year that *Brokeback Mountain* failed to achieve Best Picture, Philip Seymour Hoffman was awarded Best Actor for his depiction of the outrageously camp author Truman Capote in the film of that name. But this is rather the point: Hollywood likes to deal with sexual difference as significantly and safely *different*. *Capote* was acceptable because his camp manner fell just short of parody; *Brokeback Mountain* violated this fundamental rule by presenting two ordinary men who just happened to be in love.[75]

However, this is only half the story: for in addition to those reviewers offended by the film's subject matter, there were those outraged by what they perceived as the straightening out of Proulx's story. Daniel Mendelsohn of the *New York Review of Books* complained of the film's de-eroticization of the story combined with its marketing as a 'universal love story'.[76] This includes Focus Film's 49-page press kit which never once refers to the main characters as homosexual; choreographed photo-shoots in which the male actors were partnered with their stage wives; and a film poster, which in its 'refection' of the heads of the two lovers seems to mimic that of the heterosexual love story, *Titanic*. The press was complicit in this process of 'hetero-normalization', constantly contextualizing the love affair by reference to legendary heterosexual relationships: Rick Moody in *The Guardian* drew parallels with *Romeo and Juliet*; the *Christian Century*'s John Petrakis invoked *Wuthering Heights*; while Carrie Rickey of the *Philidelphia Inquirer* offered *Tristan and Isolde*. Perhaps most pertinently, in *USA Today* Mike Clark described the film as an 'unfulfilled Wyoming love story', before adding, 'but this time, we don't mean Alan Ladd and Jean Arthur in *Shane*'.[77] Effectively, the film producers and critics did what guardians of the cowboy myth have been doing for generations: they desexualized him, alienating those gay critics who heralded its progressive contents. Thus, the film succeeded in alienating both conservative and gay critics, leading to the debacle of Oscar night, and Jack Nicholson's more than eloquent – 'Woaa!'

Proulx's cowboys are confused young men who want to be Shane, but instead create a version of western masculinity that is nostalgically puerile and deeply conflicted. Nowhere is this confusion clearer than in their sexual development, for which Jack Schaefer's character, despite all his macho posturing, provides a remarkably poor role model. In her *Wyoming Stories* Proulx holds up the distorting mirror to Shane to reveal the dark underbelly of his swaggering machismo. He is transformed into the grotesque figure of Rasmussen Tinsley, his sexual prowess reduced to perverse self-exposure, and Diamond Felts, whose insular and violently misogynistic version of cowboy masculinity leaves him as disfigured on the inside as Rasmussen is on the outside. In 'Brokeback Mountain' Proulx lifts the lid on a mythology that promotes male relationships at the expense of the female and domestic, yet violently condemns sexual intimacy among men. This is not simply Proulx's 'gay cowboy story', a label that diminishes its wider implications, but a natural step in the evolution of her interest in the way in which landscape and mythology can distort sexual identity (a theme introduced in the first of her *Wyoming Stories* – 'The Half-Skinned Steer'). Above all, Proulx's cowboys are crushed by their attempts to find accommodation with the legacy of the West; it is, as we have seen, a fate shared by many of Proulx's characters, who find themselves struggling to live up to the archetype that governs their sense of identity. Nowhere is this dislocation more profound than in Proulx's representation of the cowboy's high plains nemesis, the Indian, to whom we turn next.

5

Indians

'This land is full of ghosts and spirits. It speaks to me more than any other place I've ever been', Proulx claimed after her move to Wyoming.[1] One suspects that primary among such ghosts, in a landscape eloquent with a history of conflict and suffering, are the voices of Wyoming's Native Americans: Red Cloud, Sitting Bull and those Cheyenne who fought on the Powder Valley Trail. It is a familiar experience for anyone travelling through a landscape that resonates with its Indian past, their existence transcribed into the maps of the white settlers – the Grand Tetons, Black Hills – and the cultural imagination. In her novel *Postcards*, a disorientated Loyal Blood is at one stage depicted alone in a mountainous landscape carved as much by the American imagination as by 'ancient water'. The sandstone has been 'irradiated' by the hypnotic chants of the Indian war dance, the air echoing to the hoof beats of 'Red Horse, Red Cloud and Low Dog' as they swept down upon the 'astounded faces of Fetterman, Crook, Custer, Benteen, Reno' (276). He hears an 'Indian singing from the Rosebud Reservation' and thinks that it is 'the howling of the wind', while on the radio, in ironic juxtaposition, he listens to 'I'm Proud to Be an American' (308–9). These are Proulx's ghost voices.

And ghost voices they remain in Proulx's contemporary Wyoming, their presence signalled by their absence but captured in the traces left behind: the petroglyphs and arrowheads that stimulate the creative imagination. The Native Americans we have encountered so far in this study exist on the periphery of her *Wyoming Stories*: the archetypal marauding Red Indian conjured up by an unscrupulous businessman to alter an uneconomic route ('The Sagebrush Kid', *FJW*), or the savage Ute evoked by a confused hunter to explain the gruesome death of a female settler ('Them Old Cowboy Songs', *FJW*). The contemporary Native American characters that form the focus of this chapter remain, like their historical forebears, marginal, which is particularly surprising considering Wyoming's Native population is more than twice the national average. When they do appear, their stories form a subplot designed to explore aspects of the main narrative. Only one story has a strong Native American character and examines themes of assimilation and the loss of cultural heritage found in other Native American literatures, 'The Indian Wars Refought' (*BD*). Elsewhere in Proulx's fiction, their transience and marginality is their story. In 'The Governors of Wyoming' (*CR*), *Postcards* and *That Old Ace in the Hole*, Native Americans are transformed into silent, Indian hitchhikers who drift aimlessly into the pages of her narratives, their very condition a symbol of generations of geographical and cultural displacement.

Yet despite their fleeting appearance, Proulx actually has a great deal to say about Native Americans; but there again, so does everybody. The Native American equivalent of the Marlboro Man is the suffering Indian staring majestically across the desert, immortalized in Maynard Dixon's *What an Indian Thinks* (1912) and recycled in countless tacky reproductions. His silence is convenient because, like the continent from which he takes his name, it allows others to speak for him. Thus, the Native American exists in the popular imagination as a patchwork of cliché that tells us more about the preoccupations of white society than the subject itself. From the beginning, Leslie Fiedler reminds us that there was a determination to contextualize the continent's inhabitants within European history. He was aligned with the Celts of Ireland, the lost tribes of Israel, and even refugees from Atlantis. Indeed, it is in his confrontation with the Indian, Fiedler argues, that 'the European becomes the "American" as well as the Westerner'.[2] When Columbus arrived in 1491, his appellation 'Red Indian' demonstrates once again the expectation that, regardless of geographical fact, the indigenous population were to be props employed in a European narrative. The Native American poet Simon Ortiz pokes fun at this element of wish fulfilment in his poem 'Indians' Wanted', which repeatedly asserts that 'Indians were what people in Europe wanted to believe'. The belief was so strong that 'soon even "the Indians" believed there were "Indians"', an observation that humorously alerts the reader to the complex relationship between identity and cultural expectation.[3]

If being an 'Indian' is to be the victim of bad geography, then the supposedly more culturally sensitive term 'Native American' reinforces the misconception that the continent's indigenous population was homogenous and waiting to be written into somebody else's history. French philosopher Michel Montaigne's conception of the 'Noble Savage' living in a 'state of nature' was being lampooned as early as Shakespeare's *The Tempest*, but the myth that Native Americans were a small, Stone Age group of nomads subsisting on buffalo hunting has persisted. The reality, Proulx argues, is more nuanced:

Instead of a few wandering tribes in a vast, untamed wilderness, which is what I learned as a child, there was a large population of many, many tribes who practiced advanced agriculture and deliberate control of wild animals, made landscape modifications through fire and irrigation, built a variety of houses and shelters, in the southwest erected enormous building complexes and supported sophisticated religions and mythologies.[4]

When Proulx talks of ghosts, one suspects that it is just as much these pre-contact peoples as Red Cloud that dominates her historical imagination. Much of her work in the Red Desert with archaeologist Dudley Gardner has sought to piece together the lives of these ancient tribes.[5] Their presence is inscribed in the landscape: the petroglyph stands in the shadow of the petrol station, the hieroglyph next to the hacienda. Indeed, the view from the living room of her Bird Cloud home includes a limestone cliff over which, archaeological evidence suggests, a bison drive may have occurred in ancient days. The discovery of tipi rings and arrowheads while excavating the house's foundations suggests that she is living on a site haunted by Wyoming's Native past, a sense she seems to acknowledge through the evocative name Bird Cloud.[6]

It is the ghosts of these ancient peoples that Proulx brings to life in the imaginative exercise, 'Deep-Blood-Greasy-Bowl' (*FJW*). Australian novelist Delia Falconer considered this 'the collection's most engrossing and deeply moving story', largely because it is atypical of Proulx's grimy social realism.[7] The story is neither engrossing nor deeply moving, indeed it is not really a story at all (there is little attempt at developing either sympathetic characters or a complex plot), but a fictional imagining. In this context, however, it is of great significance because it challenges all our preconceived notions concerning Native Americans, in the process releasing them from the nostalgic label of the Indian.

'Deep-Blood-Greasy-Bowl'

Central to its success is Proulx's ability to evoke a credible ancient ancestor – not simply a cowboy in furs, but a character who behaves and thinks in ways different to our own. There are a few anachronisms – time is measured in terms of weeks, seasons and years; women have husbands, are accoutred with 'deerskin bags' and calculate the skins needed for their tipis as if they were measuring up for curtains – but generally Proulx succeeds in presenting a people more spiritually attuned to their environment (131).

In his novel *The Inheritors*, Nobel Prize winning author William Golding depicts a world seen through the eyes of Neanderthal man. His approach is largely conceptual; his interest is in the processes by which his characters make sense of the world around them. Proulx's vision is more poetic, her distant progenitors are, as she makes clear, 'exquisitely sensitive to nuances of the natural world: strong clouds rubbing against the sky like a finger drawn over skin, the quiver of a single blade of grass in calm air showing subterranean movement' (124). When seen through their eyes, the division between the animate and inanimate breaks down and metaphorical language springs back to life: clouds cease to be gaseous and resolve themselves into something solid; a river becomes a living organism with a 'choked' mouth; and it is not simply a figure of speech to suggest that coyotes argue (123). Their eyes are sharp – when gazing into his camp from a height, the young hunter, Small Marmot, can pick out 'the fringe of shining hairs outlining a puppy's ears'; their hearing is so acute that silence is transformed into a positive entity; and their sense of smell is such that they can detect a storm coming in from the sea from 'the briny smell of seaweed' (128, 124).

Throughout, Proulx seamlessly interweaves man with landscape: 'Some men went to the chert vein that erupted along a ridge beyond the sand dunes, worrying the desirable nodules coated with white calcareous cortex from the earth' (127). The participants remain indistinguishable from each other and, through a process of personification, from the landscape. The earth is a giant, complete with backbone and veins, the chert a bloody eruption from a vein that provides the 'nodule' – a growth which will give the primitive men tools for further bloody slaughter. They are also a people practising a primitive form of religion based around the incantations of the shaman and the symbolism of the 'Deep-Blood-Greasy-Bowl'. (This represents an artefact that has been squeezed out of more familiar depictions of the West, the revelation that it had 'come to them in the distant past' pushing our temporal boundaries of what might be considered 'western' back even further (128).) Significantly, though its function is to catch the blood of slaughtered bison, it represents a spirituality that works in accordance with, rather than superimposing itself upon, the natural environment. The bison and hunters are conceived of as part of a wider cycle controlled by the seasons. Individual characterization is kept to a minimum, partially, one suspects, to prevent anachronistic emotional development, but mainly to emphasize the shared consciousness of the hunters with each other and with the bison. Men who were boys during the last hunt intuit the arrival of a new herd made up of their offspring, an intuition shared by the magpies and ravens which scavenged the bones of the last hunt: 'No one doubted that the birds remembered the last drive and would aid them in the next one' (131).

To the hunters, the bison are not simply prey, but a spiritualized herd that have been roaming the earth gradually making their way to this date with destiny (124). Accordingly, the herd is described throughout in terms that suggest its homogeneity: initially it is depicted using verbs emphasizing its liquidity (it is a 'black mass pouring out of their deep hole into sunlight'); in the latter stages it becomes 'a vast living animal with hundreds of legs' (125, 130).

Yet despite this spiritualization, Proulx does not spare the readers' sensibilities during her description of the slaughter. There is an improbable 'cartoon moment' when the bison lurch over the edge of the cliff and are momentarily suspended by the image of their running legs. It is a visual paradox augmented by the alliterative deployment of consonants usually associated with rapidity and lightness of movement to describe their headlong plummet – 'falling, flailing, flying' – brought to an abrupt halt with the percussive 'bellows of broken bison' (130, 131). From then on, all is blood. But it is a slaughter still underpinned by a deep sense of spirituality. The statement 'None must live, for they would tell the secret of the invisible cliff to other bison', drifts between attribution to a character and an observing consciousness, thus reinforcing the sense that the hunters are participating in a ritual with wider implications than the immediate hunt (131). As men, women and boys rip and devour organs from the still living animals, Proulx makes clear that the combination of blood and ritual 'twined' into the 'lifelong sense of existence' of those who participated. Blood becomes blood in Proulx's depiction, allowing her to establish the importance of blood and ceremony in the Native American imagination (131).

In some ways Proulx's story is an exercise in myth creation every bit as suspect as that of Columbus. Indeed, the 'red' in Red Indian seems to have shifted from a geographical confusion to the more sinister evocation of blood ritual. However, her work succeeds because it breathes life into the stony evidence of ancient hunting techniques through a combination of mysticism and blood-curdling realism. Its significance is that it challenges the parameters by which we normally conceive of Native American history while simultaneously alerting us to the importance of the imagination in the act of historical re-creation. Proulx's story prompts us to question what we mean when we talk about 'Indians'. For Indian identity has, as she makes clear in 'How the West was Spun', evolved in accordance with changing tastes among white consumers: he is the Noble Savage of the lost frontier; the savage Red Indian propagated by Bill Cody and Hollywood; the peaceful victim of Kevin Costner's *Dances with Wolves* (1988); and the environmental idealist who promises to show today's harried white population the way to serenity and health.[8] Unfortunately, the shift towards 'the Indian side', as Patricia Limerick has noted, shows a 'unitary, simple, pristine, and victimized Indian' just as un-illuminating as the old myth.[9] Thus, as Native Americans have been transformed from character to symbol it has proved difficult for both historians and writers to bring them into view.

The most sophisticated attempts at re-evaluation are works that form the corpus of any Native American literature course, works which began emerging in the civil rights era (when the Vietnam War forced Americans to appraise the country's military and colonial past), and were written by Native Americans. An explosive creative period witnessed the publication of Vine Deloria Jr's *Custer Died for Your Sins* (1969) and Dee Brown's *Bury My Heart at Wounded Knee* (1970), both of which purported to offer the Indian side of events central to the creation of American identity. During this experimental Modernist period, N. Scott Momaday produced *House Made of Dawn* (1969); James Welch, *Winter in the Blood* (1974); and Leslie Marmon Silko *Ceremony* (1977), works which introduced themes of dispossession and alienation (themes which would remain central to Native American literature to the present day), in a disruptive style that sought to keep alive the oral traditions of Native storytelling. This disruptive aesthetic persists into the early work of important Native writers such as Karen Louise Erdrich (whose *Dakotah* novels employ multiple narrators and a fragmented chronology). However, in general Native American writing has become stylistically more mainstream (diluted for a white audience, cynics argue) and more focused on issues concerning everyday lives. Sherman Alexie uses humour and satire and the same cast of hopeless misfits to explore the nihilism of reservation life in his novel *Reservation Blues* (1995); Louis Owens' *Bone Game* (1994) explores the politics of bloodlines and the intellectualization of Indian affairs within the university system; while in the novel *Dwellings* (1995), Linda Hogan re-visits the spiritual disaster of Indian removal through the lens of eco-feminism.

Although much Native American writing is rich and varied in its scope, at its core is the tragedy of the removal of a people from the land they literally worshipped. Vine Deloria Jr argues that unlike Christianity, which is portable and presents earthly existence as a vale of tears prior to elevation to the imperishable and disembodied afterlife, Native religions are fundamentally attached to the landscape.[10] Perhaps, argues Momaday, it is hardly surprising that after 'thirty thousand years of habitation' the landscape 'is integrated in the Indian mind and spirit'.[11] Forcible removal, therefore, does not simply lead to a sense of grievance but an existential crisis of identity, the psychological scars of which are experienced by today's descendants. As a result, the heroes of many Native American narratives suffer from the trauma of alienation, which can only be repaired by returning 'home' to reclaim their heritage. It is the reverse of the Turner thesis: an emphasis on finding an identity through the return home, rather than forging a new identity through conquest. In some sense, Momaday's and Silko's novels provide the blueprint for this tradition: for in both *House Made of Dawn* and *Ceremony*, the central characters, Abel and Tayo, overcome their sense of alienation and displacement in the wider world by forging a new sense of self in the land of their ancestors. It is this rupture that interests Proulx, which is perhaps unsurprising considering her insistence on the symbiotic relationship between landscape and character. When we think of the majority of her Native American characters – Joe Blue Skies, Moony Brassleg, the anonymous Indian brother in 'The Governors of Wyoming' (*CR*) – they are connected by their displacement; a feature symbolized by their appearance in the texts as hitchhikers. They are drifters cut loose from both their cultural heritage and any sense of social responsibility: they are literally and metaphorically lacking direction.

Unfortunately, as William Bevis has noted, one of the problems with heritage reclamation narratives is that they 'suggest that "identity," for a Native American, is not a matter of finding "one's self," but of finding a "self" that is transpersonal and includes a society, a past, and a place'.[12] We need to be on our guard against the notion of an 'authentic' Native American identity that exists separately from the complex negotiations that have created the 'Indian'. Sherman Alexie repeatedly addresses this problem in his work, his controversial use of the unfashionable term 'Indian' acknowledging the pervasiveness of colonial and cultural influence. In his film script for *Smoke Signals* (1998), he uses a rich vein of satire to mock the notion of identity construction, of which the following exchange between the central character, Victor Joseph, and one of his friends, is typical: 'You're always trying to sound like some damn medicine man or something. I mean, how many times have you seen *Dances with Wolves*? ... Do you think that shit is real? God. Don't you even know how to be a real Indian?'[13]

'What is a real Indian?' For Alexie, 'it's not corn pollen, eagle feathers, Mother Earth, Father Sky: It's everyday life.' And everyday life for Alexie's Indians is a bleak, self-destructive cycle of drinking, frustrated sexual relationships, fighting and early, often violent deaths.[14] These are the Indians who populate the work of Momaday, the *Dakotah* novels of Erdrich and, as will be seen, the imagination of Proulx. The statistics that underpin such representations are indeed terrifying: Indians experience twelve times the US rate of malnutrition; nine times the rate of alcoholism; seven times the rate of infant mortality; life expectancy for young men is 44.[15] And yet, according to Louis Owens, Alexie's 'real Indians' simply perpetuate the myth of the helpless, romantic victim undone by fire-water still in the process of vanishing: just as he is supposed to do.[16]

The notion of identity is complicated further by the issue of bloodlines; a theme explored by Proulx in the 'Indian Wars Refought' (*BD*). Bloodlines are important because they are an internalized symbol of the Turnerian conquest: the first trappers took Indian wives and, Patricia Riley reminds us, Thomas Jefferson and the early Christian Missionaries advocated interracial mixing as the 'bloodless' solution to the Indian problem.[17] Blood inheritance, therefore, becomes an indicator of authentic Indian identity, with nearly all tribes setting their own minimum blood quantum (usually a quarter) as an entry requirement.[18] However, as Suzanne Lundquist makes clear in her insightful discussion of this issue, this is a distinction that raises more questions than it answers: who is more 'Indian' – the 'pure blood' (a category which may be meaningless) living in New York, or the mixed-blood practitioner of Native customs living on the Pine-Ridge reservation? Alexie, as might be expected, has fun with this question, opening the story 'Lawyer's League' with the observation: 'My father is an African American giant who played defensive end for the University of Washington Huskies, and my mother is a petite Spokane Indian ballerina who majored in dance at U-Dub, so genetically speaking, I'm a graceful monster.'[19] Beneath the humour, however, he is posing the more serious question: what do we inherit with Indian blood?

The political complexity surrounding the representation of the Native American voice may explain the scarcity of Indian characters (Proulx's preferred term) in her work. When they do appear, they are lost and alienated figures freighted with cultural baggage and expectations. For, central to all the characters under consideration is the Indian identity that they both pursue and represent. Blue Skies, Proulx's most postmodern literary figure, is created from textual fragments that invite the reader to construct their own Native American narrative: is he a 'real Indian' capable of conjuring a tornado, a mental patient, or a confidence trickster exploiting his cultural heritage? In 'The Governors of Wyoming' (*CR*), Proulx uses a sordid case of contemporary paedophilia to explore the historical sexual exploitation of young Native American girls by the first settlers, in the process revisiting the binary of landscape / female exploitation. Through the behaviour of Moony Brassleg, Proulx invites us to mock the cultural innocence of her ingénue, Bob Dollar, while also exploring different conceptual approaches to spatial mapping employed by whites and Native Americans. The final story – 'The Indian Wars Refought' (*BD*) – is Proulx's most thorough exploration of Indian affairs, and focuses on a broad range of themes. Primary among them are: the relationship between appearance and reality in the construction of cultural heritage; the importance of bloodlines in moulding identity; and the negotiation between racial and familial responsibilities.

Hitchhiking with cultural baggage

The first of these characters is Joe Blue Skies, the hitchhiker who is picked up together with the sailor, Donnie Weener, by Loyal Blood in *Postcards*. Here Proulx brings together three classic wanderers: the sailor, the nomadic Indian and the cowboy. Blue Skies conforms to many of our preconceived cultural expectations: he is barely present; he sits silently chain-smoking in the back of the car making only occasional gnomic observations, singing songs and scribbling in a suitably ancient, snake skin covered book. His silence forces others to speak for him; Donnie Weener introduces him, in the process alerting the reader to the dangers of caricature and the possibility of Joe's self-conscious exploitation: 'He's Blue Skies, no shit, that's his name' (62). Such exploitation, the con-man, Weener, knows all about. The narrator is complicit in this process, continually referring to him with the definite article as 'the Indian', which evokes the literary figure found in frontier fiction, rather than the person sitting next to Loyal.

The literary Indian comes to the fore when, following the flight of Weener after he has pick-pocketed Loyal, Blue Skies appears to conjure a tornado:

> I'm singing The Friendly Song. It goes 'The sky loves to hear me.' I want to be friendly with the sky ... something twisted in the wet grass with a doomed persistence. It was a bat, injured in some way, gnashing its needle-like teeth ... 'see that,' said the Indian, pointing ... 'Tornado,' said the Indian. 'The sky loves to hear me,' he bawled. The snout swayed like a loose rope and came across the immense landscape toward them. (66)

This dramatic incident occurs in the chapter 'The bat in the long grass' – a peculiarly ambiguous title that invites the reader to make symbolic connections with the different characters. Bats are of great significance in Native American spiritualism; in the novels of Linda Hogan they become a symbol of the possibility of existing in two worlds. In *Dwellings* (1995) she explains that bats hear sounds on the edge of human consciousness, and as they throw their voice into space and wait for the echo, the landscape seems to speak through the bat.[20] The bat, therefore, is like Blue Skies, a character able to talk to the world around him. However, it is also Loyal, continually struggling against forces beyond his control, impotently gnashing his teeth but unable to escape the coming storm. The fact that the storm takes the shape of a hangman's rope, dramatizes his guilt and fear through pathetic fallacy. And yet the effects of the storm are entirely ambiguous, since our next view of the luckless Loyal is his waking up in hospital with no car, money and 'no sign of the Indian' (67). What has happened remains a mystery throughout the novel. Thus, by the time he leaves the narrative, we are unsure whether Blue Skies is a taciturn Indian who can control storms, or a confidence trickster who, in the words of the doctor treating Loyal, metaphorically 'scalps' him (67).

This ambiguity is central to Proulx's aesthetic and cultural concerns in the novel. *Postcards* is a novel of textual fragments, the clearest example being the postcards themselves, which invite the reader to construct their own narratives. This deliberately postmodern approach, which sacrifices linearity, chronology and narrative authority by forcing the reader to negotiate between different sources in order to interpret a story, is itself typical of the more experimental, subversive Native American tradition. Through a series of seemingly unconnected postcards spread throughout the novel the reader can piece together the story of Blue Skies as a successful herbalist (135), who was blinded by the storm (333), that blew Loyal's car away (323), and 'removed' the $100 bill from his shoes (253). It is a narrative that conforms to our romanticized view of Native Americans as outsiders with a special connection to nature. However, within the body of the text the reader is offered extra information which leads to another possible interpretation. In the late 1970s, Loyal finds a picture of a man called Walter Hairy Chin in a collection of discarded patient files from a mental asylum in Fargo, North Dakota, and identifies it as the Indian he picked up (276–7). So who is the man picked up by Loyal: con-man, Indian herbalist, or psychiatric patient? Or does his disruptive behaviour combined with his ability to take many forms transform him into the archetype of the 'trickster' figure in Native American writing: the aimless wanderer, liar and thief whose rich vein of magic realism demonstrates the clash between Anglo-Saxon realism and the more mystical Indian world view. We never find out, but our process of piecing together the clues offers a guide to the interpretative strategy of the novel as a whole.

Although the Indian quickly disappears from the story, he leaves his book, which takes on a textual significance all of its own. Its importance is signalled by the fact that there are three separate chapters devoted to its content, and that it is the last thing that Loyal sees through closed eyelids: 'The Indian's book falls open. He is astonished to see the pages are the great, slanting field. At the top of the field a black scribble of trees, a wall' (340). In death, the book returns Loyal to his pasture; the field he had improved over five years and which he had last seen on the fateful day when he raped and killed his girlfriend, Billy, thus precipitating his flight. On that day the pasture looks to Loyal like an open 'Bible', an image that signals the notion of godly conquest enshrined in the doctrine of Manifest Destiny (14). Billy has already become the victim of this acquisitive attitude, her remains written into the landscape, which swells to the curve of a female hip. As the Bible transforms into the Indian's book, Proulx now reminds us of all those other silent victims of pioneer conquest; a parallel that become clearer when Loyal sets out to write in it. The book offers a space to confess the truth, however we are told that 'he carried the Indian's book around with him for years before he started to write in it' (106). Before then he reads, but can make little of the Indian's pen and Ink drawings and arbitrary lists, even though through them we can chart the Native American experience of first contact, persecution, flight and disaster; a list that mirrors Loyal's recent experience. Ironically, Loyal can only make sense of a reference to 'scalpings', which contextualizes the Indian within a narrative framework with which he feels comfortable. Eventually he sets out to write:

> On the page for Birthdays the Indian had written. 'My son Ralph born Aug 12 1938 died diarrea Aug 11 1939. ... Loyal crossed out the Indian's notations. On the Birthday page he wrote his own name and birth date, then those of his family. ... Tentatively, barely pressing the pencil against the paper, he wrote 'Billy', but erased it a minute later... . When he turned the light out he saw the blue night fitted into the rectangles of the window glass, the crumpled earth glowing with phosphorescent metals, the blurring wind and stars. The Indian's book. His book. (108-9)

Loyal appears to have approached the book in the spirit of the confessional, but he is unable to write Billy's story; instead he writes his own history over that of the Indian, thus eliding two elements of western exploitation. The landscape, women and Native Americans were all victims of white conquest, their histories silenced and written over. When he turns out the light, the world has changed: the sky has become imprisoned behind the bars of the window, and the land a repository of shiny metals to be exploited. And yet in the deliberately vague pronoun 'His' there is some ambiguity as to who is the possessor of book and by extension the land. Loyal has inscribed his story over it, and yet there seems to be some deeper resonance that suggests it still belongs to the Indian. This ambiguity opens up the irony of the hitchhiking Indian: he is not the romantic nomad, but a character dispossessed of the land that gave his life a meaning, but which remains unintelligible to Loyal.

The second hitchhiking Indian is the young boy picked up by Shy Hemp in 'The Governors of Wyoming' (*CR*). Despite being one of the first acts chronologically, the meeting is plotted towards the end of the story and makes clear a paedophile subplot running through the text. The Indian is spotted wading through the 'Waist-High Grass' that gives this section of the story its title; he is a pastoral wanderer who is, by his own admission, 'goin nowhere' (271). When Hemp turns around to pick him up, Proulx prepares us for a world turned upside down. As with Blue Skies, Proulx emphasizes the awkwardness of the initial encounter through the Indian's silence, a meeting during which she also allows the landscape to introduce the twin themes of sexual and ecological exploitation with which the story will be concerned: 'The sky showed a scraped nakedness, hard, and with a stain along the south-west horizon from the Utah refineries' (271). Proulx elides these themes further through the agency of the Indian, whose close connection to the landscape (he smells of 'grass and crushed leaf') gives him a heightened sensitivity to the needs of those, like Shy Hemp, whose name suggests an aversion to the natural. The Indian's intuition is made brutally clear in Hemp's blurted request for 'A girl. Thirteen. To fuck. He would pay' (272). It is a request which, as with Billy, makes clear the connection between sexual and geographical exploitation.

In this story, however, what is important is that the female victim is Native American. Hemp's taste for young Indian girls is, like the behaviour of all Proulx's sexual misfits, traced to a seminal event in his childhood. Hemp recalls an incident during a visit to the memorial to Portuguee Phillips (a memorial raised following the massacre of Fetterman's troops in 1866) with the family of a Native American classmate, 13-year-old Nikole Angermiller. During the return trip, drowsing in the back of an old sedan, his head full of Indian history and 'Who Shot the Sheriff' on the radio, he is brought to his first orgasm by the young Nikole. As he later reflects on the incident: 'she had hurled him into corruption, but who had thrown her into the pit?' (256). Proulx's uncomfortable answer is her brother. Hemp's paedophilia is also the product of his marital frustration, a situation fraught with irony. He may have abandoned the ranching lifestyle, but he still looks like a cowboy and clearly embraces its element of sexual dominance. Unfortunately he cannot dominate and 'ride' his wife, Roany (a name that suggests horse). She is an outsider who loves the cowboy in Hemp and quickly realizes the exploitative potential of the western mythology that her husband rejects and sets up a store selling western paraphernalia. Unable to control his wife, Hemp turns to the anonymous and more pliant Native American, carrying out his affair in the kind of 'natural' landscape that purifies the act by evoking a pastoral state (265). However, this is just another form of exploitation which reveals the dark underbelly of the western myth propagated by his wife.

This exploitative irony is given a different dimension when we recall that Hemp is not merely a reluctant cowboy, but an eco-terrorist with a stated aim of returning the range to the 'state of nature' before the arrival of the white man. The conquest did not simply bring about the appropriation and exploitation of the land, but also its female inhabitants. William Kittredge tells us in his essay 'White People in Paradise' that 'in the fur-trapper days, it is said, Indian women were so incessantly raped by white men that they resorted to a strategy called "going for sand". When trappers showed up those women would go to the creeks and pack their vaginas with sand.'[21] Significantly, Proulx argues, the exploitation was not only sexual. Trappers often used liaisons with Indian women to find out the location of the best trapping sites, and male relations were only too ready to sell the services of female family members. She cites Richard Irving Dodge's observation, made in his largely sympathetic study *The Plains of North America and its Inhabitants* (1876), that 'when the trapper was an institution of the plains, he did not consider his outfit complete, unless he had one or more Indian wives'. Although, Proulx infers from this account, 'many trappers had long and apparently happy liaisons with Indian women', she is also clear that these bucolically entitled 'country marriages' masked a pattern of exploitation which was repeated in subsequent generations.[22] It is an uncomfortable exploitative truth made apparent in the behaviour of the brother in Proulx's story, who is only too willing to sell the services of his sister to Hemp. Hemp's eco-terrorism, therefore, is not driven by environmental concerns as much as guilt. In seeking to return the landscape to its condition before the arrival of the trappers (discussed in 'Ranchers'), he is seeking to remove all exploitative elements, most notably himself.

The final Indian hitchhiker is the shambling figure of Moony Brassleg, picked up by Bob Dollar in *That Old Ace in the Hole*. In this encounter, Proulx returns to the theme of the legacy of displacement. For Brassleg may appear directionless, but he has lessons to teach Bob and by extension the white middle classes, about finding their way. When Bob slows down to pick up this mysterious figure, we are aware that his views on Indian history have been moulded by a combination of his reading of the 1845 expeditionary account of Lieutenant James William Albert (which offers a romanticized vision similar to Montaigne's evocation of the 'Noble Savage'), and the bloody description of Comanche atrocities recorded in the diary of a young pioneer who moved West in 1878: 'They got hold of a clock salesman last year, cut open his stomach, pulled out his guts a ways, tied em to the horn of his saddle and whacked the horse' (63, 76). Thus, when Bob picks up the old Indian carrying his possessions in a single sack, he expects an encounter which has some resonance with either the 'noble' or 'bloodthirsty' savage. That Brassleg fulfils neither, remains silent and feigns sleep, is a source of disappointment. However even his silent presence brings about a perceptual change in Bob:

> Bob, somewhat annoyed, as he had expected conversation in return for the ride, drove on, the telephone poles striking across the plain near

the road, the wires rising and falling in long swoops. He was in sand sage and dune country … . It was impossible not to think of blowing dust gradually covering everything, the fine dirt settling in layers, the thickening layers … covering the bones of dinosaurs, the houses of men, the trails and roads, building up inch by inch, foot by foot, millennium after millennium, the multiple pasts of the scarred landscape gone and forgotten. (286)

The narrator draws out the uneasiness of the situation by contrasting Bob's need to engage in phatic talk with Brassleg's comfortable silence, cultural stereotypes that are picked up in the 'telephone poles' that border the road. They remind us of a civilization intent on personal communication over vast distances, contrasted with one that values silence as a sign of self-control, dignity and reverence. The Native American writer Charles Alexander Eastman recalls in his memoir *The Soul of the Indian: An Interpretation* (1911) boyhood lessons in the art of silence, which was considered by his people the cornerstone of character. Eastman, a physician who attended the dying at Wounded Knee, is controversial within the Native American community: he worked tirelessly to bring Native culture to the wider world, but stands accused of playing to stereotypes in order to do so. Once again, therefore, we are left to wonder whether Brassleg's feigned sleep is the result of fatigue or the necessity to perform; whichever, though it irritates Bob, it conforms entirely to cultural expectations. In this uncomfortable silence we travel through a landscape which reminds us of the impermanence of those who dwell upon it, and that just as Native American culture has vanished with little trace, the western culture of Bob Dollar will one day be buried in sand. As a result of such contemplation they seem to arrive both geographically and chronologically in the short-grass landscape of Indian Country – something that Brassleg senses intuitively: 'Most there, ain't we?' (286).

But where 'there' might be remains another point of cultural contrast. One of Bob's first questions to Brassleg was the cheery, 'Where are you from?' (286). He was hoping to elicit a tribal affiliation that would have enabled him to make the bridge between the Indian of his imagination and the man sitting beside him. He finds the response, Oklahoma, entirely unsatisfactory. But the comic answer masks a serious point; as a descendant of a displaced tribe he is from nowhere. Furthermore, as Bob finds to his exasperation, Brassleg's concept of where he is going differs greatly from his own. For whereas Bob expects an exact location – a house or street – Brassleg has no map, just an imaginative grasp of his destination (the house of his daughter), built on his reading of the landscape. This conceptual approach to the landscape finds resonance with US travel writer William Least Heat-Moon's idea of deep mapping, explored in his book *PrairyErth (a deep map)* (1991). The text chronicles his perambulations through Chase County, Kansas, during which he exposes the limitations of western mapping in favour of just wandering. To wander is to allow the boundaries between geographic coordinates and temporalities to dissolve, to break boundaries and re-connect with a less superficial map: 'Whenever we enter the land, sooner or later we pick up the scent of our own histories, and when we begin to travel vertically, we end up following road maps in the marrow of our bones and in the thump of our blood.' It is an internalized map, he claims, inscribed in the DNA of Native Americans who enjoy a symbiotic relationship with the landscape, without the politically motivated impulse towards division that underlies Western cartographic practice.[23]

Unfortunately, this conception is so alien to both Bob and the reader that we begin to doubt the existence of the destination and by extension the daughter. Therefore, when Brassleg's daughter does appear, we are forced once again to reinterpret the story by inspecting our prejudices. Shirley Mason, as her name suggests, is an anglicized Native American; a nurse who, ironically, specializes in the care of the elderly. Part of this assimilation is that she understands the importance of maps and knows how to give Bob directions he will understand. It is a cultural evolution that extends to her domestic affairs: she knows the direction of her own life, which is a rejection of the reservation in favour of conformity to white working patterns. This, however, is also combined with a nostalgic recreation of traditional living within the confines of her own home. Vine Deloria Jr calls this process 'retribalisation', a process which marks not an evasive nostalgia for a vanished past but a confidence among Native Americans to resist total assimilation within the white hegemony.[24] Mason's house may appear conventional on the outside, but the interior offers a Native American approximation of a pioneer log cabin, complete with mesquite fire, Indian paintings done by Brassleg and a couple of rocking chairs. It appears as a home for the displaced. In this environment the family eat traditional elk roast and Bob Mason – a retired teacher – explains how Brassleg is to instruct them in traditional ceremonies and herbal remedies. In these surroundings Brassleg comes into his own and reverses the traveller and guide roles assumed thus far. For when, lulled by the familial atmosphere, Bob draws parallels between their experience and his own feelings of displacement, it brings a withering response from Brassleg:

> But you are lucky. There are chances for you, a white young man. How you like it on the reservation, forty to eighty-five percent unemployment, no jobs at all, no money to get out, no school, nothing but get drunk,

make babies, use the ADC check for bottle? Young men there do not think, What am I going to be in my life? Answer: a drunk, die young and miserable, leave damaged children behind. They think, How long will I live? (294)

This is the apocalyptic vision of reservation life presented by Erdrich and Alexie. Kittredge draws attention to a spate of young male suicides in Wyoming's Wind River Reservation in 1985, which prompted the population to make a conscious effort to re-learn the ceremonies and traditions of their ancestors.[25] To some extent Bob Mason, 'a recovering alcoholic', is following this process of re-tribalization in an effort to give his life a new direction. However, there is theatricality about the evening that puts us on our guard: Bob Mason's aphoristic, faux-Indian register characterized by an unusually contorted syntax – 'Did you not bring your medicine bag?' – narrowly avoids parody; and the traditional Indian paintings produced by Brassleg – one depicting an empty field with two arrow shafts – may seem 'full of meaning' to Bob, but appear clichéd to the reader (292, 3). Proulx seems to be warning us that her Native American characters, like her cowboys, are just as susceptible to participation in caricatured versions of themselves. Thus, when Bob leaves with Brassleg's gnomic advice – 'you will have to find your way alone. Maybe this uncle you speak of will help you' – ringing in his ears, he is bemused to observe him settling down to watch television. Brassleg, like Blue Skies, seems to occupy two worlds, but here they are contrived to deliberately thwart our expectations: he is both shaman and consumer of pulp culture (294).

'The Indian Wars Refought'

In each of the above works, Proulx's Indians are transients whose role is to question cultural expectations, whether those of other characters, the reader, or even their own. Here, as in Anglo history in general, their stories form only a marginal part of the larger narrative. 'The Indian Wars Refought' (*BD*), however, is devoted entirely to questions of cultural identity, assimilation and lost heritage. The story focuses on the relationship between the well-to-do widow of a rich lawyer, Georgina Crawshaw, and the surprise choice for her second marriage, her much younger ranch foreman, Charlie Parrott (part Oglala Sioux, but, as his name suggests, a good mimic). He was brought up on a reservation, but after a couple of failed marriages and the birth of a now estranged daughter, Linny, he has chosen to conceal his background. When Linny decides to join the newlyweds, Proulx carefully teases out the tensions that arise when romance combined with affiliations of blood and cultural heritage are brought into conflict. These tensions are cast into sharp relief, and also contextualized within wider Native American history, by Linny's discovery of the last surviving copy of Bill Cody's lost film of the massacre of Wounded Knee in 1876. The film becomes the Story's overarching metaphor, allowing Proulx to explore the legacy of white atrocities on contemporary Anglo-Indian relationships; the connection between the individual and their heritage; and the role of the imagination and authenticity in historical recreation.

The beginning of the story seems bizarrely disconnected from the rest, but it sets out to warn us of the danger of appearances: a central theme in the narrative that follows. The opening sentence – 'ONE SUMMER DAY AROUND THE TURN OF THE LAST century' – offers a mixture of specificity and vagueness that establishes verisimilitude while also drawing attention to its fictionalization (17). It is an ambiguity traced in the architecture of the Brawls building itself, the narrative adopting a guidebook register to describe a classical frontage which proves to be as false as lawyer Brawls' teeth, or, indeed, the character himself. For however carefully Proulx traces three generations of the Brawls' legal practice, describing his legal assistance to Bill Cody within the context of real historical events such as the Teapot Scandal and the Depression years, Brawls himself is fictional (19). Furthermore, despite always being lawyers, their association with Bill Cody signals the attachment of the Brawls clan to a theatrical version of the West. They consider themselves ranchers, give themselves suitably western names, and wear cowboy regalia in the office. This is both part of an invented history and a potent business strategy: everybody in Wyoming trusts a cowboy. The brief history of the Brawls family, therefore, not only establishes an emotional counterpoint to that of Linny, but also introduces the combination of imagination and historical fact that are central to the construction of an authentic heritage.

This process is, of course, dramatized by Cody's project of the 'historical recreation' of the battle of Wounded Knee: a seminal moment in the creation of Native American identity. The fact that the film is lost and that so little is known about its content makes it the ideal focus for the theme of myth creation. This process begins within the narrative itself, with Proulx's elision of real and fictional characters and events mirroring Cody's own habit of grafting faux narratives over authentic props. The facts of the film are that it was made by Essaney and released in August 1914. It was variously called *Wars of Civilization* (a title not only breathtaking in its historical and cultural insensitivity, but ironic considering the apocalypse that had just been unleashed in Europe); the more culturally affirmative *The Last Great Battle of the Sioux; From the Warpath to the Peace Pipe* (a title that announces the film's happy ending, which shows contented Indian farmers bringing in their crops); and *Buffalo Bill's Indian Wars* (a title that appears to acknowledge its own theatricality). Proulx plumbed for *The Indian Wars Refought*, probably because its vagueness allows it to be transposed onto the different battles fought within her text.[26]

From the start, Cody was keen to portray his film as historically accurate, which implied authentic props. He petitioned Secretary of War, Linley M. Garrison, to release the necessary cavalry regiments, and the Secretary of the Interior, Franklin Lane, to authorize the participation of about one thousand Sioux. The advisor on historical accuracy was the US commander at the original massacre, Lieutenant General Nelson Appleton Miles, who was also a cast member. Miles appears in Proulx's narrative as a character 'fussy about accuracy', but like Cody this obsession does not extend to moral responsibility (a letter of the time reveals that 'Gen. Miles would not allow them to show the women and children in the fight and that was left out'[27]), but rather the more practical consideration of representing the correct number of troops in authentic uniforms (34). That Cody should create the appropriate numerical impression by marching the same soldiers past the camera repeatedly allows Proulx to send out a warning concerning the blurred distinction between appearance and reality. In this case, despite appearances to the contrary, the camera really does lie. Proulx returns to this complex theme through her inclusion of an opening night review of the film which is of questionable authenticity. Significantly, the author is less concerned with the film's contents, which are brushed over, but with the 'very wonderful' quality of the 'realism' achieved by the relatively new invention of the moving picture (34). He remains blissfully blind to the central irony of this praise: that white technology led to the destruction of the Indians and now, with Indian participation, it is bringing their destruction back to life and preserving it in perpetuity.

This irony was not lost on a very different kind of reviewer, Chauncey Yellow Robe, a Sioux whose mother was niece to Sitting Bull, and whose criticisms of Cody are articulated by Linny in the story. Yellow Robe served as a consultant on films that he believed portrayed Native Americans in a sympathetic light, the best known being *Silent Enemy* (1929). The film sought to re-create the lives of the Ojibwa Indians before the arrival of the white settlers, and was introduced by a prologue written and spoken by Yellow Robe in which he addresses the issue of authenticity raised by the film's docudrama approach. He asks the audience to regard the performers not as actors, but as people revisiting their heritage, noting that while the white man has all but destroyed their civilization, the white man's technology, ironically, will bring it back to life. In this sense, the camera is not a 'Silent Enemy' but a 'Silent Friend'. His insistence on impartiality means that he was a lifelong critic of Cody's Wild West shows and also the public desire for lurid depictions of Indian savagery. The review quoted by Linny is an adaptation of his 1914 essay 'The Menace of the Wild West Show' in which he claims that Cody's attempt to achieve 'historical preservation' was a 'disgrace and injustice to the Indian race'.[28]

Yellow Robe's scornful dismissal suggests that Linny's decision to destroy the film without viewing it is intellectually sound and perhaps even morally virtuous. Having read Dee Brown's seminal *Bury My Heart at Wounded Knee* (1970), she believes that the film will show 'an Indian dragging a soldier from a horse, some fake hand-to-hand fighting, Indians poking two white captive women with a stick, the Gatling and Hotchkiss guns spraying, and everywhere Buffalo Bill peering into the distance' (38). Destruction, therefore, is an act of purification, which protects her newly acquired Indian identity from further stereotyping, while also preventing yet another white person (Georgina owns the films) profiting from the misery of what she now identifies as her own people. This, at least, is one Indian war that will not be refought.

Proulx, however, presents her decision as culturally myopic. To begin with, Brown's revisionist work is not without critics regarding its impartiality. Some historians argue that his determination to correct an injustice clouded his historical judgement, the result being a highly sentimental account, based on selective and un-cited sources, which is as suspect as Cody's.[29] Furthermore her action fails to take into account the willingness of Native Americans to take part in Cody's shows in general and the film in particular. Years after the event, Edward Owl King defended his participation in the film claiming: 'The Indians without thinking went ahead and performed in the ways that were directed by some of the white people, not truthfully but just the way they wanted it presented in the pictures. That tells the wrong story.'[30] Here, once again, there is a determination to present Native Americans as puppets rather than active agents, combined with a failure to acknowledge the complexity of Native American participation in their own fictionalization. The difficulties in presenting the 'right story' are brought into sharp relief by the history of another survivor of the original massacre who enjoyed a long association with Cody, the Lakota shaman Black Elk. Black Elk's importance to the Native American community rests on a series of interviews given to the academic John G. Neihardt, published under the title *Black Elk Speaks* (1932). Long considered the seminal guide to Native spirituality and rituals, more recent scholarship has emphasized the collaborative nature of the project. Black Elk's words were translated by his son, transcribed by Neihardt's daughter, then edited and organized by Neihardt himself. Neihardt stands accused of producing a composite Indian for white audiences, a process with which Black Elk, bearing in mind his relationship with Cody, was actively complicit. Thus, the interpretation of this most 'authentic' of Native American texts – a 'Bible of North American tribes' according to Vine Deloria Jr – has become a site of cultural struggle between Native American academics: another Indian war refought.[31] Linny's destruction of Cody's film unseen signals her blinkered belief in the 'right story' distilled from cultural interplay. By exposing the 'reel Indians' to sunlight she offers not illumination but contamination. Her mistake is her failure to engage in the complex business of heritage reclamation.

The war that is fought in Proulx's narrative focuses on the domestic struggle between blood ties and romantic love, and between cultural heritage and economic pragmatism: the tension explored in the central family triangle. Although Proulx's main concern is Linny's discovery of her roots, it is prefaced by the compressed histories of both the Brawls' family and Georgina Crawshaw. Whereas the former are artificial, Georgina really is ranch-born and raised, thus bringing a degree of authenticity to the Brawls' ranching ambitions. She comes from a line of horse breeders, a trade constructed upon the careful nurturing of bloodlines, and her speciality is polo ponies. It is a form of horsemanship even further removed from the utility of ranch work than the highly theatrical sport of rodeo, which once again questions our notions of what constitutes an authentic western heritage. This issue is thrown into sharp relief when Georgina's husband, Sage, is killed, leading to calls for her to maintain the tradition: 'I mean, there's *history* there. You got a responsibility' (24). The statement prepares us for the struggle between Charlie and Linny over Indian history, by reminding us that Charlie has a responsibility to his Indian heritage. In choosing to marry her much younger Native American ranch foreman, Georgina is rejecting her heritage in terms of race, age and class. She is also rejecting polo, a sport not played by Native Americans, for a different kind of riding: one in which Charlie, with 'buttocks like cantaloupes', excels (24).

Any possibility of this relationship working comes to an end with the arrival of Linny, a 'pure Nevada hellcat', who has walked out on her alcoholic mother with the vague idea of straightening herself out (25). Initially her interest in bloodlines and inheritance is purely mercenary: she realizes that Georgina is getting on and with no heirs the ranch will pass to Charlie and then to her. She concludes that he 'had played the sexual attraction card well. She understood the game', as he did: 'They were a pair' (28). Initially, Linny is ignorant of her heritage and the fact that her dysfunction may also be a blood inheritance from the atrocities visited upon her ancestors.

An interesting text in this context is Janet Campbell Hale's autobiography *Bloodlines: Odyssey of a Native Daughter* (1993). The daughter of an alcoholic father and abusive mother, she initially disinherits her Indian heritage, bleaching her skin to fit in. However, a visit to the battlefield of Bear Paw (where the Nez Percé led by Chief Joseph were crushed by General Howard) re-awakens her interest in her roots while also suggesting that her family dysfunction may have been inherited from such atrocities. It is a seductive narrative, but also fraught with danger, because it suggests that finding one's self is easily confused with finding a more glamorous, transpersonal Indian identity.[32]

This is the problem that Proulx explores through Linny's cultural awakening. She is disappointed by her father's rejection of his Indian past. He claims 'I been de-Indianized' – a process that began when his parents named him 'Charlie' rather than 'Stands Lookin' Sideways or Big Dick', because 'they saw how the world was going' (39–40). For Charlie his Indian heritage is part of his past to be kept under check, and an exotic component to be exploited in his relationship with Georgina. Indeed, so successful is he at parroting other cultures that Georgina, who is a good judge of bloodlines, believes that his heritage may be Mexican. Despite his outward equanimity, however, the narrative makes clear that inside the injustices of his ancestral past are bubbling away like a kettle. It is Linny's desire to discover her Indian heritage that 'raise[s] the lid' on his own (39).

Central to Proulx's narrative is the fact that Linny's heritage is not part of *her* past, but part of her present reading of Dee Brown's account of Wounded Knee. For her the battle is not simply an historical event that has become a symbol – potent but static – of white oppression; it is a human catastrophe recreated vividly in her imagination as though 'it happened last week' (43). It is here, through this act of imaginative recreation, that Proulx brings together the two threads of Linny's domestic struggle and Cody's film, reminding us that cultural heritage is as much an imaginative act as a historical fact. The importance of the imagination is reinforced through the shifting significance of Wounded Knee within the narrative. As Charlie drives Linny off to the reservation to discover her roots, he pats her 'still unwounded knee' in a gesture of affection, which implies that the 'wound' will come when she discovers the truth of reservation life (45). For Linny's version of Indian history is peopled with heroic figures like Crazy Horse and Sitting Bull in the shadow of whom her father's accommodation with white society is to be dismissed as weak (44). Charlie, however, recognizes her cultural recreation as just as distorted as Cody's, more a lifestyle choice based on the commodification of Indian heritage than a realistic appraisal of reservation life: 'I'm guessin you want a do the whole thing, don't you – sweat lodge, beaded moccasins, get yourself a pretty Indian name, find a good-lookin Indian stud, and get yourself a rez life?' (40). The reservation is for Charlie what it was originally designed for: a prison. His memories echo the words of Moony Brassleg: 'He recalled the awful boredom of the place, the hopeless waiting for nothing', and he notes rather cynically that Linny 'would get involved, and after a few years of passionate activism she might fall away from it and end up on urban sidewalks in the company of street chiefs and hookers' (43, 44). This, we can conclude, is the 'Indian war refought' every day in reservations across America.

Proulx's Indian characters are recognizably Proulxian; their stories are not a footnote to the *Wyoming Stories*, but a nuanced exploration of the collection's central themes. Perhaps this is unsurprising. For despite their marginality within her various subplots, their story grows out of their forcible removal from the land, a thematic concern that has been central to Proulx's naturalist fiction from *Postcards* onwards. In her fiction they are wanderers carrying a 'deep map' of their ancestral lands, a palimpsest beneath the interstates and shopping malls of contemporary Wyoming, which leads them back to their 'heritage'. But quite what constitutes authentic Indian heritage is what is at stake in these stories: at its darkest it is a map that charts a geography and history of exploitation that is continually resurfacing in the dysfunctional lives of contemporary Indians. More generally, heritage reclamation becomes a means of 'finding oneself' – or, at least, 'a self'. For stripping away the generations of cultural influence that have gone into making the 'Indian' to reveal the 'real' as opposed to the 'reel' Native American proves problematic. Notions of 'authenticity' and 'artificiality' are, as they are in many of the *Wyoming Stories*, central to these stories; Proulx's Indians are presented as victims not simply of a white hegemony, but, like her pioneers, ranchers and cowboys, an inability to distinguish between authenticity and cultural cliché. They are, in this sense, 'Indians' – composite characters that embody Wyoming's continual process of negotiation with its mythical past.

6

Losers

'Proulx's Wyoming is a place where everything is unravelling', writes Geraldine Bedell of the *Wyoming Stories*: 'The economy, family, old ways. New people – the rich who buy up ranches and the poor who come for the methane gas work and live in trailers – move in and make more or less laughable attempts to understand the place. Proulx is a poet of bewildered people lost in a landscape.'[1] Proulx's Wyomingites are indeed lost: lost in a geographical landscape that punishes the unwary; lost in a cultural landscape that ridicules western values; lost in an economic landscape that stretches beyond state borders. It 'is deliciously ironic and very sad', Proulx observes, that Wyomingites continue to believe in 'the independent rural life', but feel powerless because 'they can't see who's making the rules and the economic strategies' that govern their lives.[2] They are lost, in effect, in modernity.

Proulx's Wyoming is full of victims: previous chapters have focused on the pioneer victims of a hostile landscape; cowboys living in the shadow of the Marlboro Man; Indians dispossessed of their land and heritage; and ranchers trapped between nostalgia and global economic forces. This last group provides a painful contrast to the characters that form the focus of this chapter. For although Proulx's small, independent ranchers suffer dirt poverty, their battle with environmentalists and corporate capitalists fits into a pioneer narrative of struggle against insurmountable odds which reinforces rather than diminishes their cultural identity. This chapter focuses on those sons and daughters who, for whatever reason, never inherit the family ranch and end up in dead-end jobs. These are Proulx's losers: they may cherish their freedom, but they are also aware that in severing their connection with the land they have lost an important aspect of their western identity. Leecil Bewd, who has a cameo in 'The Mud Below' (*CR*), provides the blueprint. He is the ranch son who loses out to inheritance tax and the banks, but keeps his western identity alive through the rodeo circuit. In a telling symbolic transformation, Proulx allows rodeo to change from an affirmation of cowboy identity to a metaphor demonstrating the difficulties of survival in a turbulent global economy. Life for Leecil becomes a 'dirty ride' of 'goin a funerals, hospitals, divorce court and real estate closins', events that mark his descent into 'The Mud Below' (*CR*, 62–3).

Bad Dirt is full of victims like Leecil, the very name of the collection suggesting the detritus left out during the construction of a successful economic and cultural identity. They are remnants from a bygone economic age; dispossessed of their ranches they find themselves plummeting towards economic failure, drink and the trailer park. The real bad dirt in *Bad Dirt*, however, is a loser of a different kind: the trailer-trash roughneck following Wyoming's numerous coal and gas booms. Trailer parks lie on the edge of the city and also on the edge of public morality, their residents stigmatized as losers in a culture that conflates economic failure with failure of aspiration and determination. They provide Middle America with an opportunity to observe a contemporary version of Leslie Fiedler's wilderness 'other' (the primitive outsider who offers an animalistic version of the civilized self), or Julia Kristeva's 'abject' (the dirt poor social elements excluded to keep the cultural body clean), which both appals and fascinates in equal measure.[3] Hence, trailer trash shows fill the airwaves, the residents paraded through daytime reality TV shows like participants in a Victorian freak show. The men are depicted as drunken, angry and violent, making up for their poverty with a runic system of Wagnerian overstatement – monster trucks, guns and WLF wrestling; their large, sweat-panted wives, often with a brood of delinquent kids on welfare in tow, are accused of multiple crimes of taste, predatory sexuality, and Elvis adulation.[4]

This is a very different Wyoming to that presented in Gretel Ehrlich's *The Solace of Open Spaces* and in the *Wyoming Stories* discussed so far. This Wyoming is underpinned by harsh economic realities, which Proulx explores in the essays 'Wyoming the Cowboy State' and 'Opening the Oyster'. She argues that the State legislature has used tax incentives to encourage rich outsiders and real-estate agents to purchase uneconomic ranches in the hope of bringing in much-needed ready-cash. Furthermore, she also accuses the State of using the tax system to encourage mining companies in the hope that they will provide work to, among other groups, displaced ranch hands. Unfortunately, though the negative effects of this policy are clear in the visual and air pollution, the economic benefits are questionable.[5] She allows her character Wade Walls (the shadowy eco-terrorist cowboy of 'The Governors of Wyoming' (*CR*), to condemn Wyoming as a '97,000-square-mile dog's breakfast of outside exploiters, Republican ranchers and scenery':

> He knew about the place, the fiery column of the Cave Gulch flare-off in its vast junkyard field, refineries, disturbed land, uranium mines, coal

mines, trona mines, pump jacks and drilling rigs ... all disguised by the deceptively empty landscape ... He knew all about the state's lie-back-and-take-it income from federal mineral loyalties, severance and *ad valorem* taxes, the old ranches bought up by country music stars and assorted billionaires acting roles in some imaginary cowboy revue, the bleed-out of brains and talent, and for common people no jobs and a tough life in a trailer house. (235–6)

Not only does the boom-and-bust economic cycle associated with energy extraction destabilize the local economy, but, as Beth Loffreda has observed, increased mechanization, combined with the tendency of companies to import their workforce, also means that the promise of local employment has not been fulfilled (in the ten years from 1987–97, coal production increased by 110 per cent while employment decreased by 1 per cent). Wyoming has been transformed into little more than a resource colony, with profits syphoned off elsewhere and little investment in long-term infrastructure such as roads, parks and schools. As a result, Wyoming is home to some of the poorest workers in the US (Wyoming's average wage was fifth lowest in the US in the 1990s), who are left bringing up families in dirt poor conditions (30 per cent of school children qualify for assisted lunches). The social consequences can be devastating: Wyoming experiences high levels of drug usage (teenagers are twice as likely as the national average to have used methamphetamine), and it was ranked eighth in the table of domestic violence in the US in 1997.[6]

Picking their way through the 'dog's breakfast' of Wyoming's economic mismanagement are Proulx's losers: the dispossessed ranch sons and incoming roughnecks condemned to tough lives in trailer homes with no prospects. Their narratives are located at the intersection between global economics and small-town western culture, and reflect the difficulty of adapting a cowboy culture marinated in nostalgia to the realities of the global marketplace. The first section of this chapter offers a brief discussion of those ranch sons and daughters whose stories clearly exemplify this struggle, while also inviting readers to re-evaluate their own vision of what constitutes the authentic West. It begins with 'Job History' (*CR*), which, as the title suggest, offers a pared-down 'history' of a couple's turbulent working lives, while simultaneously exploring the survival of western regionalism in the interconnected, postmodern world. The humorous antics of Deb Sipple in 'The Trickle Down Effect' (*BD*) enable Proulx to draw a contrast between the 'cowboy capitalism' of Ronald Reagan's presidency and the community values of the West. In 'Florida Rental' (*BD*), Proulx transforms the struggle between a rancher and his trailer neighbour into a re-enactment of Wyoming's Johnson County War, in the process exploring who owns the cultural capital of the West. The chapter then moves to a more detailed discussion of two stories that contextualize the economic failings of the central characters through references to Darwinian notions of 'adaptation' and 'the survival of the fittest'. In 'A Lonely Coast' (*CR*) Proulx explores the dysfunctional lives of a group of waitresses whose drug abuse and predatory sexuality are vindicated by a dissipated and feminized form of the cowboy myth. In 'The Wamsutter Wolf' (*BD*) Proulx transforms the 'wolf' of the title into a group of trailer-trash roughnecks, to explore the notion of winners and losers (and whether one can be both at the same time) in the economics of the New West.

Small-town losers

Proulx's intention in 'Job History' is announced in the title, which not only petitions the reader to approach the text as 'history' rather than 'fiction', but also puns on the biblical 'Job': a man made to suffer by God. And Leeland Lee, the story's central protagonist, certainly suffers, the repetition in his surname drawing attention to his fruitless attempts to shelter from the economic storms that surround him. Proulx adopts a present-tense reportage, which conveys the fast-paced immediacy of the modern world, without the overt intrusion of a narrative consciousness. The characters are two-dimensional and never speak (part of the convention that makes it representational history rather than fiction), their lives reduced to the minimum as they reel from one catastrophe to the next.[7] Lee is a ranching son who in former days would have been riding the range, but instead finds himself living with his young family in a 'trailer on Poison Spider Road, jammed between two rioting neighbours' (92). He is, however, determined to succeed in the modern economy and turns his hand to a series of entrepreneurial projects. Unfortunately they all fail due to factors beyond his control: a winter freeze decimates his hog farm; a new interstate highway takes customers away from his fledgling garage concern; and the recession kills off his embryonic butchering and freezing operation. His offer of a 'local ranch supply store that saves a long drive into town' fails when it becomes apparent that, ironically, people 'relish the long drive to a bigger town where they can see something different' (93).

This is not, however, simply an account of one man's economic struggle; it is a story that asks how regional identity can be preserved in a postmodern West flattened by international commerce and the interstate. A job as a long distance lorry driver allows him to hit the trail like the footloose, fancy-free cowboy of his imagination, but his wife and family mean that he is always circling his home town of Unique. So much for the brave cowboy in the postmodern world; he married too young and now has domestic responsibilities. Furthermore, his journeys also prove to him the irony of the name Unique, for according to Lee 'every place is the same', with similar chain stores crowded on identical High Streets (95). And yet, Proulx argues throughout the story, what remains singular about Unique, and by extension the West, is that despite the obvious impact of global economic markets, it seems remarkably isolated from the outside world. Proulx emphasizes this isolation through the inclusion of a number of radio references to major news stories of the twentieth century that seem to have no effect on the lives of the inhabitants; indeed, it is clearly a piece of Proulxian irony that the characters are too busy struggling to make a living to pay attention to the world that is shaping that struggle. What remains regionally distinctive in Proulx's story is a consciousness of difference (reinforced in a studied invocation of a western past) combined with a shared elusive entity that could be called 'a western way of life'.

Deb Stipple, like Leecil Bewd and Leeland Lee, is the ranching son bereft of the ranch, his tale of economic frustration compressed into a whirlwind backstory:

> It had been easy when he was a kid lording it over his two sisters, enjoying the run of the ranch he'd believed would some-day be his, getting first pick of the horses ... But as he moved into his mid-twenties the easy edges fell off. The ranch had gone to the Elk Tooth bank ... [and] in a search for the famous solace of open spaces he'd built up a drinking habit ...
> So went the cycle of Deb Sipple's years measured in bar bills and small work. ('The Trickle Down Effect', *BD*, 49–50)

By the time the story opens he has been married and divorced twice, a 'sorry shit' drifting from trailer to trailer. Sipple, whether he knows it or not, is a player in an economic system that goes well beyond Wyoming borders. Its presence is both localized and caricatured in the description of his spending in one of Elk Tooth's three bars as Wyoming's very own 'trickle down effect' (50). This is a humorous reference to Reagan's right-wing economic model of the 1980s, which advocated the encouragement of wealth creation by entrepreneurs (in contrast to tax and spend methods of wealth distribution), in the belief that money trickles down to the poorest. Ironically, Reagan, a former screen cowboy, projected himself as the real-life embodiment of the tough straight-talking Marshall Johnson from *Law and Order* (1953) – riding into town to clear up the malaise of civil rights unrest, urban chaos and student disquiet to speak up for ordinary folk. What he promised was 'boom time' for 'go getting' entrepreneurial talent.[8]

Slovenly Sipple provides a corrective to this cowboy capitalism, not simply through his failure, but also his success. Proulx's tone throughout is light; Sipple is typical of the working class male presented in television sit-coms such as *All in the Family*, in which men are lazy buffoons, lost in a world of complex economic forces and dominant women. His successful entry into the cutthroat world of capitalist supply and demand (exploiting his ownership of Elk Tooth's only flatbed truck to demand an excessive transport fee from a desperate rancher, Fiesta Punch) is treated as screwball comedy rather than social commentary. Yet Proulx is making serious points regarding the economics of the New West. To begin with, as Daniel Schweitzer has observed, Sipple's drunken drive from a bar in Minnesota to Wyoming (a distance of over 650 miles) is narratively compressed into the space of a few cigarettes and beers, thus reinforcing the interconnectedness of the New West (56).[9] Furthermore, a disastrous harvest does not necessarily imply disaster for the farmer; help is available at the end of a phone. Help may be easily summoned, but Sipple's monopoly of ownership allows him to exploit his economic advantage in accordance with the 'go getting' rhetoric of Reaganomics, but in contrast to the cardinal western rule of helping a friend in need. Fiesta Punch condemns his dealing by evoking 'the spirit a Butch Cassidy' – but this suggests a more glamorous form of daylight robbery involving anonymous banks rather than ordinary people (54). In effect, his behaviour highlights the tension at the heart of Reagan's attempts to play the cowboy president: while his political rhetoric tells us that a cowboy doesn't shoot first, his economic rhetoric encourages us to shoot first, and with a big gun!

The barmaid who serves Sipple his beers and coined the phrase Wyoming's 'trickle down effect' is Amanda Gribb, who is herself engaged in a bitter economic struggle with external forces. In a contemporary retelling of the Johnson County War of 1892 (which pitted Wyoming's homesteading nesters against the original cattle barons, culminating in a bitter showdown at Dog Ear Creek), Proulx pitches feisty Amanda Gribb, living in a trailer on Dog Ear Creek, against local rancher, Otis Wainwright Rench. Nightly, his cowboys cut the fences around her trailer so that the cattle can take advantage of her carefully tended garden, until she hits upon the solution of introducing alligators into the stream that borders their territory as a deterrent. This is more than simply a humorous tale of female ingenuity overcoming bullying chauvinism; it is another invitation to assess the economic landscape of the New West. All is not as it seems in this uneven struggle: Rench is not a small, independent rancher, but fronts a conglomerate out of Denver. He simply mobilizes cowboy rhetoric and an appeal to Wyoming's free-range past to satisfy the economic need to feed his herd cheaply. It is Gribb, by contrast, a single, female vegetarian living in a trailer, who demonstrates fabled western qualities of grit and determination.

Gribb also displays a nostalgic attachment to Wyoming's western past. She loves the sawdust and sweat of Pee Wees (the bar where she works), and objects when the owner installs a big colour television so that his patrons can watch football. However, whoever has the money controls the future, and, as his decision to show re-mastered DVDs of 1950s football games demonstrates, he also controls the past. It is a lesson that Bill Cody taught the West a hundred years ago. Proulx goes on to explore the full implications of this hard truth through her inclusion of the personal history of one of the cowboys employed to repair the cut fences surrounding Amanda's trailer. June Bidstrup, as we have seen in the chapter 'Cowboys', conforms so clearly to everybody's notion of what a cowboy should look like that he is invited to Hollywood to star in a new movie. Ironically, the movie offers a new angle on the Johnson County War, in which it is not 'big rancher greed and dominance' that force the homesteaders from the land, but a tornado (211). It is a historical reworking that once again emphasizes the role of money and imagination in the creation of 'history'. In a further irony, Bidstrup fails to get the part because he does not fit Hollywood's vision of an authentic screen cowboy, and so returns to Elk Tooth to string fences for Amanda in a contemporary and 'authentic' version of the war.

It is a war that Amanda wins because she understands more quickly than Rench the interconnectedness of the contemporary West, both geographically with other regions and notionally with its various pasts. For Rench, the West is caught in aspic: it is a land of free-range cattle with no place for isolated trailer trash like Amanda. But her rental solution reinforces the truth revealed by Sipple, that the contemporary West is not isolated but part of a global communications network, with help at the end of a mobile phone. What is more, Amanda's method of cattle control is not only humorous, but also reminds us that our vision of what constitutes the authentic West is constructed by TV Westerns rather than the 'natural' ecosystem. It is the same point that Proulx was making through 'Down Under Wyoming' in 'The Half-Skinned Steer' (*CR*). If cattle, relative newcomers to the West, are to be considered a 'natural' part of the western landscape, why not, the narrative asks, trailer parks?

'Florida Rental' is an amusing update of a familiar struggle in Proulx's work: whose story defines the West? Amanda Gribb is little more than a caricature of the pioneer values of pluck and ingenuity repackaged in a trailer park; Rench is a caricature capitalist behind a cowboy mask. Gribb and Sipple may be economic victims, but Proulx's tone is humorous. This is very different to her treatment of the barmaids working behind the counter of the Golden Buckle in 'A Lonely Coast' (*CR*), feisty women who prove less successful at reconciling dead-end jobs with their vision of western freedom. In this story caricature gives way to developed characters full of inner conflicts and contradictions; screwball is replaced by black humour; satire gives way to gritty social realism. Indeed, in both 'A Lonely Coast' and 'The Wamsutter Wolf' (*BD*) – the trailer-trash story discussed at the end of this chapter – it is clear that Proulx is seeking to elicit neither laughter nor pity from her reader, rather the dominant mood is despair. The characters in these stories share no coherent vision of a settled future, their frustrations leading to lives of drug abuse, violence and unfulfilling sexual encounters. Throughout, their self-destructive impulses are encouraged and endorsed by a dissipated cowboy mythology.

In terms of both content and style, these stories come closest to the kind of minimalist realism dominating the American short story market in the 1980s and 90s. The critic Bill Burford coined the term *Dirty Realism* to describe these 'low-rent tragedies about people who watch daytime television, read cheap romances or listen to country and western music'.[10] Although the label is in many ways a marketing gimmick, it describes a style of writing that illuminates Proulx's own venture into the dirt. These are pared-down stories characterized by linguistic economy (Carver's minimalism providing a model), present-tense immediacy (many have the hallmarks of confessions), and an emphasis on the impact of consumer clutter. The men in these stories tend to be emotionally stunted, their identity challenged by a feminized consumer society from which they feel alienated and for which they have contempt. The women tend to be similarly lost; freed from the oppression of an overbearing patriarchy and the expectations of motherhood, they are caught in the trap of unfulfilling work and short-term relationships. It is their voices that we hear in the stories of Jayne Phillips, Bobbie Anne Mason and Ellen Gilchrist, and also in the work of western writer Pam Houston. All are concerned with the female experience, often adopting female narrators (or at least strong female focalizing agents), whose tone, despite differences in geography, class and age, is detached, bordering on resigned. These deadpan voices echo through the various narrators in Phillips' *Fast Lanes* (1987) (women living dysfunctional lives who are trying to switch to the slow lane), and also Gilchrist's *Drunk with Love* (1986) (in which women break free from a rigid southern matriarchy only to fall in love with the wrong kind of men).

Pam Houston picks up the theme of dysfunctional relationships in her first collection of stories, *Cowboys Are My Weakness* (1992), which is of particular interest when considering Proulx's characterization in 'A Lonely Coast'. Houston's feisty female narrators seem to combine feminist credentials with a pathological desire for the wrong type of highly masculine man represented by the postmodern cowboy, a paradox that they narrate with a tone of resigned wisdom. Their tragedy is that their cowboy ideal is controlled by a western ethos that measures masculinity through sexual conquest and which is compromised by ideas of 'monogamy' or 'commitment'. When the latter seems imminent, Houston's men ride off into the sunset, literally in the case of the collection's title story. And, as we look at this story more closely, after the despairing narrator has watched her man (who 'looked like a cowboy' but turned out to be 'just a capitalist with a Texas accent who owned a horse') disappear, she hits the road and heads for Cody, Wyoming. As she listens to country music on the radio she reflects that 'the men in the songs were all either brutal or inexpressive and always sorry later. The women were victims, every one.'[11] They are sentiments that could be articulated by the narrator of 'A Lonely Coast'.

'A Lonely Coast'

Proulx's anonymous, female first person narrator interweaves two separate but thematically related stories. The main narrative focuses on her friend Josanna Skiles (cook at a local bar) and her lover Elk Nelson and their deaths in a mindless act of road rage. The second narrative concerns the end of her nine-year marriage to the unfaithful Riley and her subsequent removal to a junk trailer in the aptly named Crazy Woman Creek drainage. She herself remains in the shadows, identified only through her roles as rancher, wife and waitress; she is the passive observer (literally) of her husband's infidelity with a 15-year-old ranch hand and the bar-room antics of her friends. The former experience informs the tone of despair and black humour with which the story is narrated as she attempts to make sense of the disastrous lives of those that surround her. Though detached, her tone suggests world-weary intimacy; she extrapolates a dark message from her narrative that is delivered to an imaginary 'friend' (230). Furthermore, though she is depressingly regional in her outlook (her one out of state experience recalls a visit to a bleak stretch of sea described as the lonely coast (214)), she, like many of the female narrators discussed above, exhibits a contemplative turn of mind that leads her easily from the trivial to deeper existential problems. We see this quite clearly in her reflections on the 'lonely coast' of the title (discussed in 'Landscape'). Though the props are awkwardly contrived (human consciousness reduced to a lighthouse and a stubby cluster of yellow plants), her homespun conclusion – that both the landscape and people are engaged in a process of change that leaves the latter little opportunity to shape their own lives – is bleakly Darwinian. It is the full implication of this insight that Proulx explores in her story.

Proulx picks up related Darwinian themes in the highly compressed backstory that introduces the central character: Josanna Skiles. Her parents owned a ranch 'south of Sundance with a long-shot view of the Black Buttes', from which she escaped to become a cook in a local restaurant (212). Her grandfather went off to World War Two as part of the 115th Powder River Cavalry, a name that evokes skirmishes with Red Cloud, but he is appalled to discover that jeeps and desk jobs had replaced their horses. While he is away, it is found that the cattle are afflicted with a gene for dwarfism, transforming the stock into tiny replicas of a western herd. Through this curious account, Proulx reinforces the twin Darwinian themes of adaptation and inheritance and poses significant questions concerning the West's failure to adjust to a changing world. For, as the world around adapts, sending men to war in tanks rather than on horses, the western gene pool, undercut by a stoical resistance to change, shrinks: literally. Faced, upon his return, with a visible diminishment of the western myth, the grandfather can only respond by drowning himself in a river whose rivulets are also drying up. Josanna's observation that 'her people had always taken the gritty way' serves to underline the bankruptcy of an inheritance in which fabled cowboy grit now condones suicide (213). If this is the response of the war-veteran grandfather, what chance has the granddaughter, condemned to a dead-end life of waitressing, of coming to a meaningful accommodation with her western past? And what chance has she got, chasing after her cowboy ideal amidst Wyoming's ever shrinking gene pool of 'twist-face losers', to build a meaningful relationship? (221).

The women in this story are all refugees from 'rough marriages full of fighting and black eyes and sobbing imprecations', whose determination not to be victims leads to a feminine interpretation of the cowboy myth constructed around their drunken nights at the Golden Buckle (216). Their adaptive task, however, is made difficult because of their role selling tacky versions of the West to tourists. Josanna cooks Japanese food at the 'Wig-Wag Lodge', a theme bar ornamented with western memorabilia. The owner, Jimmy Shimazo, was a boyhood internee in Heart Mountain, Wyoming, who stayed on after the war to exploit Wyoming's nostalgic vision of itself. He is a model of adaptation, combining a westerner's craving for the exotic with their nostalgia for their past.[12] His success, however, makes it difficult for Josanna and her friends to reconcile the hopelessness of their economic present with the glamour of their western inheritance. What emerges is a highly eroticized cowboy identity in which women take control. The 'lonesome cowboy' is degraded into an advert in the 'lonely hearts', a victim of their predatory bar-room trawls on Saturday night. As they squeeze into the cowboy wardrobe of skinny blue jeans and tight boots, and adopt the suitably western phrases of 'sieving' and 'cutting out' to apply to the stray men picked up in bars, it is clear that this is not a feminized version of the cowboy myth, but an ultra-masculine version appropriated by women (212, 7).

The men they choose bring nothing but trouble. As one of the trio observes: 'If it's got four wheels or a dick you're goin a have trouble with it, guaranteed' (216). The narrator's reflective turn of mind offers a more nuanced explanation for the emotional limitations of Wyoming's men, which has implications for the trilogy as a whole. Men, she observes, are always operating on an instinctual level: 'Wyos are touchers, hot-blooded and quick, and physically yearning. Maybe it's because they spend so much time handling livestock.' The instinct to stroke and caress also leads to 'the lightning backhand slap' (216). Sex and violence emerge from the same root, sometimes seeming to blur into one another. Effectively, a life around stock has left Wyoming's men emotionally stunted; it is in the genes. The evidence for this is all over the *Wyoming Stories*: thrice married Mero Corn can never quite escape the image of his father's girlfriend on all fours whinnying like a horse; Diamond Felts rides women like he rides bulls; and Ennis del Mar can only conceive of family life as a cowshed full of calving heifers. In this story, the connection is made even more explicit through the infidelity of the narrator's husband, Riley, which takes place in a cattle shed during calving. The births are difficult because the calves are too large for the heifers due to their impregnation by the neighbour's big Saler bull. Proulx's symbolism emphasizes the irresponsibility of men determined to live according to the eroticized element of the cowboy legacy without other aspects of its moral code. Riley takes his cue from the bull and wants to impregnate the whole herd; as he confesses later: 'I seen my chance and I taken it' (213). His irresponsibility is underlined by the fact that, like the bull, he is too big for the girl; it is her first time and she is covered in blood. It is the women who suffer the consequences; the heifer that they were helping has been left to die with the calf inside her, an act of emotional dereliction that the narrator puts on a par with his betrayal.

Elk Nelson, like Riley, is part of a diminishing gene pool determined to take advantage of the hyper-masculinized vision of the cowboy legacy. He is a drifter who had 'worked oil rigs, construction, coal mines, loaded trucks', but every Saturday night he carries the gun-toting, cowboy swagger which proves irresistible to women – particularly Josanna (217). With his arrival, the brassy individual, who took pot shots at her ex-husband, disappears and is replaced by a submissive woman who allows Elk to place his 30-.30 in the gun rack of her truck without a murmur: a symbol of submission more potent than the wedding vows. His presence helps her to make sense of her own relationship with her western past. Because she now has her cowboy, there is no need for her to play the role; she can simply subsume her character in his. What she demands in return is loyalty. Unfortunately, in cowboy terms this is only applicable to a cause, a horse or a 'pardner', none of which apply to Josanna. Domestic loyalty is an anathema, which, as Pam Houston's narrator notes of all those cowboy songs, is the tragedy of women (and men in the case of Jack Twist) who fall in love with cowboys. It is impossible to domesticate the mythic cowboy without destroying the myth, a paradox that Josanna seeks to resolve at the story's denouement.

Half of the story is focused on the events leading up to and including the climactic final scene, the details of which are recorded from the limited perspective of the narrator as she works behind the bar. From this position she describes 'women with eyebrows like crowbars, the men covered with bristly red hair, knuckles the size of new potatoes, showing the gene pool was small and the rivulets that once fed it had dried up' (221). Among them is Elk Nelson; he is dressed like Shane, but behaves like Coldpepper's Saler bull, intent on impregnating the whole herd. On this night, however, we are warned through the contrivance of a roaring 'fireball' that the combustible Josanna will explode. The fireball brings closure to the extended fire metaphor that has held the narrative together (this began with the comparison of Josanna to a burning house and continued through descriptions of the smouldering resentment of her friends) and is used to illuminate, in Gothic fashion, the Golden Buckle's collection of western memorabilia. It is a piece of melodrama that reminds us of the explosive western legacy underpinning the drama about to unfold. It is entirely appropriate, therefore, that the story's climax should be a pointless act of road rage, reported in the action-packed style of a Western shoot-out. The narrator is withdrawn from the action, leaving a fragmentary account of newspaper cuttings, police reports and witness accounts for the reader to piece together. According to the narrator, Josanna had confronted the lonely coast of her own despair and found it easy to 'yield up to the dark impulse' (230). Whether she also kills Elk is left for the reader to decide. Symbolically, his murder reinforces the notion that it is impossible to domesticate the cowboy without destroying him. However, to kill the cowboy is to destroy the mythic symbol that provides Josanna and her friends with their identity. It is, therefore, symbolically, suicide. Thus, having dispatched Elk, she turns the gun on herself: 'her people had always taken the gritty way' (213).[13]

Elk represents a character-type seen infrequently in Proulx's Wyoming: the roughneck outsider prepared to adapt cowboy mythology to his own predatory needs. He is marginal in 'A Lonely Coast', but takes centre stage in 'The Wamsutter Wolf', in which Proulx turns to the roughnecks following Wyoming's various oil and gas booms. This story offers another slice of gritty social realism underpinned by broader Darwinian themes. The wolf of the title, a once feared but now endangered predator, provides the perfect symbol to explore the theme of adaptation among winners and losers in the postmodern economic landscape.

'The Wamsutter Wolf'

Proulx sets out this theme early in the story during a discussion between the central protagonist, Buddy Millar, and the conservative parents who have dismissed him as one of life's losers. They hold out the example of his brother, Zane, a biologist and expert on wolves, who is doing his bit to 'preserve the balance of nature' (144). In addition to offering a grating brotherly comparison, the discussion reveals their belief in a world held in benign '*balance*' in which winners and losers are distinguished by hard work. Their decision to take a Saga Cruise dodging icebergs in the Arctic is a deliberate challenge to a philosophy that suggests that, like the sinking of the Titanic, disaster comes from bad luck. Significantly, Zane offers the Darwinian counterpoint: nothing is balanced in either the natural or economic world, but both exist in a state of perpetual struggle as species continually adapt in order to gain advantage over competitors.[14] He likens the struggle for existence to playing poker with a constantly changing pack of cards and players in a house that is being demolished. This is easily illustrated by the plight of Wyoming's indigenous wolf (the Rocky Mountain), which was once a successful lone predator until it was wiped out by the more ubiquitous pack wolf – the Canadian Grey. It failed to adapt and is now on a losing streak and, like the Dodo before it, is in danger. By extension, trailer-trash losers, like those we meet later in the story, are victims of a failure to adapt to the contemporary economic world, an indictment that fits in with the Reaganomics of Buddy's parents. However, within the body of narrative, Craig Deshler (the story's other 'wolf man') offers a different version of the fate of the Rocky Mountain wolf. He argues that there was no such catastrophe because the supposed predator and victim are, in fact, the 'same animal' (159). Thus, Proulx's central metaphor invites us to make a much more considered distinction between evolutionary winners and losers, between predators and victims, between loners and pack animals – and whether we can be one while seeming the other.

This distinction offers the context for Proulx's story, in which rebellious Buddy, who considers himself a lone wolf, turns his back on stifling Middle America to take to the dirt roads in search of the authentic Wyoming. Proulx's interest is the outsider unable to read his surroundings, a favoured narrative device in the *Wyoming Stories* in which characters find it difficult to distinguish between authentic experiences and models of cultural expectation, particularly when, like the wolf, their identity can be blurred. We have met Buddy's type before, notably in the character of Snipe in 'Heart Songs' (*Heart Songs*). Snipe is a young, urban musician who goes into the woods in search of 'authentic' backwoods music, which he believes he has found in Eno, Fat Nell and the Hillbilly tunes of the Twilight family. His shallowness is clear from his determination to exploit their music through record contracts, even while he is marvelling at their unique talent. Yet this is a story about a city boy who strays out of his depth. When he makes a pass at the vocalist, Fat Nell, believing that she is Eno's daughter rather than wife, the violence that has been lurking beneath the surface throughout the story explodes. The Twilights suddenly appear to Snipe as they long ago appeared to the reader, a family reminiscent of the hillbillies in James Dickey's *Deliverance*, a cruel patriarchy whose gene pool dried up long ago.

Like Snipe, Buddy presents himself as a man of the world, a dirt tracker actively in search of the 'bad dirt' that characterizes the authentic Wyoming of his imagination (143). He ignores the main roads (which suggest social conformity), preferring the back tracks around Baggs and Wamsutter, which act as a palimpsest of the region's history. Here, on roads that Proulx describes elsewhere as redolent of Wyoming's Indian and pioneer past, he can believe that he is striking out and following the 'ghostly ruts' of the old Overland Trail (164).[15] This pioneer optimism is sorely tested when, after days of aimless driving, he pitches up at the trailer park town of Wamsutter. Wyoming novelist Alexandra Fuller describes the ambience of Wamsutter as 'like waking up the morning after with a beer hangover'.[16] Even Buddy recognizes it as a 'desperate place', comprising 'hundreds of trailers' around 'a strip of gas stations and convenience stores' (148). To the reader it seems a fitting epitaph for an American dream predicated on movement in hope. To Buddy, however, it is 'the real Wyoming – full of poor, hard-working transients, tough as nails and restless, going where the dollars grew' (148). This may be a trailer court, but to him its residents encapsulate the optimism lost from Wyoming's pioneer past. He is in for a rude awakening.

This process begins with the dismantling of his belief in the independent pioneer. Most pioneers, as was seen in the chapter 'Pioneers', were victims of unscrupulous companies prepared to take advantage of their optimism. In her essay 'Inhabitants of the Margins', Proulx gives an account of a scheme operated by the 'The Triad Land Company' 25 miles south of Wamsutter in 1977. Their 10-page 'Fact Sheet' promised high yield crops from the 40-acre 'ranches', a claim condemned by Wamsutter locals, who scoffed at the idea of farming on such *bad dirt*. Nevertheless, 18 families moved in, but found that 'there was no electricity, no water, no town, no school bus service. The dust-laden wind blew constantly', leading most to move out and the scheme to eventually collapse.[17] It is the empty trailer of such a pioneer family that Buddy discovers during an early reconnaissance of the park that he is to make his home. In it he finds a newspaper cutting from 1973, which records the family's pleasure upon arrival: 'This is our dream come true', claims the father, 'to own our own ranch. We're the new pioneers' (150). Unfortunately, the development never materializes, the 'pioneers' are left stranded and the ruined trailer becomes a testament to the ruthlessness of corporate wolves. The cynical crayon addition 'Dad says' to the article reminds us that for Proulx the real victims were the women and children dragged in the wake of male optimism. As Buddy looks closer he recognizes the trailer he is renting. The 'Dad' has now joined the corporate wolf pack, while the cynical daughter is the fat girl in 'grimy sweatpants' who is happy to introduce customers to their modest homes because she never shared her father's delusions (148).

So what are we to make of the descendants of these disillusioned pioneers? A snakebite injury leads Buddy to a period of convalescence during which the next-door trailer becomes the focus of his scrutiny. The Wham family and mountain man Craig Deshler are introduced to us through Buddy's eyes and accordingly they conform to the poor but hard-working transients of his imagination. With photographic lyricism he details their movements in a manner that suggests an entomologist discovering a new species. They are categorized as 'Fat Wife', 'Old Dad' and 'Big Boy', the latter a bow hunter whose slaughtered antelopes feed the family barbeques. 'So far, so good', he concludes: these are the authentic pioneer descendants that he was searching for. However, this is a story about misreading and prejudice, failings exhibited by Buddy but also by the reader. For we are only able to laugh at Buddy's romantic notions because we are acculturated to perceiving trailer parks in a certain way. William Kittredge's description of a trailer park around Evanston in 1981 reminds us of the full horror: 'Easy money, followed by large numbers of people, gambling, prostitution, sewage problems, and all the macho you could hope for ... undermining respect for what might be called the "civilised virtues" of home.'[18] This is 1981, but he could be describing a frontier town of 1881. But that is the point: roughnecks are the new 'trailer-park cowboys', their masculine excess vindicated by a western culture suspicious of books, banter and bathing. Of the gas boom around Wamsutter in the early 1980s, he is scathing: 'It lasted three years. They're still getting over it.'[19]

Proulx is not offering a corrective to Kittredge. She is not an apologist for America's trailer communities, and elsewhere in her fiction she has been quick to seize upon the symbolic opportunities afforded by its vulgar stereotypes to represent a nation that has lost its moral compass. At the end of the novel *Postcards*, for example, she depicts the young Kevin Witkin (who like Loyal before him has committed rape) hiding in a trailer park, existing on a diet of pizza and pornography:

> Down in the trailer park the skirl of motorcycle wheelies in dirt. Busted-muffler trucks. The fucking trailer church with its tin steeple … Noise was driving him crazy … Cacophonous symphony of slamming doors. Shouting women, children crying and calling. Saturday afternoon target practice. Assorted trucks, cars, motorcycles, snowmobiles, three-wheelers, ATVs. (337)

In a narrative that has already transformed the journey West in hope to a flight East in fear, the trailer park provides an apt and conclusive symbol of the failure of the American Dream. Proulx makes this clear by siting the park on Loyal's pasture, land nourished into fruitfulness in a symbolic re-enactment of the original conquest. When he flees, the land is transformed into a trailer park. By the 1960s it looks like a cemetery (indicating the death of a certain pastoral affiliation with the land (151)), by the 1980s it has become the dystopia described above. This is where Kevin holes up after his own crime of sexual violence; there is no need to go on the run like Loyal: here, he fits right in.

Rase and Cheri Wham would also fit right into this trailer dystopia; they are trailer-trash grotesques whose full horror is relayed to us through Buddy's description of the interior of their trailer. As Cheri proceeds to change a diaper a few inches from Buddy's coffee mug, his averted gaze records:

> Wads of trodden gum appeared as archipelagos in a mud-coloured sea while bits of popcorn, string ends, torn paper, a crushed McDonald's cup, and candy wrappers made up the flotsam. An electric wall heater stuck out into the room. On top of it were three coffee mugs, two beer cans, several brimming ashtrays, a tiny plastic fox, and a prescription bottle. Through the amber plastic of the bottle he could see the dark forms of capsules. (153–4)

There is no need for the narrator to broach the subject of broken dreams, or the existence of winners and losers in life's evolutionary poker game: it is captured in this description. It certainly isn't what Buddy was looking for: he wanted 'bad dirt' not besmeared diapers. And yet, though he remains the focalizing agent throughout the scene, the narrative tone is ambivalent: there is neither bohemian idealization nor smirking voyeurism, simply the cataloguing of the objects upon which his gaze rests. Thus, though the reader is horrified by the abject state of the Wham family, the real object of censure and derision is Buddy, who, on first contact with the authentic 'bad dirt' of his imagination, is so disgusted that he rushes back to his own trailer and 'quickly made his bed and washed the dishes lest he become like them' (155).

Buddy's reaction guides us to Proulx's real target in this story: middle-class voyeurs in search of a bit of rough. There is, as *Vogue* columnist Margo Jefferson has noted, a form of 'trailer chic' clearly exhibited in a taste for chunky costume jewellery and the kind of black and white photography that fills art galleries.[20] Capturing the dirt poor on film is a subject of great interest to Proulx: she has written positively on Carl Mydans' photographic record of family life during the Great Depression; Richard Avedon's no-nonsense portraits of working people collected in *In the American West* (1985); and Andrea Modica's photographs of the trailer community of *Treadwell* in rural New York (1996) – of which more in a moment. She has also explored the more exploitative aspect of artistic voyeurism in the short story 'Negatives' (*Heart Songs*), in which two middle-class, middle-aged homosexuals move to a rural idyll in search of the authentic America. While Buck B. admires the landscape, photographer Walter Welter goes in search of the 'down and dirty', and finds it in the figure of Albina Muth:

> They saw her at the mall supermarket standing in line with children clustered on the cart like flies, or carrying bags of beer and potato chips out to a pickup truck in the parking lot. Her children, with thick-lidded eyes and reptilian mouths, sat in the bark-strewn truck bed rolling empty soda cans. (172)

The rural poor seen through Walter's eyes are chain-smoking consumers of beer and chips with reptilian children. Albina emerges in Walter's dinner party stories as an entirely fictional creation of his prejudice: a welfare fraudster married to a wife-beater with the remnants of a vestigial tale. When they agree a photo-shoot (she wants something cute or maybe sexy), he insists on photographing her naked in an abandoned poorhouse. As he poses her in increasingly degrading positions, it is quite clear that she is generating both erotic arousal and also latent sexual hostility. And this is the 'negative' aspect of Walter's art; he is not interested in capturing the image of Albina as much as exercising through her the sadistic fantasies suggested by his name and her social class. For him she is the trailer-tramp of pulp fiction transformed into art for middle-class titillation.

The photographs of Mydans, Avedon and Modica are, as Proulx makes clear, different because as photographers they carefully navigate between controlling agent and voyeuristic detachment. Mydans' compositions, she claims in her introduction, succeed because he avoids transforming his subjects into a propaganda coup for his employers (The Farm Security Administration), while simultaneously avoiding the temptation to over-sentimentalize the suffering witnessed. He manages to capture the essence of any situation by 'getting inside what he saw'.[21] These sentiments are repeated in her review of *Treadwell*, in which she notes that 'Modica has a strong eye for the human condition ... She sees, and shows us how to see, a kind of beauty in mean lives.' Modica's subjects are plump, tattooed bodies depicted amidst dirty mattresses and torn curtains, but there is not the contempt exhibited by Welter. Indeed, as Proulx observes, at times their poses seem to evoke those of classical forms, their tattered clothes lending ironic nobility.[22] Avedon's photographs openly challenge the image the West has of itself, replacing handsome cowboys and noble ranchers with blood-splattered slaughterhouse workers, women truckers, drifters and roughnecks. Their scratched, scraped and mangled bodies are a testament to 'tough lives lived in tough places'. The reaction of westerners, Proulx records in her review of the collection, was one of fury: they saw the dirt but not the stern beauty.[23] Clearly, we might conclude: 'Reality has never been much use out here.'

The photographic precision apparent in the description of the Whams' trailer seems to offer an antidote to, rather than play upon, the caricature of trailer-trash slovenliness brought to us through the cluttered set of *Roseanne* or the Heffernans' living room in *King of Queens*.[24] This is an Avedon photograph translated into words; if we are horrified by the description it is not because of any manipulation on Buddy's part (he is too incapacitated by his own rude awakening to make a judgement), but because of the abject nature of what he records. The same is not true, however, of the description of Rase Wham, who is introduced to Buddy on the following day at a drunken barbeque. Once again the scene is viewed through Buddy's eyes, but by this time he has made the necessary perceptual adjustment in relation to his hosts. There is no middle ground in his imagination and the figure of Rase he now perceives is a nightmare caricature of trailer-trash toughness:

> Rase came slouching over, stuck out a blood-crusted hand. There was the familiar shaved bullethead, the wide neck and great swollen mounds of muscle. Rase Wham's face was scarred, and there were tattoos of barbed wire, fanged snakes, and an AK–47 spitting red bullets on his arms. (156)

Rase is the real 'bad dirt' – the big bad wolf of his childhood imagination – who is made all the more dangerous because he is the volatile and dissatisfied leader of a pack who wishes he was single. Even Buddy can see the danger. Except that once again, he is wrong. Buddy's problem in this story is that Rase changes from the hard-working transient of his Romantic imagination to the trailer-trash bully of his nightmares without ever coming into view as a more complex character. The real danger in this story of misconceptions is not Rase, but Craig – the indigenous Wyoming wolf man.

Craig Deshler is a complex figure: Rase can only conceive of him as a character sprung from his childhood: 'He's the real thing, sleeps on the ground, tracks lions, cooks cowboy coffee.' Deshler himself seems only concerned with how others see him: 'Everybody tells me I was born a hundred years too late … I should a been a mountain man, they tell me. I'm a throwback and proud of it' (156, 157). He sees himself as a glamorous figure in the mould of Claude Dallas, a contemporary mountain man who became a western hero in 1986 when, following his murder of two game wardens, he managed to evade the police for a year in the sagebrush of Idaho. Deshler's eulogy to Claude Dallas suggests he is not immune to the confusion between authenticity and cultural cliché, but rather than a weakness it becomes part of his adaptive armoury. Predictably, Buddy is drawn to his sinister 'air of surety'. However, this only lasts as long as their first conversation, after which Buddy dismisses him as a bore (with a voice like an outboard motor) and a phoney, who has made more concessions to the modern age – Power Wagon, rifle, watch – than he cares to dwell upon (156, 158). This is not Grizzly Adams, but a man whose appalling flatulence smells like 'raw skunk' (157). Once again, Buddy has got it wrong.

Deshler may be a bore, but he is dangerous; his concessions to the modern world simply demonstrate his adaptability. His true threat is revealed not in his homage to Claude Dallas, but in his observations concerning wolves. 'I look at a wolf, I look at myself', he claims in a moment of rare self-deprecation: he does not mean the big, bad fairy tale wolf that crunches the bones of children who refuse to sleep; that is the violent, roughneck cliché who is Rase (who later breaks his son's arm for just this reason (159)). In reality he is announcing the presence of Wyoming's most adaptable predator, the Rocky Mountain wolf, which has survived precisely because everybody thinks that it has disappeared. Though everybody dismisses Deshler as an exotic but lone crank, he is in fact a pack wolf looking for a mate. He further contextualizes this need within his own mountain-man culture, according to which he is not the isolated hermit typified by Grizzly Adams, but a figure on the lookout for his own Indian squaw. Thus, when he teaches Rase's young son Lye to howl like a wolf, he is figuratively baptizing him into his wolf pack with Cheri as his mate: no wonder Rase is jumpy around Craig (159).

Cheri, however, has her own agenda. She has clearly chosen Buddy to replace Rase, luring him to stay the night to protect her from her marauding husband and waiting until he is asleep before making her advances. In his sleepy state Buddy succumbs because he initially mistakes her for an attractive waitress who had recently served him in a local bar; a mistake that underlines Cheri's claim to be Wyoming's most adaptable predator. Nature is not balanced or benign, and Buddy, who had sought to act morally ('Cheri, I don't want to tell you how to run your life but you got a think about the kids' (167)), is betrayed by his own sexual urges as 'his traitorous body went for the jackpot' (168). The collapse of any semblance of moral authority is reinforced by the narrative's careful detailing of the morning after. As Buddy looks through the trailer's tiny window he notes that amidst the streaks of dawn sunlight, 'there was a tumbled mass of indigo and salmon cloud to the east. The faded rabbitbrush lashed in the blustery wind' (169). The negative violence implied by the verbs amplifies and compromises the beauty of the composition: nature's violence is sublime in its beauty. Not so the activities that have taken place inside the trailer, Buddy's 'stained, bagging underwear' signalling that he has traded 'bad dirt' for 'trailer grime' (168).

The scene is now set for a suspenseful denouement: Buddy has slept with the wife of a known psychopath, whose powerful father 'could sweep the dirt under the rug' (173). He sleeps with a gun, but when he takes 'bad dirt tracks' now they all seem to lead back to Wamsutter, an indictment of his earlier footloose Romanticism. The positive result of his experience is that he now realizes that he is not the lone wolf that he imagined himself to be. He reconciles himself with his family and re-joins the pack. He even phones his brother Zane – the only real lone wolf in the story – and asks him about a job on fishing boats: a definitive break with a life of bad dirt roads (174). (Typical of Buddy's tendency to broad generalizations, he believes that because Zane lives in Alaska he must be on the coast.) When Buddy eventually runs into Deshler for the last time, he finds himself 'looking into the mountain man's eyes' where a 'hard, alpha stare' has taken the place of the old 'merry twinkle'. Rase's fate remains a mystery, but we are led to believe, through the innocent observations of Vernon Clarence, that Craig has fed him to the wolves. It is a supposition that Buddy seems to intuit, hence his acknowledgement: 'I see you got your own pack now' (176).

Proulx's losers are the casualties of economic change, condemned to life in a trailer park and a complex negotiation with the region's western heritage. But what constitutes the West is up for grabs in a postmodern economy in which the story the region tells itself can be bought and manipulated by big money. Throughout these stories Proulx exposes politicians, corporate ranchers and Hollywood directors who continue to emphasize the heritage of the region while exploiting it economically. Her losers are a combination of those who fail to adapt to the realities of global economics (the ranch sons and daughters who never inherit); those characters for whom the adaptation of the western myth is a travesty (the waitresses of the Golden Buckle Bar); and those incomers trapped in Wyoming's boom-bust economic cycle (the trailer roughnecks following the oil strikes). They are all losers in Zane Millar's existential poker game, not because they have bad cards, but because they fail to adapt their play to the cards dealt. The only success in this chapter of failure is the mountain man throwback, Craig Deshler, and his adaptive success derives from his appearing to be a loser.

Conclusion

This book began with the Disney-style parade of archetypal cowboys, Indians and pioneers watched by Gilbert Wolfscale; an image that seems to symbolize Proulx's Wyoming. The *Wyoming Stories* peek behind the folksy charade to reveal the grim reality of a community struggling to adapt the legacy of the West to postmodern economic realities. It is a task made difficult by the influx of rich outsiders determined to live out western fantasies which condemn locals to the role of stage props, and the arrival of corporate giants eviscerating both the landscape and a way of life behind a mask of cowboy rhetoric. Proulx's success in this collection is that she reanimates a traditional form of regional writing while avoiding returning to Wyoming's nostalgic past, or wallowing in its dysfunctional present. She creates a Wyoming that exists as a series of connections – geographical, historical, cultural, economic and aesthetic; a Wyoming that may appear disconcerting to the reader in search of a traditional story of the West (a unified narrative of struggle and conquest), but one entirely in keeping with the postmodern denial of the sweeping linear narrative. Indeed, her collection sets out to warn against the narrowness and partiality of this approach, encouraging the reader to acknowledge that the contemporary West is a region in which the trailer park stands in the shadow of the Grand Tetons and the Wal-Mart cashier stands in the shadow of Shane. One story that explores the theme of linearity versus connectedness while simultaneously suggesting what Proulx means by the 'Wyoming' of the *Wyoming Stories* is 'Family Man' (*FJW*). Set in the Mellowhorn Retirement Home, where cowboys come to die, the story challenges both the characters and our own preconceptions of the West, suggesting an alternative vision that provides an apt conclusion for this particular story and for the trilogy as a whole.

'Family Man' is a story about telling stories, particularly the stories we tell about the West. The central character is the aging Ray Forkenbrock, who is prompted by his granddaughter, Beth, to tell the story of his days as a cowboy. At its heart is the secret that he has borne for years, that his father, a travelling salesman for whom he protests undiminished love, was a polygamist with families all over the state. In many ways the behaviour Forkenbrock Senior acts as a parody of Turner's thesis that Americans were created by western conquest: he conquers sales regions and produces Americans everywhere! Ray's broken confession is interwoven with the stories of various staff members, fragments through which Proulx explores the brutality of family relationships and the implications of belonging to a broader family group. The narrative reprises many familiar Proulxian themes: the constructed nature of the West; the burden of the myth; the importance of landscape. Central to the story, however, as it was to the collection's curtain raiser, 'The Half-Skinned Steer', is the unreliability of memory due to its selectivity and repression when creating a linear narrative, both individually and as a community.

The Mellowhorn is where old and New West collide. From the beginning, the constructed nature of the region is foregrounded by its ersatz interior décor. It is 'a rambling one-story log building identifying itself as western' through 'furniture upholstered in fabrics with geometric "Indian" designs, lampshades sporting buckskin fringe' and 'walls hung [with] Mr Mellowhorn's mounted mule deer heads and a two-man crosscut saw' (3). It is the kind of home to which Bill Cody would have retired. While most of the residents consent to Mr Mellowhorn's patrician belief that the final years should be spent in a hedonistic whirl of smoking, drinking and lascivious television, Ray sits apart, staring out of the window (5). He is part of the old West, an archetypal cowboy with eyes of 'the palest, palest blue, the colour of ice chipped with a pick', which are fixed not on daytime television, but on the landscape and weather (4). However, what he sees through the window of the overheated care home is a feminized landscape in which 'bunchgrass showed up like bleached hair', the sky appears 'milk-white', and a stock pond shimmers like the bottom of zinc sink (3–4). 'Nothing in nature', we are told, 'seemed more malign to Ray Forkenbrock than this invisible crawl of weather.' The weather, through pathetic fallacy, represents his own crawl towards death and contrasts with the sublime harshness that killed an old horse catcher met in his youth (7). His death, for a man steeped in cowboy folklore, seemed 'more honourable' than the infantilization of the Mellowhorn (8).[1]

When Beth asks Ray to tell his story, therefore, she is expecting an uplifting cowboy tale that approximates with her Hollywood-inspired imagination. The story that is told, like so many in the collection, dismantles both our and her nostalgic vision of Wyoming's past. Ray's narrative starts promisingly enough with the evocation of 'the noiselessness of his youth' before 'traffic and leaf blowers and the boisterous shouting of television' (13). But this pastoral idyll is not Ray's memory, but Beth's romantic interpretation. By contrast, his account of growing up in 'Coalie Town' is a catalogue of transgressive family relationships with which the reader of the rest of the collection will be familiar: the Dolan brothers who continually try to kill each other; Ray's ambivalence to the mysterious death of his brother; his sexual experience with a girl already sexualized by her brother and stepfather

(16, 19). This catalogue of dysfunction reinforces a theme running through the trilogy: that tough lives lived in harsh, isolated conditions do not necessarily lead to the moral elevation implied by western mythology; rather they lead to the reverse.

Significantly, Ray's broadly chronological approach is continually punctuated by seemingly irrelevant histories, through which device Proulx highlights the selection and repression common to the construction of all narratives. Beth's continual pausing and rewinding of the tape transforms this mental process into a physical symbol. Ray's broken confession is also interwoven with the stories of Mellowhorn staff members, through which the reader is reminded of Ray's participation in the interconnected relationships making up the present. The narrative makes this clear through Ray's conversation with one of the care assistants, Berenice Pann, in which she highlights their connection through their low-paid jobs: he 'cowboyed, ran wild horses, rodeoed, worked in the oil patch, sheared sheep, drove trucks, did whatever', while she has been a 'waitress, day care, housecleaning, Seven Eleven store clerk' (5). Further connections are revealed through her boyfriend, Chad Grills, who is related to the Bledsoe family, for whom Ray cowboyed. This connection, however, is broken when she splits with Grills following his failure to stand up to a group of roughnecks in an argument during one of their Sunday drives.[2]

The scene itself, though seemingly unimportant in the narrative, allows Proulx to explore the role of the geography of the newly interconnected West in forging a regional identity. Chad and Berenice get lost driving on 'the new, unmarked roads the [gas] companies had put in' – what Proulx describes in *Red Desert* as 'a cat's cradle of connecting tracks that seem to go nowhere' (25).[3] This is a far cry from the landscape remembered by Ray, and 'getting lost where you had been born, brought up, and never left was embarrassing' (26). The real force of the scene, however, emerges in an angry altercation with a road crew (who suspect them of being environmentalists), during which Chad asserts: 'I live in this county. I was born here. I got more rights to be on his road than you do', an outburst which is met with the sneering response: 'I don't care if you was born on top of a flagpole' (28). In a sense the worker is right, geography does not make westerners. How can it when they get lost? How can it when these desiccated dirt roads bear no resemblance to the landscape both they and the reader regard as western?

Ray's identity is intimately linked to his identification with the brutal landscape and the dignity of the dying horse catcher. It is the stuff of cowboy myth and an easy replacement for a father who turns out to be a disappointment. However, Proulx's narrative has sought to disrupt such nostalgia by reminding us of Ray's role in other networks. The purpose of this becomes clear through the introduction to the Mellowhorn of Forrie Wintka, 'the first female he had ever plowed', 70 years previously (19). Wintka attempts to re-forge their connection through the memory of a 'teacher that got froze in a blizzard looking for her cat', a deliberately feminine version of the horse catcher's death. However, this does not fit into Ray's masculine conception of the West and has been forgotten (18). Not so Wintka, who through her conjugation of selves – 'Forrie Wintka, a.k.a. Theresa Worley a.k.a Terry Dolan and, finally, as Terry Taylor' – becomes a physical reminder that in Wyoming 'everything you ever did or said kept pace with you right to the end' (20, 19). When Wintka falls into the Grand Canyon on a Mellowhorn 'adventure weekend', it is not simply a personal disaster, but, as Daniel Schweitzer makes clear, the loss of part of the network of associations that makes up Ray's story (20).[4] This moment of realization leads to the much richer understanding that a personal history, and by extension that of the whole community, is not a linear declension from a single memory, or even the memory of a single person, but is the product of interaction within a network.

Ray's moment of clarity offers an apt conclusion to the story and, in foregrounding the importance of interconnectedness, the *Wyoming Stories* as a whole. For readers approaching the *Wyoming Stories* expecting, like Beth recording Ray, to hear a story of the West, Proulx's trilogy can be disorienting. This study has suggested that Proulx's Wyoming is less a geographical region than a group of intersections. To some extent this is because she is working within the genre of the short story collection, a form which she has likened to a 'house of windows, each opening onto different but related views'.[5] The optical metaphor is apt, and is reinforced throughout the collection by her insistence on the narrow-mindedness of those characters – Mitchell Fair, Buddy Millar, Old Red and, of course, Ray – intent on observing the West through a single window. Proulx's Wyoming also exists at the intersection of a number of literary genres – dirty realism, lyrical pastoralism, dime store cowboy, magical realism, classical tragedy and fairy tale (often more than one within the same story) – which have the effect of disrupting a narrow narrative perspective.

The Wyoming that emerges from the *Wyoming Stories* is the product of an interconnectedness that gives a shifting sense of the region through time. It may be locatable on a map, but it comprises fictional and real towns within a landscape described in the kind of detail that convinces the reader of its verisimilitude while drawing attention to it as cultural product. Geography is no longer a static means of defining a region, but a palimpsest revealing a legacy of human interaction. We are never allowed to forget that where ranches and trailer parks now stand, Indians once camped and the sea once lapped. Her fictional towns also lie at the intersection of small-town America with global capitalism, their High Streets a combination of local shops, global chains and western theme stores designed to sell a commodified version of the West back to itself. On its streets historical figures rub shoulders with fictional characters and domestic dramas are played out against a backdrop of reported global events. And yet for all the reference to the outside world and its clear impact on the lives of her characters, Proulx's Wyoming seems curiously detached and timeless. The trilogy may end in Iraq, but we are back on the Frontier. This is largely because her characters spend their time looking backwards, contextualizing contemporary struggles within the notional behaviour of the western archetypes – cowboy, Indian, pioneer, rancher – that govern their identity. It is their attempts to adapt idealized role models to the contemporary world that bends them out of shape and produces the grotesque caricatures that inhabit so many of the stories. Essentially, Proulx's Wyoming is a narrative creation that reminds us of the tenuousness of the distinction between 'fiction' and 'reality' and proves the wider implications of the collection's tagline: 'Reality's never been of much use out here.'

Since the completion of the *Wyoming Stories*, Proulx's fictional interest has retreated back to the forests from which she emerged to take advantage of Wyoming's sight lines. *Rough Deeds*, trailered in a short story of the same name published in the *New Yorker* in June 2013, is set in Quebec's forests in the first half of the eighteenth century and follows the fortunes of two French immigrants and their descendants. Proulx's account of the inspiration for the project sounds strikingly familiar to readers acquainted with her description of her arrival in Wyoming:

> About fifteen years ago, back in my driving days, when I crossed the continent by different routes, I passed through a scrap of a town on Michigan's Upper Peninsula. It was a scrubby place with a single building, a derelict all-purpose store, and on a hillside of bushes and weeds I saw a sign saying something to the effect that on this spot the century before grew the greatest white-pine forest in the world. Nothing was left of that forest except the sign, and that was when I began to think about writing a novel intertwined with the history of deforestation.[6]

Proulx once again seems to have stumbled upon a landscape commensurate to her creative talents. She claims that what interests her is not the morality of the situation, but the sweep of interlinking cultures – French, Chinese, Dutch, British, and various American states – brought together by the trees. Like Wyoming, Newfoundland or the Texas Panhandle, the historical Quebec she presents is a region in which people are trying to hold on to traditional ways of life against the threats of an increasingly interconnected world. She records a time of land grabs, violence, and 'rough deeds', combined with a sense 'that something irreplaceable was disappearing'. Another *Lost Frontier* ...

Notes

Introduction

1. David Thomson, 'The Lone Ranger', *The Independent on Sunday* (30 May 1999); http://www.independent.co.uk/arts-entertainment/the-lone-ranger-1096783.html [accessed 3 September 2013].
2. Nicci Gerrard, 'The Inimitable Annie Proulx', *The Observer* (13 June 1999); http://www.guardian.co.uk/theobserver/1999/jun/13/featuresreview.review [accessed 7 September 2013]. Ros Wynne-Jones, 'Happier to Write than Love', *The Independent on Sunday* (1 June 1997); http://www.independent.co.uk/opinion/happier-to-write-than-love-1253675.html [accessed 10 September 2013].
3. Katharine Viner, 'Death of the Author', *The Guardian* (6 June 1997), Section 2, 2.
4. Aida Edemarian, 'Home on the Range', *The Guardian* (11 December 2004); http://www.guardian.co.uk/books/2004/dec/11/featuresreviews.guardianreview13 [accessed 12 September 2013].
5. Annie Proulx, 'Blood on a Red-Carpet', *The Guardian* (11 March 2006); http://www.guardian.co.uk/books/2006/mar/11/awardsandprizes.oscars2006 [accessed 4 September 2013].
6. An excellent account of Proulx's early writing life is available in Karen Rood's *Understanding Annie Proulx* (Columbia: University of South Carolina Press, 2001).
7. Wynne-Jones, 'Happier to Write than Love'.
8. Tim Gautreaux, 'Behind Great Stories there are Great Sentences', *The Boston Globe* (19 October 1997), 4.
9. 'An Interview with Annie Proulx', *Missouri Review* 22:2 (Spring 1999), 84–5; http://www.missourireview.com/content/dynamic/view_text.php?text_id=877 [accessed 4 September 2013].
10. Interview, *Missouri Review*.
11. 'A Conversation with Annie Proulx', *The Atlantic Online* (12 November 1997); http://www.theatlantic.com/past/docs/unbound/factfict/eapint.htm [accessed 3 September 2013].
12. Christopher Cox, 'An Interview with Annie Proulx', *The Paris Review* 188 (Spring 2009); http://www.theparisreview.org/interviews/5901/the-art-of-fiction-no-199-annie-proulx [accessed 11 September 2013].
13. Sybil Steinberg, 'E. Annie Proulx: An American Odyssey', *Publishers Weekly* 3 (June 1996), 57–8 (57).
14. Yi-Fu Tuan, *Space and Place: The Perspective of Experi*ence (Minneapolis: University of Minnesota Press, 1997), 184.

15 For an excellent study of characters' blindness to landscape see Margaret E. Johnson, 'Proulx and the Postmodern Hyperreal', in Alex Hunt (ed.), *The Geographical Imagination of Annie Proulx: Rethinking Regionalism* (Lanham, MD and Plymouth: Lexington, 2009), 25–38.
16 William Fox, *The Void, the Grid, and the Sign: Traversing the Great Basin* (Reno: University of Nevada Press, 2000), 55, 53.
17 Annie Proulx (ed.), *Red Desert: History of a Place* (Texas: University of Texas Press, 2009), Introduction, 77–81 (78).
18 Tom Rea, 'The View from Laramie Peak', in Michael Shay, David Romtvedt and Linn Rounds (eds), *Deep West: A Literary Tour of Wyoming* (Wyoming: Pronghorn Press, 2003), 283–8 (283–4).
19 Ibid., 284.
20 *Owen Wister Out West: His Journals and Letters*, ed. Fanny Kemble Wister (Chicago: University of Chicago Press, 1958), 31.
21 See 'The World without a West' in Leslie Fiedler, *The Return of the Vanishing American* (London: Paladin, 1968).
22 Leo Marx, *Machine in the Garden* (New York: Oxford University Press, 1964), 113–14.
23 Henry Smith Nash, *Virgin Land: The American West as Symbol and Myth* (Cambridge, MA: Harvard University Press, 1950), 17.
24 Theodore Roosevelt, *The Winning of the West* (1889–96). For a perceptive analysis of the impact of both Lewis and Clark see Karen Jones and John Wills, 'Lewis and Clark: Mapping the West', in *The American West: Competing Visions* (Edinburgh: Edinburgh University Press, 2009), 21.
25 See Karen Jones and John Wills, 'Frontier Germ Theory', *The American West*, 51.
26 Nash, *Virgin Land*, 291.
27 See Richard Slotkin, *Gunfighter Nation: The Myth of the Frontier in Twentieth-Century America* (New York: Atheneum, 1992), 55. For excellent discussion see Jones and Wills, *The American West*, 47–8.
28 Philip Deloria, *Indians in Unexpected Places* (1st edn 1999; Lawrence: University Press of Kansas, 2004), 60.
29 Jean Baudrillard, *America* (London: Verso, 1989), 32.
30 Richard White, 'Frederick Jackson Turner and Buffalo Bill', in James R. Grossman (ed.), *The Frontier in American Culture: An Exhibition at the Newberry Library – Essays by Richard White and Patricia Nelson Limerick* (California: University of California Press, 1994), 7–65 (34).
31 Slotkin, *Gunfighter Nation*, 69.
32 See Gary Scharnhorst, '"All Hat and No Cattle": Romance, Realism, and Late Nineteenth-Century Western American Fiction', in Nicolas Witschi (ed.), *A Companion to the Literature and Culture of the American West* (Oxford: Blackwell Publishing, 2011), 281–96 (283).
33 See Jim Kitses, *Horizons West* (London: Thames and Hudson and British Film Institute, 1969), 11.

34 See 'Cowboy Presidents and the Political Branding of the American West', in Jones and Wills, *The American West*, 93-4.
35 Wister, *Roosevelt: The Story of a Friendship* (New York: Macmillan, 1930), 31. Quoted in Jones and Wills, *The American West*, 93.
36 Bernard DeVoto, 'Birth of the Art', *Harper's Monthly* (December 1955), 9-12 (9). See also David B. Davis, 'Ten-Gallon Hero', *American Quarterly* 6:2 (Summer 1954), 111-25 (115).
37 Wallace Stegner, 'History, Myth and the Western Writer', in *The Sound of Mountain Water* (1st edn 1969; Harmondsworth: Penguin, 1997), 191.
38 See Jones and Wills, *The American West*, 231-2.
39 William Kittredge, *Owning it All: Essays* (Port Townsend, WA: Graywolf Press, 1987), 171.
40 Mark Horowitz, 'Larry McMurtry's Dream Job', *New York Times on the Web*; http://www.nytimes.com/books/97/12/07/home/article2.html [accessed 9 August 2013].
41 'Biography', 20 December 2005; http:// www.annieproulx.com/bio.html [accessed 3 April 2010].
42 'More Reader than Writer: A Conversation with Annie Proulx', *Wyoming Library Roundup* 5-8 (7) (Autumn 2005); http://www-wsl.state.wy.us/roundup/Fall2005Roundup.pdf [accessed 9 September 2013].
43 Acknowledgements, *Close Range*, 8.
44 See resulting collection, *Trails: Towards a New Western History*, ed. Patricia Nelson Limerick, Clyde A. Milner II and Charles E. Rankin (Kansas: University Press of Kansas, 1991).
45 Turner has always had critics. Bernard DeVoto used *Harper's Magazine* either side of the war to denounce the pioneer myth as corporate looting. See John L. Thomas, *A Country in the Mind: Wallace Stegner, Bernard DeVoto, History, and the American Land* (New York and London: Routledge, 2002), 91-2.
46 Roland Barthes, *Mythologies* (1st edn 1957; London: Paladin, 1973), 143, quoted in Neil Campbell, *The Cultures of the American New West* (BAAS Paperbacks) (Edinburgh: Edinburgh University Press, 2000), 6.
47 In conversation with Jim Robbins, *Last Refuge: The Environmental Showdown in Yellowstone and the American West* (New York: Morrow and Co., 1993), 254-5.
48 Neil Campbell, *The Rhizomatic West: Representing the American West in a Transnational, Global, Media Age* (Lincoln: University of Nebraska: 2008), 35.
49 Robert Athearn, *The Mythic West in Twentieth-Century America* (Lawrence: University Press of Kansas, 1986), 274.
50 Campbell, *Cultures*, 20-3.
51 Annie Proulx, 'Wyoming: The Cowboy State', in John Leonard (ed.), *These United States: Original Essays by Leading American Writers on Their State within the Union* (New York: Thunderer's Mouth Press, 2003), 495-508 (500).

52 Stegner, *Mountain Water*, 20.
53 See Jack Hitt, 'Where the Deer and the Zillionaires Play' *Outside Magazine* (October 1997), 122–234; http://www.outsideonline.com/outdoor-adventure/Where-the-Deer-and-the-Zillionaires-Play.html?page=all [accessed 4 September 2013].
54 Elaine Showalter, *A Jury of her Peers: American Women Writers from Anne Bradstreet to Annie Proulx* (New York: Alfred A. Knopf, 2009), 508.
55 Joyce Carol Oates, 'In Rough Country', *New York Review of Books* (October 2008); http://www.nybooks.com/articles/archives/2008/oct/23/in-rough-country/?pagination=false [accessed 3 September 2013].
56 Campbell provides an excellent discussion of McCarthy's cowboys and the western imagination, *Cultures*, 24.
57 Proulx, 'The Cowboy State', in J. Leonard (ed.), *These United States*, 496.
58 Patricia Nelson Limerick, quoted in Hitt, 'Zillionaires', *Outside Magazine*.
59 Annie Proulx, *Bird Cloud: A Memoir* (London: Fourth Estate, 2011), 127.
60 Jack Lessinger, 'Creating Penturbia', in *Penturbia: Where Real Estate Will Boom After the Crash of Suburbia* (Seattle and Washington: SocioEconomics, Inc., 1991), 236–44 (239–40).
61 Warren Adler, 'The State of the Cowboy State in the New Millennium', in M. Shay, D. Romtvedt and L. Rounds (eds), *Deep West*, 263–70 (267–8).
62 Robbins, *Last Refuge*, 212.
63 Tim Sandlin, 'How Place Affects My Subject Matter', in M. Shay, D. Romtvedt and L. Rounds (eds), *Deep West*, 432–4 (433).
64 Hitt, *Zillionaires*, 232.
65 For an excellent study of Proulx's depiction of landscape and western culture see Anthony Rudolph Magagna, 'Placing the West: Landscape, Literature, and Identity in the American West', unpublished PhD dissertation (University of California, 2008), 172–3. Also see excellent discussion of the hyperreal in Johnson, 'Proulx and the Postmodern Hyperreal', in Hunt (ed.), *The Geographical Imagination*, 25–38.
66 Liza Nicholas, *Becoming West: Stories of Culture and Identity in the Cowboy State* (Lincoln: University of Nebraska Press, 2006), xiii.
67 See Jones and Wills, *The American West*, 305.
68 Beth Loffreda, *Losing Matt Shepard: Life and Politics in the Aftermath of Anti-Gay Murder* (New York: Columbia University Press, 2000), 60.
69 JoAnn Wypijewski, 'A Boy's Life: For Matthew Shepard's Killers, What Does it Take to Pass as a Man?', *Harper's Magazine* (September 1999), 7; http://WWW/READINGS/10–05_Toolbox/Wypijewski_Boys_Harper's_Sept1999.pdf [accessed 12 September 2013].
70 Annie Proulx, *Accordion Crimes*, 456.
71 Interview, *Missouri Review*.
72 Interview with Edemariam.
73 See in particular Terrence Rafferty, '*Bad Dirt*: A Town with Three Bars', *New York Times* (5 December 2004); http://query.nytimes.com/gst/fullpage.

html?res=9B0CEFDA143EF936A35751C1A9629C8B63&pagewanted=all [accessed 3 September 2013].
74 Gretel Ehrlich, *The Solace of Open Spaces* (Harmondsworth: Penguin, 1985), 6.
75 In interview with Gregory L. Morris, *Talking up a Storm: Voices of the New West* (Lincoln: University of Nebraska Press, 1995), 65–80 (72).
76 For a fascinating study of the language of Westerns see Jane Tompkins, *West of Everything: The Inner Life of Westerns* (New York and Oxford: Oxford University Press, 1992), 47–67 (49–51).
77 Interview, *Wyoming Library Roundup*.
78 Annie Proulx, 'How the West was Spun', Review essay of exhibition exploring the heroic myths of the American frontier, Compton Verney, Warwickshire. *The Guardian: Saturday Review* (25 June 2005); 4–6; http://www.guardian.co.uk/books/2005/jun/25/featuresreviews.guardianreview24 [accessed 3 October 2013].

Chapter One

1 'More Reader than Writer: A Conversation with Annie Proulx', *Wyoming Library Roundup* 5–8 (7) (Autumn 2005); http://www-wsl.state.wy.us/roundup/Fall2005Roundup.pdf [accessed 9 September 2013].
2 Annie Proulx, 'Dangerous Ground', in Timothy R. Mahoney and Wendy J. Katz (eds), *Regionalism and the Humanities* (Nebraska: University of Nebraska Press, 2008), 6–25 (9).
3 See Richard Etulian, *Re-imagining the Modern American West: A Century of Fiction* (Arizona: University of Arizona Press, 1996), 84; Richard Slotkin, *Gunfighter Nation: The Myth of the Frontier in Twentieth-Century America* (New York: Atheneum, 1992), 253.
4 An Interview with Annie Proulx', *Missouri Review* 22:2 (Spring 1999), 84–5; http://www.missourireview.com/content/dynamic/view_text.php?text_id=877 [accessed 4 September 2013].
5 Proulx, 'Dangerous Ground', 7, 18, 12. (Proulx's italics)
6 See Hal Crimmel, 'The Apple Doesn't Fall far from the Tree: Western American Literature and Environmental Literary Criticism', in N. Witschi (ed.), *Companion to American West*, 367–77 (369).
7 Michael Kowalewski, 'Writing in Place: The New American Regionalism', *American Literary History* 6:1 (Spring 1994), 171–83 (173–5). Cheryll Glotfelty and Harold Fromm (eds), *The Ecocriticism Reader: Landmarks in Literary Ecology* (Athens, GA: University of Georgia Press, 1996), xxiii.
8 Ibid., 175.
9 Aida Edemarian, 'Home on the Range', *The Guardian* (11 December 2004); http://www.guardian.co.uk/books/2004/dec/11/featuresreviews.guardianreview13 [accessed 12 September 2013].

10 Proulx, 'Dangerous Ground', 21.
11 The narrator is caretaker for a country property for an alcoholic city stockbroker and his estate agent friend who dresses like a cowboy. His position is a moral dilemma: he loves nature, but when they visit (their unnaturalness underlined by a taste for gay child pornography) he is forced to witness their mindless destruction of the landscape.
12 Proulx, 'Dangerous Ground', 22.
13 Marilynne Robinson, *Housekeeping* (1st edn 1981; London: Faber and Faber, 1985), 178.
14 See Ivan Doig, *This House of Sky: Landscapes of a Western Mind* (1978) (San Diego, New York and London: Harcourt Brace and Company, 1992), 22–3.
15 Proulx, 'Dangerous Ground', 10.
16 W. J. T. Mitchell proposes similar arguments in *Landscape and Power* (Chicago: University of Chicago Press, 1994), 2.
17 Proulx, 'Dangerous Ground', 11.
18 Mark Klett, *Revealing Territory* (Albuquerque: University of New Mexico Press, 1992), 10. Quoted in Neil Campbell, *The Cultures of the American New West* (Edinburgh: Edinburgh University Press, 2000), 74.
19 Proulx, 'Dangerous Ground', 19.
20 Ibid., 13.
21 Ibid., 14.
22 Willa Cather, *O Pioneers!* (1st edn 1913; Nebraska: University of Nebraska Press, 1992), 21.
23 See Margaret E. Johnson, 'Postmodern Hyperreal', in Alex Hunt (ed.), *The Geographical Imagination of Annie Proulx: Rethinking Regionalism* (Lanham, MD; Plymouth: Lexington Books, 2009), 25–38.
24 Annie Proulx, 'The Bunchgrass Edge of the World', *CR*, 131; acknowledgements, *Close Range*, 9.
25 Willa Cather, *My Antonia* (1st edn 1914; London: Virago Classics, 1983), 7.
26 Alan Weltzien, 'Annie Proulx's Wyoming: Geographical Determinism, Landscape, and Caricature', in Hunt (ed.), *Geographical Imagination*, 99–112 (100).
27 'An Interview with Annie Proulx', *Missouri Review* 22:2 (Spring 1999), 84–5; http://www.missourireview.com/content/dynamic/view_text.php?text_id=877 [accessed 4 September 2013].
28 Rick Bass, 'Where the Sea Used to Be', in *The Sky, The Stars, The Wilderness* (Boston and New York: Houghton Mifflin, 1998), 49.
29 Beth Loffreda, *Losing Matt Shepard: Life and Politics in the Aftermath of Anti-Gay Murder* (New York: Columbia University Press, 2000), 165, 166.
30 'A Conversation with Annie Proulx', *The Atlantic Online* (12 November 1997); http://www.theatlantic.com/past/docs/unbound/factfict/eapint.htm [accessed 3 September 2013].
31 Weltzien provides an excellent interpretation of this scene, 'Proulx's Wyoming', in Hunt (ed.), *Geographical Imagination*, 106–7.

32　Annie Proulx, 'Forts Halleck and Fred Steele', in A. Proulx (ed.), *Red Desert: History of a Place* (Texas: University of Texas Press, 2009), 283–92 (284).
33　Proulx, 'Halleck and Steele', *Red Desert*, 284; 'Inhabitants of the Margins', *Red Desert*, 306.
34　Proulx, 'Halleck and Steele', *Red Desert*, 285.
35　For a perceptive and more in-depth discussion of this issue see Milane Duncan Frantz, 'My Heroes Have Always been Cowboys: The De-romanticising of the Cowboy Mythology in Annie Proulx's *Close Range*', MA dissertation (University of Houston, 2007), 89, 109.
36　There is an excellent analysis of this story by Ryan D. Poquette, particularly the main themes of memory and sexual repression, available in E-Notes; http://www.enotes.com/topics/half-skinned-steer/themes#themes-themes [accessed 3 September 2010].
37　Frantz, 'My Heroes', 13.
38　Daniel Schweitzer provides an excellent exploration of this scene, particularly the musical misunderstanding, in '"Reality's Never been of Much Use Out" Where? Annie Proulx's *Wyoming Stories* and the Problems of Neoregionalism', MA dissertation (University of South Dakota, 2011), 20.
39　Bénédicte Mellion, 'Unreal, Fantastic and Improbable Flashes of Fearful Insight in Annie Proulx's *Wyoming Stories*', available at www.benemeillon.com/.../Unreal-Fantastic-and-Improbable-Flashes-of-F [accessed 12 September 2013].
40　Ellen Boyd, 'Oral History and Revenge in Annie Proulx's "The Half-Skinned Steer"', *Forum: University of Edinburgh Postgraduate Journal of Culture and The Arts* 13; http://www.forumjournal.org/site/issue/13/ellen-boyd [accessed 23 August 2013].
41　An excellent discussion of Proulx's use of imaginative maps is to be found in Carol L. Joyner's 'Cultural Mythology and Anxieties of Belonging: Reconstructing the "Bi-cultural" subject in the fiction of Toni Morrison, Amy Tan and Annie Proulx', unpublished PhD Dissertation (University of London, 2002), 296–8.
42　Gary Snyder, *The Practice of the Wild: Essays by Gary Snyder* (San Francisco: North Point Press, 1990), 154.
43　Annie Proulx, *Bird Cloud: A Memoir* (London: Fourth Estate, 2011), 183–4.
44　Annie Proulx, 'The Wer-Trout', *Heart Songs* (1988) (London and New York: Harper Perennial, 2006), 133.

Chapter Two

1　See Richard Etulain, *Re-imagining the Modern American West: A Century of Fiction, History, and Art* (Tuscon: The University of Arizona Press, 1996), 49.
2　Annie Proulx, 'Traversing the Desert', in A. Proulx (ed.), *Red Desert: History of a Place* (Texas: University of Texas Press, 2009), 253–65 (254, 258).

3. Wallace Stegner, *Where the Bluebird Sings to the Lemonade Springs* (Harmondsworth: Penguin, 1992), 70.
4. Annie Proulx, 'Dangerous Ground', in Timothy R. Mahoney and Wendy J. Katz (eds), *Regionalism and the Humanities* (Nebraska: University of Nebraska Press, 2008), 6–25 (17).
5. Wallace Stegner, *Big Rock Candy Mountain* (1st edn 1943; New York: Penguin Books, 1991), 83.
6. Teresa Jordan, *Cowgirls: Women of the American West* (Lincoln and London: University of Nebraska Press, 1992), xxvi.
7. Patricia Nelson Limerick, *The Legacy of Conquest* (New York and London: W. W. Norton and Company, 1987), 48.
8. Susan Armitage, 'Through Women's Eyes: A New View of the West', in Susan Armitage and Elizabeth Jameson (eds), *The Women's West* (Norman and London: University of Oklahoma Press, 1984), 9–18 (9).
9. See Lilian Schlissel, *Women's Diaries of the Westward Journey* (1st edn 1984; New York: Schoken Books, 2004), 14.
10. See T. A. Larson, *Wyoming: A Bicentennial History* (New York: W. W. Norton and Company, 1977), 78–9.
11. Julie Roy Jeffrey, *Frontier Women: The Trans-Mississippi West 1840–1880* (New York: Hill and Wang, 1979), xv–xvi.
12. From the Western *The Santa Fe Trail* (1940) directed by Michael Curtiz.
13. David Potter, 'American Women and American Character', in Barbara Welter (ed.), *The Woman Question in American History* (Hinsdale, IL: The Dryden Press, 1973), 117–32 (120).
14. Page Smith, *Daughters of the Promised Land: Women in American History* (Boston: Little, Brown, 1970), 223–4.
15. Katherine Harris, 'Homesteading in Northeastern Colorado, 1873–1920: Sex Roles and Women's Experience', in S. Armitage and E. Jameson (eds), *The Women's West*, 165–78 (174, 171).
16. Sandra L. Myres, *Westering Women and the Frontier Experience, 1800–1915* (Albuquerque: University of New Mexico Press, 1982). See in particular, 6–7, 11, 269–70.
17. Elizabeth Jameson, 'Women as Workers, Women as Civilisers: True Womanhood in the American West', in S. Armitage and E. Jameson (eds), *The Women's West*, 145–64 (154).
18. Peggy Pascoe, 'Western Women at a Cultural Crossroads', in P. N. Limerick, C. A. Milner II and C. E. Rankin (eds), *Trails: Towards a New Western History* (Kansas: University Press of Kansas, 1991), 40–58 (45).
19. Louise Westling, *The Green Breast of the New World: Landscape, Gender, And American Fiction* (Athens, GA: University of Georgia Press, 1996), 5–6.
20. Annette Kolodny, *The Lay of the Land: Metaphors as Experience and History in American Life and Letters* (Chapel Hill: University of North Carolina Press, 1975), 8–9, 102, 28.

21 Iowa seems to have been particularly attractive to German settlers. See Leland Sage, *A History of Iowa* (Ames: Iowa State University, 1974), 93.
22 See also her 'Rural German-Speaking Women in Early Nebraska and Kansas: Ethnicity as a Factor in Frontier Adaptation', *Great Plains Quarterly* 1:1 (1989), 239–51 (248, 241); http://digitalcommons.unl.edu/cgi/viewcontent.cgi?article=1389&context=greatplainsquarterly [accessed 3 September 2013].
23 Annie Proulx, 'The Union Pacific Railroad Arrives', *Red Desert*, 293–6 (293).
24 John McPhee, *Rising from the Plains* (New York: Farrar, Straus and Giroux, 1986), 59.
25 Annie Proulx, *Bird Cloud: A Memoir* (London: Fourth Estate, 2011), 139.
26 Proulx, 'Union Pacific', *Red Desert*, 293.
27 Limerick, *Legacy*, 125.
28 Henry Smith Nash, *Virgin Land: The American West as Symbol and Myth* (Cambridge, MA: Harvard University Press, 1950), 123.
29 Proulx, *Bird Cloud*, 139.
30 Dee Brown, *The American West* (1st edn 1995; London: Pocket Books, 2004), 140.
31 Quoted in Dudley Gardner, 'The Union Pacific, the Chinese, and the Japanese', *Red Desert*, 297–304 (299).
32 Quoted in John L. Thomas, *A Country in the Mind: Wallace Stegner, Bernard DeVoto, History, and the American Land* (New York and London: Routledge, 2002), 120–1.
33 Interview with Elizabeth Simpson, quoted in Simpson's *Earthlight, Wordfire: The Work of Ivan Doig* (Moscow, ID: University of Idaho Press, 1992), 147.
34 William Kittredge, 'White People in Paradise', *The Next Rodeo: New and Selected Essays* (Saint Paul, MN: Graywolf Press, 2007), 168.
35 Gretel Ehrlich, *The Solace of Open Spaces* (Harmondsworth: Penguin, 1985), 9.
36 Annie Proulx, 'Red Desert Ranches', *Red Desert*, 317–27 (319).
37 Ehrlich, *Solace*, 9.
38 Proulx, *Bird Cloud*, 33.
39 David Fenimore, 'Folksinging in the West, 1880–1930', in N. Witschi (ed.), *A Companion to the Literature and Culture of the American West* (Oxford: Wiley-Blackwell, 2011), 316–35 (326–7).
40 Annie Proulx, 'How the West was Spun', *The Guardian: Saturday Review* (25 June 2005), 4–6.
41 Karen Jones and John Wills, 'Women in the West: The Trailblazer and the Homesteader', in Jones and Wills, *The American West: Competing Visions* (Edinburgh: Edinburgh University Press, 2009), 136.
42 Jameson, 'Women as Workers', 151–2.
43 Stephen Abell, 'Woebegone in Wyoming', *Times Literary Supplement* (12 September 2008), 22.

44 T. A. Larson, *History of Wyoming* (1st edn 1965; Lincoln and London: University of Nebraska Press, 1978), 399.
45 Ibid., 416.
46 Ibid., 407–8.
47 Proulx, 'Dangerous Ground', 17.
48 *The Family Flivvers to Frisco* (1927). Quoted in Marguerite S. Shaffer, 'Western Tourism', in William Deverell (ed.), *A Companion to the American West* (Oxford: Blackwell Publishing, 2004), 373–89 (381).
49 Quoted in R. H. Burns, A. S. Gillespie and W. G. Richardson, *Wyoming's Pioneer Ranches* (Laramie: Top-of-the-World-Press, 1955), 554.
50 Larson, *History*, 416. This acreage is half that proposed by congressman Frank Mondell in his 1913 law.
51 Ibid., 412.
52 John Rolfe Burroughs, *Where the Old West Stayed Young* (New York; Morrow, 1962), 332–3. Proulx cites this book a number of times in *Red Desert*.
53 Annie Proulx, 'Inhabitants of the Margins', *Red Desert*, 305–9 (308).
54 Annie Proulx, 'Horse Bands of the Red Desert', *Red Desert*, 329–38 (332).
55 Ibid., 331.
56 Ibid., 331.
57 See Jack Lessinger, 'Creating Penturbia', in *Penturbia: Where Real Estate Will Boom After the Crash of Suburbia* (Seattle and Washington: SocioEconomics, Inc., 1991), 239–40. William Kittredge, 'The Last Safe Place', *Time Magazine* (6 September 1993), 27.
58 Anthony Rudolph Magagna, 'Placing the West: Landscape, Literature, and Identity in the American West', unpublished PhD dissertation (University of California, 2008), 158.
59 Magagna provides perceptive interpretation of this scene, 'Placing the West', 161.
60 Jean Baudrillard, *America*, trans. Chris Turner (New York and London: Verso, 1988), 6.
61 Proulx, 'Dangerous Ground', 18.
62 William Kittredge, 'Drinking and Driving', *The Next Rodeo*, 125–41 (128).
63 Benjamin Markowitz, 'Weighed Down by Past', *The Daily Telegraph* (12 December 2004); www.telegraph.co.uk/culture/books/3633197/Weighed-down-west.html#? [accessed 3 September 2013].

Chapter Three

1 Jim Robbins, *Last Refuge: The Environmental Showdown in Yellowstone and the American West* (New York: Morrow and Co., 1993), 262.
2 Patricia Nelson Limerick, *The Legacy of Conquest* (New York and London: W. W. Norton and Company, 1987), 158.

3 William Kittredge, *The Next Rodeo: New and Selected Essays* (Saint Paul, MN: Graywolf Press, 2007), 51–66 (59).
4 Edward Abbey, 'Even the Bad Guys Wear White Hats: Cowboys, Ranchers and the Ruin of the West', *Harper's* (January 1986), 51–5. Quoted in Limerick, *Legacy*, 157.
5 Limerick in interview with Robbins, *Last Refuge*, 255.
6 John L. Thomas, *A Country in the Mind: Wallace Stegner, Bernard DeVoto, History, and the American Land* (New York and London: Routledge, 2002), 138.
7 Neil Campbell, *The Cultures of the American New West* (Edinburgh: Edinburgh University Press, 2000), 53.
8 Sharman Apt Russell, *Kill the Cowboy: A Battle of Mythology in the New West* (Lincoln: University of Nebraska Press, 2001), 12.
9 Richard White, *It's Your Misfortune and None of My Own: A New History of the American West* (Norman: University of Oklahoma Press, 1991), 613.
10 Robbins, *Last Refuge*, 92, 86, 80.
11 Geraldine Bedell, 'Roaming in Wyoming', *The Observer* (12 December 2004); http://www.guardian.co.uk/books/2004/dec/12/fiction.features [accessed 16 September 2013].
12 Clive Sinclair, '*Bad Dirt*: Home on the Range', *The Independent* (31 December 2004); http://www.independent.co.uk/arts-entertainment/books/reviews/bad-dirt-wyoming-stories-2-by-annie-proulx-6155346.html [accessed 25 November 2013].
13 Anthony Magnana offers a perceptive reading of Wolfscale's bemused alliances, 'Placing the West: Landscape, Literature, and Identity in the American West', unpublished PhD dissertation (University of California, 2008), 198–9.
14 See Beverly Stoltje, 'Making the Frontier Myth: Folklore Process in a Modern Nation', *Western Folklore* 46:4 (1987), 235–53 (239).
15 Richard Slotkin, *Gunfighter Nation: The Myth of the Frontier in Twentieth-Century America* (New York: Atheneum, 1992), 546.
16 Milane Duncan Frantz, 'My Heroes Have Always been Cowboys: The De-romanticising of the Cowboy Mythology in Annie Proulx's Close Range', MA dissertation (University of Houston, 2007), 90–1.
17 Teresa Jordan, *Cowgirls: Women of the American West* (Lincoln and London: University of Nebraska Press, 1992), xv.
18 Annie Proulx, *Accordion Crimes* (1996) (London and New York: Harper Perennial, 2006), 482.
19 Robbins, *Last Refuge*, 95.
20 Frantz makes this observation, 'My Heroes', 109.
21 Matthew Cella, *Bad Land Pastoralism in Great Plains Fiction* (Iowa City: University of Iowa Press, 2010), 182–3.
22 Elizabeth Abele, 'Westward Proulx: The Resistant Landscapes of *Close Range: Wyoming Stories* and *That Old Ace in the Hole*', in A. Hunt (ed.),

The Geographical Imagination of Annie Proulx: Rethinking Regionalism (Lanham, MD and Plymouth, Lexington Books, 2009), 113–25 (121–2).
23 John Brinckerhoff Jackson, *Discovering the Vernacular Landscape* (New Haven: Yale University Press, 1984), 89.
24 Karen Jones and John Wills, *The American West: Competing Visions* (Edinburgh: Edinburgh University Press, 2009), 110–11.
25 Annie Proulx, 'How the West was Spun', *The Guardian: Saturday Review* (25 June 2005), 4–6; http://www.guardian.co.uk/books/2005/jun/25/featuresreviews.guardianreview24 [accessed 3 October 2013].
26 Frantz, 'My Heroes', 49.
27 Ibid., 50.

Chapter Four

1 Annie Proulx, 'How the West was Spun', *The Guardian: Saturday Review* (25 June 2005), 4–6; http://www.guardian.co.uk/books/2005/jun/25/featuresreviews.guardianreview24 [accessed 3 October 2013].
2 David. T. Courtwright, *Violent Land: Single Men and Social Disorder from the Frontier to the Inner City* (Cambridge, MA: Harvard University Press, 1996), 88.
3 Theodore Roosevelt, *Ranch Life and the Hunting-Trail* (New York: Century Co., 1899), 55–6.
4 Owen Wister, 'The Evolution of the Cowboy', *Harper's* 91 (September 1895), 602–17 (604).
5 William Dale Jennings, *The Cowboys* (New York: Bantam Books, 1972), 224.
6 Zane Grey, *Riders of the Purple Sage* (1st edn 1912; Lincoln: University of Nebraska Press, 1994), 272. Quoted from David Fenimore, '"A Bad Boy Grown Up": The Wild Life behind Zane Grey's Westerns', in David Rio, Amaia Ibarraran, José Miguel Santamaria and M.a Felisa López (eds), *Exploring the American Literary West: International Perspectives* (Universidad del Paris Vasco: 2006), 57–68 (64).
7 William Savage Jr, *The Cowboy Hero: His Image in American History and Culture* (Norman and London: University of Oklahoma Press, 1979), 101.
8 Milane Frantz provides an excellent analysis of this story: 'My Heroes Have Always been Cowboys: The De-romanticising of the Cowboy Mythology in Annie Proulx's Close Range', MA dissertation (University of Houston, 2007), 31–2.
9 Frantz, 'My Heroes', 11.
10 Ibid., 26–7, 45.
11 Anthony Rudolph Magagna, 'Placing the West: Landscape, Literature, and Identity in the American West', unpublished PhD dissertation (University of California, 2008), 174–5.
12 Elizabeth Atwood Lawrence, *Rodeo: An Anthropologist Looks at the Wild and the Tame Rodeo* (Knoxville: University of Tennessee Press, 1982), 48–9.

13 Ibid., 28.
14 Ibid., 193.
15 Savage, *Cowboy Hero*, 104.
16 Alfred Kinsey, Wardell Pomeroy and Clyde Martin, *Sexual Behaviour in the Human Male* (Philadelphia and London: W. B. Saunders, 1949), 457, 459.
17 Annie Proulx, *That Old Ace in the Hole* (1st edn 2002; London and New York: Harper Perennial, 2004), 138.
18 John D'Emilio and Estelle Freedman, *Intimate Matters: A History of Sexuality in America* (Chicago: University of Chicago Press, 1988). Proulx alludes to their collation of 'Poetic fragments' which illuminate not only the tenderness of men who love 'in the way men do', but also the dangers of the bunkhouse: 'Young cowboys had a great fear / That old studs once filled with beer / Completely addle' / They'd throw on a saddle, And ride them on the rear.' Quoted in 'How the West was Spun', *The Guardian: Saturday Review* (25 June 2005), 4–6.
19 Vito Russo, *The Celluloid Closet: Homosexuality in the Movies* (New York: Harper and Row, 1985), 81. See also Chris Packard, *Queer Cowboys and Other Erotic Male Friendships in Nineteenth-Century American Literature* (New York: Palgrave Macmillan, 2006), 12.
20 Gary Needham, *Brokeback Mountain* (Edinburgh: Edinburgh University Press, 2010), 55.
21 Ibid., 60–1.
22 Russo, *Celluloid*, 81.
23 Larry McMurtry, 'Adapting Brokeback Mountain', in *Brokeback Mountain: Story to Screenplay* (New York and London: Scribner, 2005), 140.
24 Film versions of the novels: *Horeseman Pass By* (1961), *The Last Picture Show* (1966), and *Lonesome Dove* (1985).
25 Owen Wister, *The Virginian* (1st edn 1902; Oxford: Oxford University Press, 1998), 12, 13. William R. Handley, 'The Past and Futures of a Story and a Film', in William R. Handley (ed.), *The Brokeback Book: From Story of Cultural Phenomenon* (Lincoln and London: University of Nebraska Press, 2011), 1–23 (14).
26 Jane Tompkins, *West of Everything: The Inner Life of Westerns* (New York and Oxford: Oxford University Press, 1992), 150.
27 See Henderson website, http://www.williamhaywoodhenderson.com/ [accessed 25 September 2013].
28 Annie Proulx, Afterword, *The Power of the Dog* (1st edn 1967; Boston: Little, Brown, 2001), 278.
29 Ibid., 286.
30 William Haywood Henderson, *Native* (New York: Plume, 1993), 52–3.
31 Henderson, website.
32 Henderson, *Native*, 192.
33 Interview with Sandy Cohen: 'Annie Proulx tells the Story behind 'Brokeback Mountain'; http://www.advocate.com/arts-entertainment/

entertainment-news/2005/12/17/annie-proulx-tells-story-behind-brokeback [accessed 3 September 2013].
34 Annie Proulx, 'Getting Movied', in *Story to Screenplay*, 129–38 (135).
35 Ibid., 137.
36 Ibid., 130.
37 D. A. Miller, 'On the Universality of Brokeback', *Film Quarterly* 60:3 (Spring 2007), 50–60 (52–3). Available through JStor [accessed 12 September 2013]; http://townsendlab.berkeley.edu/sites/all/files/DA%20Miller%20On%20the%20Universality%20of%20Brokeback_0.pdf
38 Larry McMurtry and Diana Ossana, *Screenplay*, in *Story to Screenplay*, 21–97 (71).
39 Proulx, 'Getting Movied', *Story to Screenplay*, 130–1.
40 Wallace Stegner, *Where the Bluebird Sings to the Lemonade Springs* (Harmondsworth: Penguin Books, 1992), 107.
41 Helene Shugart 'Consuming Passions: "Educating Desire" in Brokeback Mountain', *Critical Studies in Media Communication* 28:3 (24 May 2011), 173–92 (182).
42 Neil Campbell, 'Brokeback Mountain's "In-Between" Spaces', *Canadian Review of American Studies* 39:2 (2009), 205–20 (207).
43 Proulx, 'Getting Movied', *Story to Screenplay*, 131.
44 Ernest Hemingway, *The Sun Also Rises* (New York: Scribner, 1926), 116.
45 Eric Patterson, *On Brokeback Mountain: Meditations about Masculinity, Fear, and Love in the Story and the Film* (Lanham, MD: Lexington Books, 2008), 78–83.
46 Ginger Jones, 'Proulx's Pastoral as Sacred Space', in Jim Stacy (ed.), *Reading Brokeback Mountain: Essays on the Stories and the Film* (Jefferson, NC: McFarland and Company, 2007), 19–28 (26).
47 Henderson, *Native*, 186.
48 Ossana/McMurtry, *Screenplay*, 53.
49 Jim Stacy makes this argument in 'Buried in the Family Plot: The Cost of Pattern Maintenance to Jack and Ennis', in J. Stacy (ed.), *Reading Brokeback*, 29–44 (41).
50 Patterson, *On Brokeback*, 28–9.
51 Gretel Ehrlich, *The Solace of Open Spaces* (Harmondsworth: Penguin, 1985), 51.
52 Ossana/McMurtry, *Screenplay*, 11.
53 Ibid., 29, 30, 59.
54 Ibid., 37.
55 Ossana, 'Climbing Brokeback Mountain', *Story to Screenplay*, 143–51 (150); Proulx, 'After the Gold Rush', *The Guardian* (23 November 2005); http://www.guardian.co.uk/world/2005/nov/23/usa [accessed 4 September 2013].
56 John Calhoun, 'Peaks and Valleys', *American Cinematographer* 87:1 (2006), 58–67 (62); http://www.ennisjack.com/forum/index.php?topic=16905.0 [accessed 3 September 2013].

57 Ossana/McMurtry, *Screenplay*, 35.
58 Ibid., 43.
59 Ibid., 66.
60 Ibid., 70.
61 Ibid., 65.
62 Ibid., 76.
63 Quoted in W. C. Harris, 'Broke(n)back Faggots: Hollywood gives Queers a Hobson's Choice', in Stacy (ed.), *Reading Brokeback*, 118–34 (129, 127).
64 Patterson, *On Brokeback*, 252–3.
65 Ossana/McMurtry, *Screenplay*, 95–6.
66 Larry McMurtry and Diane Ossana, 'Brokeback's Big Secrets', Interview with Anne Stockwell, *Advocate* (28 February 2006), 42–4 (43); Proulx, 'Getting Movied', *Story to Screenplay*, 137.
67 Roy Grundmann, quoted in Harris, 'Broke(n)back', in Stacy (ed.), *Reading Brokeback*, 130.
68 Interview with Colin Schindler, in P. Sherwell, 'John Wayne Made Real Movies: There Ain't No Queer in Cowboy', *The Telegraph* (31 December 2005). Quoted in Brenda Cooper and Edward Pease, 'Framing Brokeback Mountain: How the Popular Press Corralled the "Gay Cowboy Movie"', *Critical Studies in Media Communication* 25:3 (August 2008), 249–73 (250).
69 'The Real Cowboy Country', *Daily Telegraph* (4 March 2006), Travel Section. Quoted in Cooper and Pease, 'Framing Brokeback', 250. See Camille Johnson-Yale, 'West by Northwest: The Politics of Place in Ang Lee's Brokeback Mountain', *Journal of Popular Culture* 44:4 (August 2011), 890–907 (893–4).
70 Susan Salter Reynolds, 'Annie Proulx No Longer at Home on the Range', *The Los Angeles Times* (18 October 2008); www.latimes.com/news/nationworld/nation.la-et-proulx18-2008oct18,0,3383917.story [accessed 3 September 2013].
71 See Introduction, p. 2.
72 Bennett, 'Brokeback Mountain: Anti-Family', 2005. Quoted in Cooper and Pease, 'Framing Brokeback', 250.
73 David Kupelain, *World Net Daily* (27 December 2005); http://www.wnd.com/2005/12/34076/ [accessed 3 September 2013].
74 See Charles Eliot Mehler, 'Brokeback Mountain at the Oscars', in J. Stacy (ed.), *Reading Brokeback*, 135–51 (137).
75 Mehler, 'Brokeback Oscars', in J. Stacy (ed.), *Reading Brokeback*, 147–8.
76 Daniel Mendelsohn, 'An Affair to Remember', *New York Review of Books* (23 February 2006), 12–13 (12).
77 Rick Moody, 'Across the Great Divide', *The Guardian* (17 December 2005); John Petrakis, 'Heartbreak Mountain', *Christian Century* 123:2 (24 January 2006), 43; Carrie Rickey, 'Men in Love, and in Anguish: A Love Story of Anguish and Silence', *Philadelphia Inquirer* (16 December 2005), W3; Mike Clark, '"Brokeback" Opens New Vistas', *USA Today* (9 December 2005), E4. All quoted in Cooper and Pease, 'Framing Brokeback', 257, 258.

Chapter Five

1. Sybil Steinberg, 'E. Annie Proulx: An American Odyssey', *Publishers Weekly* 3 (June 1996), 57.
2. Leslie Fiedler, *The Return of the Vanishing American* (London: Paladin, 1968), 23.
3. Simon Ortiz, 'Indians Wanted' and 'Even "the Indians" Believed', *Out There Somewhere* (Tuscon: University of Arizona Press, 2002), 49, 50. For an excellent discussion of Indian identity, and many of the issues raised in this introduction, see Suzanne Lundquist, *Native American Literatures: An Introduction* (New York and London: Continuum, 2004), 195–7.
4. Annie Proulx, *Bird Cloud: A Memoir* (London: Fourth Estate, 2011), 165. Most critics estimate a Native population of between 850,000 and one million speaking more than 170 languages.
5. See in particular Gardner, 'Early People of the Red Desert', in A. Proulx (ed.), *Red Desert: History of a Place* (Texas: University of Texas Press, 2009), 231–7.
6. Proulx, *Bird Cloud*, 183; Preface to 'Deep Blood Greasy Bowl' (*FJW*), 123.
7. Falconer, 'Review of *Fine Just the Way It Is*', *The Age* (13 October 2008); http://www.theage.com.au/news/entertainment/books/book-reviews/fine-just-the-way-it-is/2008/10/13/1223749917539.html?page=fullpage#contentSwap1 [accessed 4 September 2013].
8. Annie Proulx, 'How the West Was Spun', *The Guardian: Saturday Review* (25 June 2005), 4–6; http://www.guardian.co.uk/books/2005/jun/25/featuresreviews.guardianreview24 [accessed 3 October 2013].
9. Patricia Nelson Limerick, *The Legacy of Conquest* (New York and London: W. W. Norton and Company, 1987), 215.
10. Vine Deloria Jr, *God is Red: A Native View of Religion* (1st edn 1972; Golden, CO: Fulcrum Publishing, 1994), 153–4.
11. N. Scott Momaday, 'A First American Views His Land', in David Landis Barnhill (ed.), *At Home on the Earth: Becoming Native to Our Place* (Berkeley: University of California Press, 1999), 19–29 (22).
12. William Bevis, 'Native American Novels: Homing In', in Brian Swann and Arnold Krupat (eds), *Recovering the World* (Berkeley: University of California Press, 1987), 580–620 (585).
13. See excellent discussion of this subject by John Warren Gilroy, 'Another Fine Example of the Oral Tradition? Identification and Subversion in Sherman Alexie's Smoke Signals', *Studies in American Indian Literatures* (*SAIL*) 13:1 (Spring 2001) 23–39 (23–5); https://facultystaff.richmond.edu/~rnelson/asail/SAIL2/131.html#23 [accessed 7 August 2013]. Discussed in Lundquist, *Native American Literatures*, 156–7.
14. Interview with John Purdy, 'Crossroads: A Conversation with Sherman Alexie', *SAIL* 9:4 (Winter 1997), 1–18 (12); https://facultystaff.richmond.edu/~rnelson/asail/SAIL2/94.html#1 [accessed 7 August 2013]. Quoted in Lundquist, *Native American Literatures*, 154.

15 See Arnold Krupat, *The Turn to the Native* (Lincoln: University of Nebraska Press, 1996), 30.
16 Louis Owens, *Mixedblood Messages* (Norman: University of Oklahoma Press, 1998), 77. Lundquist makes this argument convincingly, *Native American Literatures*, 285.
17 Patricia Riley, 'The Mixed Blood Writer as Interpreter and Mythmaker', in Joseph Trimmer and Tilly Warnock (eds), *Understanding Others* (Urbana, Il: National Council of English, 1992), 230.
18 'Who's a Native American – It's Complicated', *In America* – CNN.com. http://inamerica.blogs.cnn.com/2012/05/14/whos-a-native-american-its-complicated/ [accessed 5 July 2013].
19 Sherman Alexie, *Ten Little Indians* (New York: Grove Press, 2004), 53.
20 Linda Hogan, *Dwellings* (New York: Touchstone, 1995), 25–6.
21 William Kittredge, *The Next Rodeo: New and Selected Essays* (Saint Paul, MN: Graywolf Press, 2007), 169.
22 Annie Proulx, 'Opening the Oyster', in *Red Desert*, 339–53 (342, 352).
23 William Heat-Moon, *PrairyErth* (Boston: Houghton Mifflin, 1991), 273.
24 Vine Deloria Jr, *Custer Died for Your Sins: An Indian Manifesto* (1st edn 1969; Norman: University of Oklahoma Press, 1988), 230–2.
25 Kittredge, 'White People in Paradise', *The Next Rodeo*, 170–1.
26 American Film Institute Website 2012; http://www.afi.com/members/catalog/DetailView.aspx?s=1&Movie=1940 [accessed 15 September 2013].
27 Letter from Mrs John Brennan (wife of the superintendent at the Pine Ridge Agency) to her daughter. Quoted in Susan Forsyth, *Representing the Massacre of American Indians at Wounded Knee, 1890–2000* (Lewiston, Queenston, Lampeter: Edward Mellen Press, 2003), 193.
28 Yellow Robe, 'The Menace of the Wild West Show', *Journal of the Society of American Indians*, 2 (July–September 1914), repr. in Frederick E. Hoxie (ed.), *Talking Back to Civilisation: Indian Voices from the Progressive Era* (Boston, MA: Bedford / St Martins, 2001), 117–18 (117).
29 For critical review read Francis Paul Prucha, *The American Historical Review* 77:2 (April 1972), 589–90.
30 James McGregor, *The Wounded Knee Massacre: From Viewpoint of the Sioux* (1st edn 1940; Rapid City, SD: Fenske Printing, Inc., 1987), 108.
31 Vine Deloria Jr, Introduction to *Black Elk Speaks* (Lincoln: University of Nebraska Press, 1979), xiii.
32 See Lundquist, *Native American Literatures*, 220–5.

Chapter Six

1 Geraldine Bedell, 'Roaming in Wyoming', *The Observer* (12 December 2004); http://www.guardian.co.uk/books/2004/dec/12/fiction.features [accessed 16 September 2013].

2 Aida Edemarian, 'Home on the Range', *The Guardian* (11 December 2004); http://www.guardian.co.uk/books/2004/dec/11/featuresreviews.guardianreview13 [accessed 12 September 2013].
3 Julia Kristeva, 'Powers of Horror: An Essay on Abjection', trans. Leon S. Roudiez (New York: Columbia University Press, 1982), 4.
4 See Jim Goad, *The Redneck Manifesto: How Hillbillies, Hicks, and White Trash became America's Scapegoats* (New York, London: Simon and Schuster, 1997), 23.
5 Proulx, 'Opening the Oyster', in A. Proulx (ed.), *Red Desert: History of a Place* (Texas: University of Texas Press, 2009), 339–54 (343), Introduction, 77–81 (78), Proulx, 'Wyoming: The Cowboy State', in John Leonard (ed.), *These United States: Original Essays by Leading American Writers on Their State within the Union* (New York: Thunderer's Mouth Press, 2003), 495–508 (496).
6 Beth Loffreda, *Losing Matt Shepard: Life and Politics in the Aftermath of Anti-Gay Murder* (New York: Columbia University Press, 2000), 37–40.
7 See John Noel Moore for a perceptive analysis of the narrative style of this story. 'The Landscape of Fiction', *English Journal* 90:1 (September 2000), 146–8 (146). There is also a good analysis of the style of the story available at E-notes; http://www.enotes.com/topics/close-range/in-depth#in-depth-the-stories [accessed 1 November 2013].
8 See Karen Jones and John Wills, *The American West: Competing Visions* (Edinburgh: Edinburgh University Press, 2009), 104, 106.
9 Daniel Schweitzer, '"Reality's Never Been of Much Use Out" Where? Annie Proulx's Wyoming Stories and the Problems of Neoregionalism', MA dissertation (University of South Dakota, 2011), 54.
10 Bill Burford, Introduction to *Granta Magazine* (Summer 1983); http://www.granta.com/Archive/8 [accessed 4 September 2013].
11 Pam Houston, *Cowboys Are My Weakness* (Virago Press, 1994), 124–5.
12 In 1942 President Roosevelt ordered the internment of Japanese Americans in remote parts of the country, nearly eleven thousand were relocated to Heart Mountain in northern Wyoming.
13 Milane Duncan Frantz provides an excellent discussion of the ending, 'My Heroes Have Always Been Cowboys: The De-romanticising of the Cowboy Mythology in Annie Proulx's *Close Range*', MA dissertation (University of Houston, 2007), 59.
14 The compatibility of Darwinism with capitalist economics is acknowledged by Marx's dedication of *Capital* to the biologist.
15 Proulx, 'The Little Snake River Valley', *Red Desert*, 311–15 (313).
16 Alexandra Fuller, *The Legend of Colton H. Bryant* (Pocket Books, 2009), 94.
17 Proulx, 'Inhabitants of the Margins', *Red Desert*, 308.
18 William Kittredge, 'Overthrust Dreams', *Owning It All: Essays* (Port Townsend, WA: Graywolf Press, 1987), 114–15.
19 Kittredge, 'White People in Paradise', *The Next Rodeo: New and Selected Essays* (Saint Paul, MN: Graywolf Press, 2007), 177.

20 Quoted in Diana Kendall, *Framing Class: Media Representations of Wealth and Poverty in America* (Lanham, MD: Roman and Littlefield, 2005), 325.
21 Proulx, Introduction to *Fields of Vision: The Photographs of Carl Mydans* (The Library of Congress in association with D. Gilles, London, 2011), viii–xiii (xi, xiii).
22 Proulx, 'Reliquary', in *Treadwell: Photographs by Andrea Modica* (San Francisco: Chronicle Books, 1996), 9–12 (10).
23 Proulx, 'After the Gold Rush', *Guardian* (23 November 2005).
24 *Roseanne* (American sitcom), broadcast on ABC from October 18, 1988, to May 20, 1997; *The King of Queens* (American sitcom), broadcast on CBS from September 21, 1998, to May 14, 2007.

Conclusion

1 Proulx unearthed the image during her research for her introductory essay to *Red Desert*. It recalls the description of the 'horse catcher Tex Love, found sitting dead against a rock'. *Red Desert: History of a Place* (Texas: University of Texas Press, 2009), 77–81 (80).
2 Daniel Schweitzer provides an excellent analysis of this story in '"Reality's Never Been of Much Use Out" Where? Annie Proulx's *Wyoming Stories* and the Problems of Neoregionalism', MA dissertation (University of South Dakota, 2011), 71–5.
3 Proulx, Introduction, *Red Desert*, 78–9. Proulx also discusses the tangle of construction roads in her Introduction to Thomas Reed Petersen's (ed.), *A Road Runs Through It: Reviving Wild Places* (Boulder: Johnson Books, 2006), vii–x.
4 Schweitzer, 'Problems of Neoregionalism', 74.
5 'An Interview with Annie Proulx', *Missouri Review* 22:2 (Spring 1999), 84–5; http://www.missourireview.com/content/dynamic/view_text.php?text_id=877 [accessed 4 September 2013].
6 Interview with Deborah Treisman, *New Yorker* (June 4 2013); http://www.newyorker.com/online/blogs/books/2013/06/this-week-in-fiction-annie-proulx.html [accessed 27 October 2013].

Bibliography

Abbey, Edward, *Desert Solitaire: A Season in the Wilderness* (1st edn 1968; New York: Touchstone, 1990).
—'Even the Bad Guys Wear White Hats: Cowboys, Ranchers and the Ruin of the West', *Harper's* (January 1986), 51–5.
Abele, Elizabeth, 'Westward Proulx: The Resistant Landscapes of *Close Range: Wyoming Stories* and *That Old Ace in the Hole*', in A. Hunt (ed.), *Geographical Imagination*, 113–25.
Abell, Stephen, 'Woebegone in Wyoming', *Times Literary Supplement* (12 September 2008).
Adams, Ramon, *The Cowboy and his Philosophy* (Austin: Encino, 1967).
Adler, Warren, 'The State of the Cowboy State in the New Millennium', in M. Shay, D. Romtvedt and L. Rounds (eds), *Deep West*, 263–70.
Alexie, Sherman, *Reservation Blues* (New York: Time Warner, 1996).
—*Ten Little Indians* (New York: Grove Press, 2004).
Armitage, Susan, 'Through Women's Eyes: A New View of the West', in S. Armitage and E. Jameson (eds), *Women's West*, 9–18.
Armitage, Susan and E. Jameson (eds), *The Women's West* (Norman and London: University of Oklahoma Press, 1984).
Arosteguy, Katie, '"It was all a hard, fast ride that ended in the mud": Deconstructing the Myth of the Cowboy in Annie Proulx's *Close Range: Wyoming Stories*', *Western American Literature* 45:2 (Summer 2010), 116–36.
Athearn, Robert, *The Mythic West in Twentieth Century America* (Lawrence: University Press of Kansas, 1986).
Baile, Robert, 'Stark Tales of Wyoming by a Native Daughter', *The Boston Globe* (10 November 2008); http://articles.boston.com/2008-11-10/ae/29279050_1_bad-dirt-wyoming-swamp-mischief [accessed 21 November 2013].
Bass, Rick, *The Sky, the Stars, the Wilderness* (Boston and New York: Mariner, 1998).
Baudrillard, Jean, *America*, trans. Chris Turner (New York and London: Verso, 1988).
Bedell, Geraldine, 'Roaming in Wyoming', *The Observer* (12 December 2004); http://www.guardian.co.uk/books/2004/dec/12/fiction.features [accessed 16 September 2013].
Bevis, William, 'Native American Novels: Homing In', in Brian Swann and Arnold Krupat (eds), *Recovering the World* (Berkeley: University of California Press, 1987), 580–620.
Bolick, Katie, 'Imagination Is Everything', *The Atlantic Monthly* (12 November 1997); www.theatlantic.com/unbound/factfict/eapint.htm [accessed 28 October 2013].

Boyd, Ellen, 'Oral History and Revenge in Annie Proulx's "The Half-Skinned Steer"', *Forum: University of Edinburgh Postgraduate Journal of Culture and the Arts* 13; http://www.forumjournal.org/site/issue/13/ellen-boyd [accessed 28 November 2013].

Brown, Dee, *Gentle Tamers* (Nebraska: University of Nebraska Press, 1958).

—*The American West* (1st edn 1995; London: Pocket Books, 2004).

Burford, Bill, Introduction to *Granta Magazine* (Summer 1983); http://www.granta.com/Archive/8 [accessed 4 September 2013].

Burns, R. H., A. S. Gillespie and W. G. Richardson, *Wyoming's Pioneer Ranches* (Laramie: Top-of-the-World-Press, 1955).

Burroughs, John Rolfe, *Where the Old West Stayed Young* (New York: Morrow, 1962).

Busch, Frederick, 'A Desperate Perceptiveness', *The Chicago Tribune* (12 January 1992).

Butler, Anne, 'Selling the Popular Myth', in Clyde A. Milner II, Carol A. O'Connor, Martha A. Sandweiss (eds), *The Oxford History of the American West* (Oxford: Oxford University Press, 1996), 771–801.

Butruille, Susan, *Women's Voices from the Western Frontier* (Boise: Tamarack Books, 1995).

Caldwell, Gale, 'Wild West Transplanted to Wyoming', *The Boston Globe* (16 May 1999).

Calhoun, John, 'Peaks and Valleys', *American Cinematographer* 87:1 (2006), 58–67; http://www.ennisjack.com/forum/index.php?topic=16905.0 [accessed 3 September 2013].

Campbell, Neil, *The Cultures of the American New West* (Edinburgh: Edinburgh University Press, 2000).

—*The Rhizomatic West: Representing the American West in a Transnational, Global, Media Age* (Lincoln: University of Nebraska, 2008).

—'Brokeback Mountain's "In-Between" Spaces', *Canadian Review of American Studies* 39:2 (2009), 205–20.

Carlson, Ron, 'True Grit', *New York Times* (7 September 2008); http://www.nytimes.com/2008/09/07/books/review/Carlson-t.html?_r=1 [accessed 29 November 2013].

Cather, Willa, *My Antonia* (1st edn 1914; London: Virago Classics, 1983).

—*O Pioneers!* (1st edn 1913; Nebraska: University of Nebraska Press, 1992).

Caveney, Graham, 'Twisters in the Tale; Tall Stories Meet Big Winds and Dark Secrets in Annie Proulx's Texas: Review of *That Old Ace in the Hole*', *The Independent* (4 January 2003); http://business.highbeam.com/6001/article-1P2-1740879/books-twisters-tale-tall-stories-meet-big-winds-and [accessed 29 November 2013].

Cella, Matthew, *Bad Land Pastoralism in Great Plains Fiction* (Iowa City: University of Iowa Press, 2010).

Clark, Mike, '"Brokeback" Opens New Vistas', *USA Today* (9 December 2005), E4.

Cohen, Sandy, 'The Story behind "Brokeback Mountain"', *Associated Press* (19 December 2005); http://www.advocate.com/arts-entertainment/entertainment-news/2005/12/17/annie-proulx-tells-story-behind-brokeback [accessed 3 September 2013].

Cooper, Brenda and Edward Pease, 'Framing Brokeback Mountain: How the Popular Press Corralled the "Gay Cowboy Movie"', *Critical Studies in Media Communication* 25:3 (August 2008), 249–73.

Courtwright, David T., *Violent Land: Single Men and Social Disorder from the Frontier to the Inner City* (Cambridge, MA: Harvard University Press, 1996).

Cowley, Jason, 'Pioneer Poet of the American Wilderness', *The Times* (5 June 1997).

Cox, Christopher, Interview with Annie Proulx, *The Paris Review* 188 (Spring 2009) www.theparisreview.org/interviews/5901/the-art-of-fiction-no-199-annie-proulx [accessed 11 September 2013].

Crimmel, Hal, 'The Apple Doesn't Fall Far from the Tree: Western American Literature and Environmental Literary Criticism', in N. Witschi (ed.), *Companion to the West*, 367–77.

Cronon, William, George Miles and Jay Gitlin (eds), *Under an Open Sky: Rethinking America's Western Past* (New York: W. W. Norton and Company, 1992).

Deloria, Philip, *Indians in Unexpected Places* (1st edn 1999; Lawrence: University Press of Kansas, 2004).

Deloria, Vine Jr, *God Is Red: A Native View of Religion* (1st edn 1972; Golden, CO: Fulcrum Publishing, 1994).

Deverell, William (ed.), *A Companion to the American West* (Oxford: Blackwell Publishing, 2004).

Doig, Ivan, *Ride with Me, Mariah Montana* (New York: Atheneum, 1990).

—*This House of Sky: Landscapes of a Western Mind* (1st edn 1978; San Diego, New York and London: Harcourt Brace and Company, 1992).

Edemariam, Aida, 'Home on the Range', *The Guardian* (11 December 2004); http://www.guardian.co.uk/books/2004/dec/11/featuresreviews.guardianreview13 [accessed 12 September 2013].

Eder, Richard, 'Don't Fence Me In', *The New York Times* (23 May 1999); http://www.nytimes.com/books/99/05/23/reviews/990523.23ederlt.html [accessed 29 November 2013].

Ehrlich, Gretel, *The Solace of Open Spaces* (Harmondsworth: Penguin, 1985).

Emerson, Ralph Waldo, Address on 'Idealism', *Nature, Addresses, and Lectures* (1849) in *Ralph Waldo Emerson* (Oxford Authors Series) (Oxford: Oxford University Press, 1990), 22–9.

Etulain, Richard, *Re-imagining the Modern American West: A Century of Fiction* (Arizona: University of Arizona Press, 1996).

Falconer, Delia, 'Review of *Fine Just the Way It Is*', *The Age* (13 October 2008); http://www.theage.com.au/news/entertainment/books/book-reviews/fine-just-the-way-it-is/2008/10/13/1223749917539.html?page=fullpage#contentSwap1 [accessed 4 September 2013].

—*The Return of the Vanishing American* (London: Paladin, 1968).
Fenimore, David, '"A Bad Boy Grown Up": The Wild Life Behind Zane Grey's Westerns', in David Rio, Amaia Ibarraran, José Miguel Santamaria and M.a Felisa López (eds), *Exploring the American Literary West: International Perspectives* (Universidad del Paris Vasco: 2006), 57–68.
—'Folk-singing in the West, 1880–1930', in N. Witschi, *Companion to the West*, 316–35.
Fiedler, Leslie, *Love and Death in the American Novel* (New York: Criterion Books, 1960).
Forbis, William, *The Cowboys* (New York: Time-Life, 1973).
Fox, William, *The Void, the Grid, and the Sign* (Reno: University of Nevada Press, 2000).
Frantz, Milane Duncan, 'My Heroes Have Always been Cowboys: The De-romanticising of the Cowboy Mythology in Annie Proulx's *Close Range*', MA dissertation (University of Houston, 2007).
Gardner, Dudley, 'Early People of the Red Desert', *Red Desert*, 231–7.
—'The Union Pacific, the Chinese, and the Japanese', *Red Desert*, 297–304.
Gautreaux, Tim, 'Behind Great Stories there are Great Sentences', *The Boston Globe* (19 October 1997), 4.
Gerrard, Nicci, 'The Inimitable Annie Proulx', *The Observer* (13 June 1999); www.guardian.co.uk/theobserver/1999/jun/13/featuresreview.review [accessed 7 September 2013].
Gilchrist, Megan, *The Western Landscape in Cormac McCarthy and Wallace Stegner: Myths of the Frontier* (New York and London: Routledge, 2010).
Gilroy, John Warren, 'Another Fine Example of the Oral Tradition? Identification and Subversion in Sherman Alexie's *Smoke Signals*', Studies in American Indian Literatures (SAIL) 13:1 (Spring 2001), 23–39; https://facultystaff.richmond.edu/~rnelson/asail/SAIL2/131.html#23 [accessed 7 August 2013].
Glotferry, Cheryll and Harold Fromm, *The Ecocriticism Reader: Landmarks in Literary Ecology* (eds), (Athens, GA: University of Georgia Press, 1996).
Grey, Zane, *The Border Legion* (New York: Harper Brothers, 1916).
—*Riders of the Purple Sage* (1912) (Lincoln: University of Nebraska Press, 1994).
Grossman, James (ed.), *The Frontier in American Culture: An Exhibition at the Newberry Library – Essays by Richard White and Patricia Nelson Limerick* (California: University of California Press, 1994).
Handley, William R. (ed.), *The Brokeback Book: From Story to Cultural Phenomenon* (Lincoln and London: University of Nebraska Press, 2011).
—'The Past and Futures of a Story and a Film', in W. R. Handley (ed.), *The Brokeback Book*, 1–23.
Harris, Katherine, 'Homesteading in Northeastern Colorado, 1873–1920: Sex Roles and Women's Experience', in S. Armitage and E. Jameson (eds), *Women's West*, 165–78.

Harris, W. C., 'Broke(n)back Faggots: Hollywood Gives Queers a Hobson's Choice', in J. Stacy (ed.), *Reading Brokeback*, 118–34.

Hartigan, John, 'Unpopular Culture: The Case of "White Trash"', in *Cultural Studies* 11:2 (1997), 316–44.

Hemingway, Ernest, *The Sun Also Rises* (New York: Scribner's, 1926).

Henderson, William Haywood, *Native* (New York: Plume, 1993); http://www.williamhaywoodhenderson.com/ [accessed 25 September 2013].

Hitt, Jack, 'Where the Deer and the Zillionaires Play', *Outside Magazine* (October 1997), 122–234; www.outsideonline.com/outdoor-adventure/Where-the-Deer-and-the-Zillionaires-Play.html?page=all [accessed 4 September 2013].

Hoberman, John, 'How the West was Lost', in J. Kitses and G. Rickman (eds), *The Western Reader* (New York: Limelight, 1999), 85–92.

Holden, Stephen, 'Riding the High Country, Finding and Losing Love', *The New York Times* (9 December 2005); http://movies.nytimes.com/2005/12/09/movies/09brok.html?_r=0 [accessed 29 November 2013].

Holthaus, G. and Charles F. Wilkinson (eds), *A Society to Match the Scenery: Personal Visions of the Future of the American West* (Boulder: University of Colorado Press, 1991).

Horowitz, Mark, 'Larry McMurtry's Dream Job', *New York Times on the Web*; http://www.nytimes.com/books/97/12/07/home/article2.html [accessed 9 August 2013].

Hunt, Alex (ed.), *The Geographical Imagination of Annie Proulx: Rethinking Regionalism* (Lanham, MD: Lexington Books, 2009).

Jackson, John Brinckerhoff, *Discovering the Vernacular Landscape* (New Haven: Yale University Press, 1984).

Jameson, Elizabeth, 'Women as Workers, Women as Civilisers: True Womanhood in the American West', in S. Armitage and E. Jameson (eds), *Women's West*, 145–64.

Jeffrey, Julie Roy, *Frontier Women* (New York: Hill and Wang, 1979).

Jennings, William Dale, *The Cowboys* (New York: Bantam Books, 1972).

Jensen, Joan and Darlis Miller, 'The Gentle Tamers Revisited: New Approaches to the History of Women in the American West', *Pacific Historical Review* 40 (May 1980), 173–213.

Johnson, Margaret E., 'Proulx and the Postmodern Hyperreal', in A. Hunt (ed.), *Geographical Imagination*, 25–38.

Johnson, Susan Lee, 'Film Review *Brokeback Mountain*', *The Journal of American History* 93:3 (December 2006), 988–90.

Jones, Ginger, 'Proulx's Pastoral as Sacred Space', in J. Stacy (ed.), *Reading Brokeback Mountain*, 19–28.

Jones, Karen and John Wills, *The American West: Competing Visions* (Edinburgh: Edinburgh University Press, 2009).

Jordan, Teresa, *Cowgirls: Women of the American West* (Lincoln and London: University of Nebraska Press, 1992).

Joyner, Carol, 'Cultural Mythology and Anxieties of Belonging: Reconstructing the "Bi-cultural" Subject in the Fiction of Toni Morrison, Amy Tan and Annie Proulx', unpublished PhD Dissertation (University of London, 2002).

Kaufman, Moises, and Members of the Tectonic Theater Project, *The Laramie Project* (New York: Vintage, 2001).

Kinsey, Alfred, Wardell Pomeroy and Clyde Martin, *Sexual Behavior in the Human Male* (Philadelphia and London: W. B. Saunders, 1949).

Kitses, Jim, *Horizons West* (London: Thames and Hudson and British Film Institute, 1969).

Kitses, Jim and Greg Rickman (eds), *The Western Reader* (New York: Limelight, 1999).

Kittredge, William, 'The Last Safe Place', *Time Magazine* (6 September 1993), 27.

—*The Next Rodeo: New and Selected Essays* (Saint Paul, MN: Graywolf Press, 2007).

—*Owning It All: Essays* (Port Townsend, WA: Graywolf Press, 1987).

Klett, Mark, *Revealing Territory* (Albuquerque: University of New Mexico Press, 1992).

Kolodny, Annette, *The Lay of the Land: Metaphor as Experience and History in American Life and Letters* (Chapel Hill: University of North Carolina Press, 1975).

Kowalewski, Michael, 'Writing in Place: The New American Regionalism', *American Literary History* 6:1 (Spring 1994), 171–83.

Kupelian, David, 'Hollywood has Now Raped the Marlboro Man', *World Net Daily* (27 December 2005); http://www.wnd.com/2005/12/34076/ [accessed 3 September 2013].

Larson, T. A., *History of Wyoming* (1st edn 1965; Lincoln and London: University of Nebraska Press, 1978).

—*Wyoming: A Bicentennial History* (New York: W. W. Norton and Company, 1977).

Lawrence, Elizabeth Atwood, *Rodeo: An Anthropologist Looks at The Wild and the Tame Rodeo* (Knoxville: University of Tennessee Press, 1982).

Lehmann-Haupt, Christopher, '*Close Range*: Lechery and Loneliness out West', *The New York Times* (12 May 1999); www.nytimes.com/books/99/05/09/daily/051299proulx-book-review.html [accessed 29 November 2013].

Lessinger, Jack, *Penturbia: Where Real Estate Will Boom After the Crash of Suburbia* (Seattle, WA: SocioEconomics, Inc., 1991).

Limerick, Patricia Nelson, *The Legacy of Conquest* (New York and London: W. W. Norton and Company, 1987).

Limerick, Patricia Nelson, with Clyde A. Milner II and Charles E. Rankin (eds), *Trails: Towards a New Western History* (Kansas: University Press of Kansas, 1991).

Loffreda, Beth, *Losing Matt Shepard: Life and Politics in the Aftermath of Anti-Gay Murder* (New York: Columbia University Press, 2000).

Lundquist, Suzanne Evertsen, *Native American Literatures: An Introduction* (New York and London: Continuum, 2004).

Magagna, Anthony Rudolph, 'Placing the West: Landscape, Literature, and Identity in the American West', unpublished PhD dissertation (University of California, 2008).

Markowitz, Benjamin, 'Weighed Down by Past', *The Daily Telegraph* (12 December, 2004); www.telegraph.co.uk/culture/books/3633197/Weighed-down-west.html#? [accessed 3 September 2013].

Marx, Leo, *The Machine in the Garden: Technology and the Pastoral Ideal in America* (New York: Oxford University Press, 1964).

McMurtry, Larry, 'Adapting Brokeback Mountain', in *Brokeback Mountain: Story to Screenplay* (New York and London: Scribner, 2005).

McMurtry, Larry and Diane Ossana, 'Brokeback's Big Secrets', Interview with Anne Stockwell, *Advocate* (28 February 2006), 42–4.

McPhee, John, *Rising from the Plains* (New York: Farrar, Straus and Giroux, 1986).

Mehler, Charles Eliot, 'Brokeback Mountain at the Oscars', in J. Stacy (ed.), *Reading Brokeback*, 135–51.

Mellion, Bénédicte, 'Unreal, Fantastic and Improbable Flashes of Fearful Insight in Annie Proulx's *Wyoming Stories*'; www.benemeillon.com/.../Unreal-Fantastic-and-Improbable-Flashes-of-F [accessed 12 September 2013].

Mendelsohn, Daniel, 'An Affair to Remember', *New York Review of Books* (23 February 2006), 12–13; http://www.nybooks.com/articles/archives/2006/feb/23/an-affair-to-remember/?pagination=false [accessed 29 November 2013].

Miles, George, 'To Hear an Old Voice: Rediscovering Native Americans in American History', in W. Cronon, G. Miles and J. Gitlin (eds), *Under an Open Sky*, 52–70.

Miller, D. A., 'On the Universality of Brokeback', *Film Quarterly* 60:3 (Spring 2007), 50–60; http://townsendlab.berkeley.edu/sites/all/files/DA%20Miller%20On%20the%20Universality%20of%20Brokeback_0.pdf [accessed 12 September 2013].

Mitchell, W. J. T., *Landscape and Power* (Chicago: University of Chicago Press, 1994).

Moody, Rick, 'Across the Great Divide', *The Guardian* (17 December 2005); http://www.theguardian.com/books/2005/dec/17/featuresreviews.guardianreview12 [accessed 29 November 2013].

Moore, Caroline, 'High Prairie, Low Life: Review of *That Old Ace in the Hole*', *The Spectator* (4 January 2003); http://www.spectator.co.uk/books/20403/high-prairie-low-life/ [accessed 29 November 2013].

Morris, Gregory L., *Talking up a Storm: Voices of the New West* (Lincoln: University of Nebraska Press, 1995).

Myers, B. R., 'A Reader's Manifesto: An Attack on the Growing Pretentiousness of American Literary Prose', *The Atlantic Monthly* (1 July 2001); http://www.theatlantic.com/magazine/archive/2001/07/a-readers-manifesto/302270/ [accessed 29 November 2013].

Myres, Sandra L., *Westering Women and the Frontier Experience, 1800–1915* (Albuquerque: University of New Mexico Press, 1982).
Nash, Gerald D. and Richard Etulain (eds), *The Twentieth Century West: Historical Interpretations* (Albuquerque: University of New Mexico Press, 1989).
Nash, Henry Smith, *Virgin Land: The American West as Symbol and Myth* (Cambridge, MA: Harvard University Press, 1950).
Needham, Gary, *Brokeback Mountain* (Edinburgh: Edinburgh University Press, 2010).
Nicholas, Liza, *Becoming Western: Stories of Culture and Identity in the Cowboy State* (Lincoln: University of Nebraska Press, 2006).
Oates, Joyce Carol, 'In Rough Country', *New York Review of Books* (23 October 2008); http://www.nybooks.com/articles/archives/2008/oct/23/in-rough-country/?pagination=false [accessed 3 September 2013].
Ossana, Diana, 'Climbing Brokeback Mountain', in *Brokeback Mountain: Story to Screenplay*, 143–51.
Packard, Chris, *Queer Cowboys and Other Erotic Male Friendships in Nineteenth-Century American Literature* (Basingstoke: Palgrave Macmillan, 2006).
Pascoe, Peggy, 'Western Women at a Cultural Crossroads', in P. N. Limerick, C. A. Milner II and C. E. Rankin (eds), *Trails: Towards a New Western History* (Kansas: University Press of Kansas, 1991), 40–58.
Patterson, Eric, *On Brokeback Mountain: Meditations about Masculinity, Fear, and Love in the Story and the Film* (Lanham, MD and Plymouth: Lexington Books, 2008).
Peavy, Linda and Ursula Smith, *Pioneer Women: The Lives of Women on the Frontier* (Norman: University of Oklahoma Press, 1998).
Petrakis, John, 'Heartbreak Mountain', *Christian Century* 123:2 (24 January 2006), 43.
Pickle, Linda, *Contented among Strangers: Rural German Speaking Women and their Families in the Nineteenth Century Midwest* (Illinois: University of Illinois Press, 1996).
—'Rural German-Speaking Women in Early Nebraska and Kansas: Ethnicity as a Factor in Frontier Adaptation', *Great Plains Quarterly* 1:1 (1989), 239–51; http://digitalcommons.unl.edu/cgi/viewcontent.cgi?article=1389&context=greatplainsquarterly [accessed 3 September 2013].
Poquette, Ryan D., 'Critical Essay on "The Half-Skinned Steer"', *E-Notes*; http://www.enotes.com/topics/half-skinned-steer/themes#themes-themes [accessed 3 September 2010].
Porter, Joy, 'Historical and Cultural Contexts to Native American Literature', in J. Porter and K. M. Roemer (eds), *Cambridge Companion*, 39–68.
Porter, Joy and Roemer, K. M. (eds), *The Cambridge Companion to Native American Literature* (Cambridge: Cambridge University Press, 2005).
Potter, David, 'American Women and American Character', in Barbara Welter (ed.), *The Woman Question in American History* (Hinsdale, IL: The Dryden Press, 1973), 117–32.

Prescott, Cynthia Culver, *Gender and Generation on the Far Western Frontier* (Tuscon: University of Arizona Press, 2007).
Purdy, John, 'Crossroads: A Conversation with Sherman Alexie', *SAIL* 9:4 (Winter 1997), 1–18; https://facultystaff.richmond.edu/~rnelson/asail/SAIL2/94.html#1 [accessed 7 August 2013].
Rafferty, Terence, '*Bad Dirt*: A Town with Three Bars', *The New York Times* (5 December 2004); http://query.nytimes.com/gst/fullpage.html?res=9B0CEFDA143EF936A35751C1A9629C8B63&pagewanted=all [accessed 3 September 2013].
Rea, Tom, 'The View from Laramie Peak', in M. Shay, D. Romtvedt and L. Rounds (eds), *Deep West*, 283–8.
Reynolds, Susan Salter, 'Annie Proulx No Longer at Home on the Range', *The Los Angeles Times* (18 October 2008); www.latimes.com/news/nationworld/nation.la-et-proulx18–2008oct18,0,3383917.story [accessed 3 September 2013].
Rickey, Carrie, 'Men in Love, and in Anguish: A Love Story of Anguish and Silence', *Philadelphia Inquirer* (16 December 2005), W3.
Riley, Patricia, 'The Mixed Blood Writer as Interpreter and Mythmaker', in Joseph Trimmer and Tilly Warnock (eds), *Understanding Others* (Urbana, IL: National Council of English, 1992).
Robbins, Jim, *Last Refuge: The Environmental Showdown in Yellowstone and the American West* (New York: Morrow and Co., 1993).
Robinson, Marilynne, *Housekeeping* (1st edn 1981; London: Faber and Faber, 1985).
Rood, Karen, *Understanding Annie Proulx* (Columbia, SC: University of South Carolina Press, 2001).
Roosevelt, Theodore, *The Winning of the West*, H. Wish (ed.) (1st edn 1889–96; Gloucester: Peter Smith, 1976).
—*Ranch Life and the Hunting-Trail* (New York: Century Co., 1899).
Russell, Sharman Apt, *Kill the Cowboy: A Battle of Mythology in the New West* (Lincoln: University of Nebraska Press, 2001).
Russo, Vito, *The Celluloid Closet: Homosexuality in the Movies* (New York: Harper and Row, 1985).
Sage, Leland, *A History of Iowa* (Ames: Iowa State University, 1974).
Sandlin, Tim, 'How Place Affects My Subject Matter', in M. Shay, D. Romtvedt and L. Rounds (eds), *Deep West*, 432–4.
Savage, Thomas, *The Power of the Dog* (1st edn 1967; Boston: Little, Brown, 2011).
Savage, William, Jr, *The Cowboy Hero: His Image in American History and Culture* (Norman and London: University of Oklahoma Press, 1979).
Scharnhorst, Gary, '"All Hat and No Cattle": Romance, Realism, and Late Nineteenth-Century Western American Fiction', in N. Witschi (ed.), *A Companion Literature*, 281–96.
Schlissel, Lilian, *Women's Diaries of the Westward Journey* (1st edn 1984; New York: Schoken Books, 2004).
Schmahl, Helmut, 'Truthful Letters and Irresistible Wanderlust: The Emigration from Rhenish Hesse to Wisconsin', in Heike Bungert, Cora Lee Kluge and

Robert C. Ostergren (eds), *Wisconsin German Land and Life* (Max Karde German-American Studies: University of Wisconsin, 2006).

Schweitzer, Daniel, '"Reality's Never been of Much Use Out" Where? Annie Proulx's *Wyoming Stories* and the Problems of Neoregionalism', MA dissertation (University of South Dakota, 2011).

Shaffer, Marguerite S., 'Western Tourism', in W. Deverell (ed.), *Companion to American West*, 373–89.

Shay, Michael, David Romtvedt and Linn Rounds (eds), *Deep West: A Literary Tour of Wyoming* (Wyoming: Pronghorn Press, 2003).

Showalter, Elaine, *A Jury of her Peers: American Women Writers from Anne Bradstreet to Annie Proulx* (New York: Alfred A. Knopf, 2009).

Shugart, Helene, 'Consuming Passions: "Educating Desire" in "Brokeback Mountain"', *Critical Studies in Media Communication* 28:3 (24 May 2011), 173–92.

Simpson, Elizabeth, *Earthlight, Wordfire: The Work of Ivan Doig* (Moscow, ID: University of Idaho Press, 1992).

Sinclair, Clive, '*Bad Dirt*: Home on the Range', *The Independent* (31 December 2004); http://www.independent.co.uk/arts-entertainment/books/reviews/bad-dirt-wyoming-stories-2-by-annie-proulx-6155346.html [accessed 25 November 2013].

Skow, John, 'On Strange Ground', *Time Magazine* (17 May 1999); http://content.time.com/time/magazine/article/0,9171,990992,00.html [accessed 29 November 2013].

Slotkin, Richard, *Gunfighter Nation: The Myth of the Frontier in Twentieth-Century America* (New York: Atheneum, 1992).

—*Regeneration through Violence: The Mythology of the American Frontier, 1600–1860* (Middletown, CT: Wesleyan University Press, 1973).

Smith, Henry Nash, *Virgin Land: The American West as Symbol and Myth* (Cambridge, MA: Harvard University Press, 1950).

Smith, Page, *Daughters of the Promised Land: Women in American History* (Boston: Little, Brown, 1970).

Snyder, Gary, *The Practice of the Wild: Essays by Gary Snyder* (San Francisco: North Point Press, 1990).

Spurgeon, Sara, *Exploding the Western: Myths of Empire on the Postmodern Frontier* (Texas: Texas A&M University Press, 2005).

Stacy, Jim, *Reading Brokeback Mountain: Essays on the Story and the Film* (Jefferson, North Carolina and London: McFarland and Company, 2007).

—'Buried in the Family Plot: The Cost of Pattern Maintenance to Jack and Ennis', in J. Stacy (ed.), *Reading Brokeback*, 29–44.

Stegner, Wallace, *The American West as Living Space* (Michigan: University of Michigan Press, 1987).

—*The Big Rock Candy Mountain* (1st edn 1943; New York: Penguin Books, 1991).

—*The Sound of Mountain Water* (1st edn 1969; Harmondsworth: Penguin Books, 1997).

—*Where the Bluebird Sings to the Lemonade Springs* (Harmondsworth: Penguin Books, 1992).
Steinberg, Sybil, 'E. Annie Proulx: An American Odyssey', *Publishers Weekly* 3 (June 1996), 57–8.
Stoltje, Beverly, 'A Helpmate for a Man Indeed: The Image of the Frontier Woman', *Journal of American Folklore* 88:347 (Spring 1975), 25–41.
—'Making the Frontier Myth: Folklore Process in a Modern Nation', *Western Folklore* 46:4 (1987), 235–53.
Swaab, Peter, 'Homo on the Range', *New Statesman* (12 December 2005), 40–2; http://www.newstatesman.com/node/152202 [accessed 29 November 2013].
Thomas, John L., *A Country in the Mind: Wallace Stegner, Bernard DeVoto, History, and the American Land* (New York and London: Routledge, 2002).
Thomson, David, 'The Lone Ranger', *The Independent on Sunday* (30 May 1999); http://www.independent.co.uk/arts-entertainment/the-lone-ranger-1096783.html [accessed 29 November 2013].
Tompkins, Jane, *West of Everything: The Inner Life of Westerns* (New York and Oxford: Oxford University Press, 1992).
Tuan, Yi-Fu, *Space and Place: The Perspective of Experience* (Minneapolis: University of Minnesota Press, 1997).
Varvogli, Aliki, *The Shipping News: A Reader's Guide* (New York and London: Continuum, 2002).
Vilkomerson, Sara, 'Brokeback Encore', *The New York Observer* (12 November 2008); http://www.thefreelibrary.com/Brokeback+Encore-a01611637206 [accessed 29 November 2013].
Viner, Katharine, 'Death of the Author', *The Guardian* (6 June 1997), Section 2, 2.
Welter, Barbara (ed.), *The Woman Question in American History* (Hinsdale, IL: The Dryden Press, 1973).
Weltzien, Alan, 'Annie Proulx's Wyoming: Geograpical Determinism, Landscape, and Caricature', in A. Hunt (ed.), *Geographical Imagination*, 99–112.
Werden, Douglas, '"She Had Never Humbled Herself": Alexandra Bergson and Marie Shabata as the "Real" Pioneers of *O Pioneers!*', *Great Plains Quarterly* 7:1 (2002), 199–215.
Westling, Louise, *The Green Breast of the New World: Landscape, Gender, and American Fiction* (Athens, GA: University of Georgia Press, 1996).
White, Richard, 'Frederick Jackson Turner and Buffalo Bill', in James R. Grossman (ed.), *The Frontier in American Culture: An Exhibition at the Newberry Library – Essays by Richard White and Patricia Nelson Limerick* (California: University of California Press, 1994), 7–65.
—*It's Your Misfortune and None of My Own: A New History of the American West* (Norman: University of Oklahoma Press, 1991).
Williams, Terry Tempest, *Refuge: An Unnatural History of Family and Place* (New York: Vintage, 1991).

Wister, Owen, 'The Evolution of the Cowboy', *Harper's* 91 (September 1895), 602–17.
—*Owen Wister Out West: His Journals and Letters*, ed. Fanny Kemble Wister (Chicago: University of Chicago Press, 1958).
—*The Virginian* (1902) (Oxford: Oxford University Press, 1998).
Witschi, Nicolas (ed.), *A Companion to the Literature and Culture of the American West* (Oxford: Wiley-Blackwell, 2011).
Wynne-Jones, Ros, 'Happier to Write than Love', *The Independent on Sunday* (1 June 1997); www.independent.co.uk/opinion/happier-to-write-than-love-1253675.html [accessed 10 September 2013].
Wypijewski, JoAnn, 'A Boy's Life: For Matthew Shepard's Killers, What Does it Take to Pass as a Man?' *Harper's* (September 1999), 7; http://WWW/READINGS/10-05_Toolbox/Wypijewski_Boys_Harper's_Sept1999.pdf [accessed 12 September 2013].

Proulx

Books

(Listed in order of publication and with editions used in this book)
Heart Songs (1st edn 1988; London and New York: Harper Perennial, 2006).
Postcards (1st edn 1992; London: Fourth Estate, 2003).
The Shipping News (1st edn 1993; London: Fourth Estate, 1994).
Accordion Crimes (1st edn 1996; London and New York: Harper Perennial, 2006).
Close Range: Wyoming Stories (1st edn 1999; London and New York: Harper Perennial, 2006).
That Old Ace in the Hole (2002) (London and New York: Harper Perennial, 2004).
Bad Dirt: Wyoming Stories (2004) (London and New York: Harper Perennial, 2005).
Fine Just the Way It Is: Wyoming Stories (London: Fourth Estate, 2008).
Red Desert: History of a Place (Texas: University of Texas Press, 2009).
Bird Cloud: A Memoir (London: Fourth Estate, 2011).

Articles and essays

In *Red Desert: History of a Place*

'Forts Halleck and Fred Steele', 283–92.
'Forts of the Red Desert', 267–70.
'Horse Bands of the Red Desert', 329–38.
'Inhabitants of the Margins', 305–9.

'Introduction', 77–81.
'The Little Snake River Valley', 311–16.
'Opening the Oyster', 339–54.
'Red Desert Outlaws', 355–62.
'Red Desert Ranches', 317–27.
'Traversing the Desert', 253–65.
'The Union Pacific Railroad Arrives', 293–6.

Other articles

'After the Gold Rush', *The Guardian* (23 November 2005); http://www.guardian.co.uk/world/2005/nov/23/usa [accessed 4 September 2013].
'Blood on the Red Carpet', *The Guardian* (11 March 2006); www.guardian.co.uk/books/2006/mar/11/awardsandprizes.oscars2006 [accessed 29 November 2013].
'Books on Top', *The New York Times* (26 May 1994); http://www.nytimes.com/books/99/05/23/specials/proulx-top.html [accessed 29 November 2013].
'Dangerous Ground', in Timothy R. Mahoney and Wendy J. Katz (eds), *Regionalism and the Humanities* (Nebraska: University of Nebraska Press 2008), 6–25.
'Getting Movied', in *Brokeback Mountain: Story to Screenplay* (New York and London: Scribner, 2005), 129–38.
'How the West Was Spun', Review Essay of exhibition exploring the heroic myths of the American frontier, Compton Verney, Warwickshire. *The Guardian: Saturday Review* (25 June 2005), 4–6; http://www.guardian.co.uk/books/2005/jun/25/featuresreviews.guardianreview24 [accessed 3 October 2013].
'Urban Bumpkins', *The Washington Post* (25 September 1994); http://www.highbeam.com/doc/1P2-911232.html [accessed 29 November 2013].
'Writing in Wyoming', in M. Shay, D. Romtvedt and L. Rounds (eds), *Deep West: A Literary Tour of Wyoming* (Wyoming: Pronghorn Press, 2003), 42–6.
'Wyoming: The Cowboy State', in John Leonard (ed.), *These United States: Original Essays by Leading American Writers on Their State within the Union* (New York: Thunderer's Mouth Press, 2003).

Introductions and afterwords

Afterword to Thomas Savage, *The Power of the Dog* (1st edn 1967; Boston: Little, Brown, 2011).
Introduction to *Fields of Vision: The Photographs of Carl Mydans* (The Library of Congress in association with D. Gilles, London, 2011), viii–xiii.
Introduction to Thomas Reed Petersen (ed.), *A Road Runs through It: Reviving Wild Places* (Boulder: Johnson Books, 2006), vii–x.

'Reliquary', *Treadwell: Photographs by Andrea Modica* (San Francisco: Chronicle Books, 1996), 9–12.

Journal interviews with unnamed interviewers

'A Conversation with Annie Proulx', *The Atlantic Online* (12 November 1997); http://www.theatlantic.com/past/docs/unbound/factfict/eapint.htm [accessed 3 September 2013].

'An Interview with Annie Proulx', *Missouri Review* 22:2 (Spring 1999), 84–5; http://www.missourireview.com/content/dynamic/view_text.php?text_id=877 [accessed 4 September 2013].

'More Reader than Writer: A Conversation with Annie Proulx', *Wyoming Library Roundup*' (Autumn 2005), 5–8; http://www-wsl.state.wy.us/roundup/Fall2005Roundup.pdf [accessed 9 September 2013].

Index

Abbey, Edward 30, 96
   Monkey Wrench Gang, The 31, 86, 96
Academy Awards 2, 25, 138
Accordion Crimes 4, 18, 58, 62, 93
Adams, Robert 33
Adler, Warren 16
Adonais 126
'After the Gold Rush' 132, 180
After the West Was Won 60
Ahamkhani, Ali 101
Albert, Lieutenant James William 153
Alexie, Sherman 146, 147, 148
   Reservation Blues 146
   Smoke Signals 147
All in the Family 168
Ambush on the Pecos Trail 46
America 81–2
American Dream 75, 85, 176, 178
Anderson, Sherwood 69
   Winesburg, Ohio 38
Annales School 3, 21, 33, 56
Arcadia 125–6
Arnold, Matthew 126
   Thyrsis 126
Arthur, Jean 139
Association for the Study of Literature and the Environment (ASLE) 30
Auster, Paul 83
   Music of Chance, The 82
authenticity 11, 15, 17, 18, 23, 26, 27, 43, 74, 94–5, 118, 157–8, 160, 162, 181
Avedon, Richard 179, 180
   In the American West 132, 179
   Proulx Review 132, 180

baby boomers 15
Bad Dirt 12, 19, 20, 164
Balzac, Honoré de 79
   Père Goriot, Le 80
Barthes, Roland 13
Bass, Rick 31
   'Days of Heaven' 31
   Where the Sea Used to Be 39
Baudrillard, Jean 35, 82
   America 81–2
   Simulacrum 8, 106
Becker, Judy 132
Berry, Wendell 30
Best American Short Stories of the Century, The 46
Bierstadt, Albert 7
Big Rock Candy Mountain, The 58, 77
'Big Rock Candy Mountain' 136
Billy the Kid 43, 44, 46
Bird Cloud 15, 55, 66, 143
bison 94, 95, 144–5
Black Elk 159–60
Black Elk Speaks 159
Black Hills 10
blood imagery 35, 45, 50, 81, 85, 102
'Blood on the Red Carpet' 2
Bloodlines: Odyssey of a Native Daughter 161
Bluebeard legend 24
Bohemian Girl, The 65
Bonanza 110
Bone Game 146
Bonfils, Frederick Gilmer 74, 75
Border Trilogy 15
Brimstone Basin 11
Brinkley, John R. 62
Brokeback Mountain (film) 2, 25, 133, 137–9

awards 138
    screenplay 11, 25, 121, 123, 124, 129, 133, 134, 135, 137
'Brokeback Mountain' 25, 70, 110, 119–40
Brown, Dee 146, 159, 161
    Bury My Heart at Wounded Knee 146, 159, 161
buffalo 98
Buffalo Bill *see* Cody, Bill
Buffalo Commons policy 95
'Bunchgrass Edge of the World, The' 24, 36, 38, 39, 98, 102, 103–6
Burford, Bill 170
Burroughs, John Rolfe
    Where the Old West Stayed Young 75
Bury My Heart at Wounded Knee 146, 159, 161
Bush, George W. 10, 101
Butch Cassidy and the Sundance Kid 121

Calamity Jane 58, 93
Calamus 126
Campbell, Neil 13, 125
Canary, Martha Jane *see* Calamity Jane
Capote, Truman 123, 138
Carbon County Journal 68
Carson, Kit 11, 90
Cather, Willa 21, 29–30, 32, 35, 36, 37, 58
    Bohemian Girl, The 65
    My Antonia 59
    Professor's House, The 135
Catlin, George 108
Ceremony 31, 146–7
Charles Scribner's Sons 3
chat rooms 123
Cherokee trail 57
Cheyenne 10, 141
Cheyenne Frontier Days 17
Christianity 59

church 61
Civil War 9, 107
Claude Lorrain 126
Clift, Montgomery 120
Close Range 12, 14, 19, 123
Clough, Arthur Hugh 126
Cody, Bill 8–9, 14, 16, 18, 26, 43, 45, 57, 108, 145, 157, 158, 160, 161, 169, 186
    Indian Wars Refought, The 158–60, 161
    Wild West shows 14, 16, 18, 159
Cole, Thomas 7
Coleridge, Samuel Taylor 126
    Rime of the Ancient Mariner, The 126
Collister, Oscar 42, 43
'Colors of Horses, The' 18, 93
Columbus, Christopher 142, 145
Comanche 153
Conrad, Joseph
    Heart of Darkness 55
Contented among Strangers 63–4
Cord novels 11
Costner, Kevin
    Dances with Wolves 145
Country People 59, 63
cowboy myth 24–5, 27, 48, 71, 107, 109, 110, 112, 116–20, 124, 126, 130, 131, 133, 135, 139, 166, 170, 172–5
Cowboy Songs and Other Frontier Ballads 69
Cowboys Are My Weakness 170
Cowgirls: Women of the American West 93
Crash 2
Crazy Horse 161
Crèvecoeur, Hector 7
    Letters from an American Farmer 7
Crouching Tiger, Hidden Dragon 123
'Cult of True Womanhood' 23, 61, 69
Curtis, Tony 138

Custer, George Armstrong 8
Custer Died for Your Sins 146

D'Emilio, John 120
   Intimate Matters 120
Dances with Wolves 145, 147
Dancing at Rascal Fair 32
'Dangerous Ground' 29, 30, 31, 32, 33, 34, 82
Darwin, Charles 27, 39, 49, 57, 172, 175
'Days of Heaven' 31
'Deep-Blood-Greasy-Bowl' 25, 143–9
Deep Green 7, 96, 97
Deliverance 176
Deloria, Philip 8
Deloria Jr, Vine 146, 155, 160
   Custer Died for Your Sins 146
Denver Post 74
Depression, the 11, 74, 157, 179
DeVoto, Bernard 10, 86
dialectics 34
Dickey, James
   Deliverance 176
Dime novels 9, 11, 43, 107, 108, 109
Dirty Realism 170, 188
Disneyland 18
Dixon, Maynard
   What an Indian Thinks 142
Dodge, Richard Irving 153
   Plains of North America and its Inhabitants, The 153
Doig, Ivan 20, 32, 33, 67
   Dancing at Rascal Fair 32
   English Creek 32
   Ride with Me, Maria Montana 32
   This House of Sky 32
drug use 165, 170
Drunk with Love 170
Dude Ranches 17, 23, 93
Dwellings 146, 149

Earp, Wyatt 11
Eastman, Charles Alexander 154
   Soul of the Indian, The 154
Eclogues 126
ecocriticism 30
ecofiction 30
effeminacy 120, 134
Ehrlich, Gretel 6, 14, 54, 67, 120
   Solace of Open Spaces, The 26, 164
Electric Horseman, The 107
English Creek 32
Erben, K. J.
   Otesanek 44
Erdrich, Karen Louise 146, 147
   Dakotah novels 146, 147
Even Cowgirls Get the Blues 93
fairy tales 12, 24, 36, 42, 43, 44, 45, 49, 54, 64, 103, 105, 106, 181, 188
   imagery 49
Falconer, Delia 143
Fall, The 127
'Family Man' 185–8
Fast Lanes 170
female emancipation 24, 101
Female Malady, The 65
female suffrage 60
femininity *see also* gender 105, 106, 110, 117, 130, 188
feminist criticism 22, 32, 59, 62
fertility 63
Fiedler, Leslie 6
'55 Miles to the Gas Pump' 110
Fine Just the Way It Is 12, 19, 42
First World War 64
'Florida Rental' 27, 113, 165, 169–70
Focus Films 139
Foote, Mary Hallock 29
Ford, Glenn 120
Ford, John
   My Darling Clementine 120
Foreman, Dave 86
'Forts Halleck and Fred Steele' 42, 44, 67
Freedman, Estelle 120

Intimate Matters 120
Frontier 13, 23, 75, 77, 90, 136, 145, 149, 177
Frontier Closure 8, 11, 57, 107
   Frontier Women 60–1, 73, 75, 101, 109, 119

Garden of Eden 125–7
Gardner, Dudley 143
Garrison, Linley M. 158
gender *see also* femininity *and* masculinity 58, 59, 61
   roles 104–5
   stereotypes 104
German immigrants 63
'Getting Movied' 123–4, 125, 137
Giants in the Earth 59
Gilchrist, Ellen 170
   Drunk with Love 170
Gill, Lois 2
global economy 165, 167, 183
'Goat Gland Operation, The' 22, 58, 62–5, 81
Golding, William 144
   Inheritors, The 144
'Governors of Wyoming, The' 17, 26, 86, 96, 115, 142, 148, 151–3, 164–5
Gray's Sporting Journal 3
Great Depression *see* Depression
Great Divide 74
'Great Divide, The' 22, 23, 58, 61, 73–8
Great Divide Homestead Colony Number One 74
Great Northern Railroad 67
Great Train Robbery, The 10–11
Grey, Zane
   novels 90, 103, 109
guns 120

Hale, Janet Campbell
   Bloodlines: Odyssey of a Native Daughter 161

'Half-Skinned Steer, The' 21–2, 41, 46–51, 52, 56, 115, 140, 169, 186
Harte, Bret 29
Hawks, Howard
   Red River 120
Hawthorne, Nathaniel
   Scarlet Letter, The 127
Heart of Darkness 55
Heart Songs 3, 16, 19, 31, 55, 176, 179
'Heart Songs' 176
Heat-Moon, William Least 154–5
   PrairyErth 155
Hemingway, Ernest 20, 75, 125–6
   Sun Also Rises, The 125
Henderson, Russell 124
Henderson, William Haywood 121, 122, 126
   Native 121, 122, 124, 128
Hercules myth 126, 136
Hiawatha 75
Hickok, Wild Bill 43
Hill, James 67
Hoffman, Philip Seymour 138
Hogan, Linda 146, 149
   Dwellings 146, 149
Hoggatt, Volney 74, 75
Holladay, Ben 42, 43, 44, 45
Hollywood 25, 26, 113, 138, 145
   Westerns 86, 87, 90, 109, 120, 169
Homestead Act of 1862 65
Homestead Act of 1916 73–4
homoeroticism 25, 120
homophobia 124–5, 128, 129, 136, 138
homosexuality 25, 71, 110, 119, 120, 122, 125, 131, 132, 135, 138
'Horse Bands of the Red Desert' 77, 78
House Made of Dawn 146–7
Housekeeping 32
Houston, Pam 14, 170–1
   Cowboys Are My Weakness 170
'How the West was Spun' 24, 69, 107, 120, 145

Hud 121
Hulk 123
hyperreal 8, 16, 18, 35, 40, 104

In the American West 132, 179
Indian Wars Refought, The (film) 158–60, 161
'Indian Wars Refought, The' 12, 26, 142, 148, 156–62
Indians *see* Native Americans
Ingraham, Prentiss 9, 108
Inheritors, The 144
Intimate Matters 120
Iraq 101, 102, 189
Ives, Burl 136

Jackson, John Brinckerhoff 34, 97
James, Will 108
Jeffrey, Julie Roy 60
    Frontier Women 60
Jenks, Tom 3
'Job History' 26, 165–7
Johnson County War 124, 165, 168, 169
Johnson, Josephine
    Now in November 65

Keats, John 126
Kid, Billy the *see* Billy the Kid
Kill the Cowboy 31, 86
King, Edward Owl 159
King of Queens 180
Kingsolver, Barbara 14
Kinsey, Alfred 120, 121
kitsch 21, 36, 46, 47, 52, 56, 118
Kittredge, William 11, 12, 67, 82, 85, 152, 156
    Cord novels 11
    'The Last Safe Place' 79
    'Owning It All' 85, 177–8
    'White People in Paradise' 152–3
Klett, Mark 33
Kolodny, Annette

Lay of the Land, The 62
Kristeva, Julia 164

Ladd, Alan 11, 121, 139
Land of Many Hands 60
Land Survey 34
landscape 4, 6, 12, 19, 21, 29–56, 61, 86, 92, 98, 103, 109, 110, 114, 125, 127, 139–40, 143, 144, 152, 186, 187
Lane, Franklin 158
Laramie Republican 73
Las Vegas 104
Last Picture Show, The 121
'Last Safe Place, The' 79
Law and Order 167
Lawrence, Elizabeth Atwood 114
Lay of the Land, The 62
Ledger, Heath 137
Lee, Ang 2, 25, 123, 131, 133
    Crouching Tiger, Hidden Dragon 123
    Hulk 123
    Sense and Sensibility 123
Lessinger, Jack 16, 79
Letters from an American Farmer 7
Lévi-Strauss, Claude 9–10
    Structural Anthropology 9–10
Lewis and Clark expedition of 1804–67
Life of Oscar Collister, Wyoming Pioneer 43
Limerick, Patricia 13, 15, 59, 86, 146
Little Otik 44
Locke, John 7
Loffreda, Beth 40, 165
Logan, Alec 78
Logan, Jr, Bill 78
Lomax, John L.
    Cowboy Songs and Other Frontier Ballads 69
London, Jack 20
Lone Ranger 37, 117

'Lonely Coast, A' 21, 27, 38, 39, 40, 58, 166, 170, 171–5
Lonesome Dove series 11, 121
Longfellow, Henry Wadsworth
  Song of Hiawatha, The 75
Lopez, Barry 30

magic realism 12, 19, 21, 23, 36, 45, 91, 103, 150, 188
Mailer, Norman 20
  Naked and the Dead, The 30
Malthus, Thomas Robert 57
'Man Crawling Out of Trees' 5, 16, 22, 23, 58, 79–83
Man who Fell in Love with the Moon 122
Manifest Destiny 8, 34, 54, 62, 85, 96, 150
Maps 22, 51, 52, 141, 155
Marlboro Man 130, 138, 142, 163
marriage 79–80
masculinity *see also* gender 10, 15, 24, 75, 83, 90, 105, 108, 109, 110–12, 114, 115, 116, 119, 125, 129, 130, 188
Mason, Bobbie Anne 170
Mature, Victor 120
McCarthy, Cormac 3, 14–15, 33
  Border Trilogy 15
McCrea, Joel
  Ride in the High Country 134
McKinney, Aaron 124
McMurty, Larry 11, 12, 14, 121, 122, 124, 129, 132, 133, 134, 135, 137
McPhee, John 66
  Rising from the Plains 66
Mead, Mary 93
medical practitioners 61
'Menace of the Wild West Show, The' 159
Middle America 164, 176
Midnight Cowboy 138
Miles, Lieutenant General Nelson Appleton 158

misogyny 61–2, 64, 87, 97, 109, 115, 121, 131, 139
Missouri Review 19
Modica, Andrea 179, 180
  Treadwell 179
Momaday, N. Scott
  House Made of Dawn 146–7
Monkey Wrench Gang, The 31, 86, 96
Montaigne, Michel 6–7, 142
  'Noble Savage' 25, 142, 153
'Mud Below, The' 17, 24, 110, 112–19, 163–4
music 82
Music of Chance, The 82
Muslim women
  oppression 101
My Antonia 37, 59
My Darling Clementine 120
Mydans, Carl 179, 180
  'Proulx's Introductory Essay' 180

Naked and the Dead, The 30
Nash, Henry Smith 7
Native 121, 122, 124, 128
Native Americans 25–6, 35, 44, 96, 141–62
  land management 95
Nature Conservancy 46
'Negatives' 179
Neihardt, John G. 159–60
Nelson, Paula
  After the West Was Won 60
Nelson, Willie 107
Nevada War, The 11
'New Historians' 13
New West 85, 95–8, 166, 168
New Yorker 87, 123
Nez Percé 161
Nicholson, Jack 139
9/11 *see* twin towers
'Noble Savage' 25, 142, 145, 153
Norris, Frank 3
Now in November 65

O Pioneers 35
Oates, Joyce Carol 15
Oedipus story 49, 51
Off the Beaten Track 46
Ojibwa 158
'Opening the Oyster' 153, 164
Ortiz, Simon 142
Ossana, Diana 121, 123, 124, 129, 130, 132, 133, 134, 135, 137
Otesanek 44
Owens, Louis 146
    Bone Game 146
'Owning It All' 85

'Pair of Spurs, A' 15, 16, 17, 23, 24, 38, 91–5
Parnassus 126
Patten, Gilbert 9
People in Hell Just Want a Drink of Water' 12, 21, 34, 36–7, 109, 110–13, 119
Père Goriot, Le 80
Phillips, Jayne 170
    Fast Lanes 170
photography 33–4, 179–80
Pickle, Linda 63
    Contented among Strangers 63–4
Pietro, Rodrigo 132
pioneers 22, 39, 57–83, 105, 176–7
    female 60, 61, 64, 73, 106
Plains of North America and its Inhabitants, The 153
Popper, Deborah 95
Popper, Frank 95
'Porgeir's Bull' 46, 48
Porter, Edwin 10–11
    Great Train Robbery, The 10–11
Postcards 4, 26, 141, 142, 149–51, 162, 178
Postmodern 13, 18, 26, 33, 148, 165–7, 171, 175, 182, 185
    approaches 4, 6, 11, 150
Potter, Carroll H. 44
Power of the Dog, The 121

Practice of the Wild, The 52
prairie madonna 58–9, 69
PrairyErth 155
Professor's House, The 135
Proulx, George 68
Proulx, Roberta 68
Pryor, Beulah 61
Puritans 7

railroad companies 66
Ranch Life and the Hunting-Trail 108
ranchers 85–106
Rea, Tom 6
Reagan, Ronald 10, 27, 165, 167
Reaganomics 168, 175
Red Cloud 141
'Red Desert Ranches' 68
Red Desert: History of a Place 6, 42, 44, 187
Red River 120
Refuge: An Unnatural History of Family and Place 31
Reservation Blues 146
Rhizome 13
Ride in the High Country 134
Ride with Me, Maria Montana 32
Rime of the Ancient Mariner, The 126
Rising from the Plains 66
Robbins, Tom, *Even Cowgirls Get the Blues* 93
Robinson, Marilynne, *Housekeeping* 32
rodeo 114, 115–19, 133, 163
Rolvaag, Ole Edvart 21, 29–30, 36, 58, 65
    Giants in the Earth 59
Romanticism, European 7, 62
Romeo and Juliet 139
Roosevelt, Theodore 7, 10, 57, 101, 107, 110
    Ranch Life and the Hunting Trail 108
    Winning of the West, The 10, 57
Roseanne 180

Rough Deeds 189
roughnecks 26, 27, 165–6, 175, 177–8, 180, 183, 187
Rousseau, Jean-Jacques 7
Rubottom, Helena Thomas 12
Russell, Charles 108
Russell, Sharman Apt 86
   Kill the Cowboy 31, 86

'Sagebrush Kid, The' 12, 21–2, 42–6, 56, 141
Savage, Thomas
   Power of the Dog, The 121
Savage Jr, William 119
Scarborough, Dorothy
   Wind, The 59, 70
Scarlet Letter, The 127
Schaefer, Jack 10, 24, 139
   Shane 10, 16, 24, 110
Schlesinger, John
   Midnight Cowboy 138
Scott, Bradfield 46
Scott, Randolph
   Ride in the High Country 134
Sense and Sensibility (film) 123
Shakespeare, William
   Tempest, The 142
Shane 10, 16, 24, 110
Shane (character) 14, 24, 97, 107, 109, 112, 121, 139, 174
Shane (film) 11, 131, 139
Shelley, Percy Bysshe 126
   Adonais 126
Shepard, Matthew 124
Shipping News, The 4
Showalter, Elaine 65
   Female Malady, The 65
Sophocles 49
Sigerman, Harriet
   Land of Many Hands 60
Silent Enemy 158
Silko, Leslie Marmon 35, 146
   Ceremony 31, 146–7
Sioux 8–9, 42, 43, 158

sit-coms 168, 180
Sitting Bull 8, 141, 161
Smiley, Jane
   Thousand Acres, A 32
Smith, Henry Nash
   Virgin Land 62
Smoke Signals 147
Snyder, Gary 30, 52
   Practice of the Wild, The 52
social conditions 4
social Darwinism 8
social realism 36, 91
Solace of Open Spaces, The 6, 26, 164
songs 68–9, 70–3, 107, 127, 129, 136, 149, 171, 174
Sophocles 49
Soul of the Indian, The 154
Spanbauer, Tom
   Man who Fell in Love with the Moon, The 122
Starr, Belle 58, 93
state highway department 73
Stegner, Wallace 10, 14, 57, 75, 124
   Big Rock Candy Mountain, The 58, 77
Steinbeck, John 3, 29–30, 31
Stevens, George 11
Structural Anthropology 9–10
Suckow, Ruth
   Country People 59, 63
Sun Also Rises, The 125
Svankmajer, Jan
   Little Otik 44
symbolism 48, 114, 116, 144, 173

Tammen, Harry Heye 74, 75
Taylor, Buck 108
Teapot Scandal 157
Tempest, The 142
'Testimony of a Donkey' 16, 21–2, 41, 51–6
That Old Ace in the Hole 4, 26, 66, 95–6, 142, 153–6

'Them Old Cowboy Songs' 22, 23, 38, 58, 61, 65–73, 141
This House of Sky 32, 67
Thousand Acres, A 32
Thyrsis 126
Titanic (film) 139
'Tits-Up in a Ditch' 15, 21, 23, 24, 98–102
trailer trash 19, 58, 164, 166, 169, 170, 175, 178, 180–1
Trails: Towards a New Western History 13
Transcendentalist movement 7
'Traversing the Desert' 57
Treadwell 179
  Proulx's 'Reliquary' 180n. 22
trickle down effect 167
'Trickle Down Effect, The' 26–7, 165, 167–8
Tristan and Isolde 139
Tuan, Yi-Fu 5
Turner, Frederick Jackson 7, 8, 10, 39, 51, 57, 61, 65–6, 83, 90, 102, 107, 108, 146, 148, 185
  closure of the Frontier 8, 11, 57, 107
Turner, Ted 94
twin towers 101

'The Union Pacific Railroad Arrives' 66
United States Geologic Survey 67

Van der Water, Frederick 74
Vietnam War 90, 110, 129, 146
  veterans 91
Virgil 7
  Eclogues 126
Virgin Land 62
Virginian, The 10, 121
Virginian, the (character) 107, 109
Vivaldi, Antonio 82

Walker, Alice 135
'Wamsutter Wolf, The' 27, 166, 170, 175–83
Wayne, John 95, 103, 120, 138
Welch, James
  Winter in the Blood 146
Wells Fargo 42
'Wer-Trout, The' 55
Westerns 36, 86, 87, 90, 109, 120, 169
What an Indian Thinks 142
'What Kind of Furniture would Jesus Pick?' 18, 23, 40–1, 88–91
  reviews 89
Where the Old West Stayed Young 75
Where the Sea Used to Be 39
White, Richard 13
'White People in Paradise' 152–3
Whitman, Walt 126
  Calamus 126
Williams, Tennessee 135
Williams, Terry Tempest 14
  Refuge: An Unnatural History of Family and Place 31
Wills, John 69
Wind, The 59, 70
Winesburg, Ohio 38
Winning of the West, The 10, 57
Winter in the Blood 146
Wister, Owen 6, 10, 108
  Virginian, The 10, 121
women's magazines 61
World's Columbian Exposition (1893) 7
Wounded Knee massacre 157
Wuthering Heights 139
Wyoming Stock-Growers Association 86, 93
'Wyoming the Cowboy State' 164

Yellow Hand 9
Yellow Robe 158, 159
yuppies 96

www.ingramcontent.com/pod-product-compliance
Lightning Source LLC
Chambersburg PA
CBHW062141300426
44115CB00012BA/2001